Holiday Decorating For Dummies®

FEB 2 8 2004

Things to Put in Your Decorating Stash

If you're looking for quick and easy ways to fill in blank spaces, add to your current holiday decorations, or just want additional items to spruce up your holiday, keep some of these items on hand:

- **Ribbons:** All sizes and holiday colors. Use ribbon as fillers and decorative accents to home décor items.

- **Vases, bowls, or baskets:** Have a variety on hand to use for simple arrangements of flowers, fruit, food items, or utensils for buffets.

- **Accent pillows:** Keep a few standard-sized accent pillows in your stash so that you can add them to a sofa or window seat, or throw them on the floor for additional seating. If you want to save space, invest in one set and purchase or make slipcovers in holiday colors to switch out every season.

- **Fruit:** Place fruit (either real or fake is fine) in bowls, make topiaries with them, or wire them into garland. Fruit is an easy addition to add to any holiday or special occasion setting.

- **Flowers/foliage:** Have both fresh and faux plants, blooms, and single stems handy to easily arrange here and there at the holidays. Purchase seasonal blooms mentioned in each chapter to decorate for the holidays. Insert them into wreaths, place bunches in vases, or place potted plants or blooming bulbs in a space that needs a quick touch-up.

- **Books:** Add a few handsome bound books to your stash. Use them to raise or lower arrangements, photo frames, or other accessories.

- **Candles:** Keep a few neutral-colored candles in pillars, votives, tealights, or tapers to add temporary lighting for any special occasion.

- **Fabric remnants, linens:** Use fabric remnants and table linens to add splashes of color to holiday buffets or table settings. Don't worry about hemming remnants, simply fold the puddled edges underneath for a quick solution.

- **Trays:** Use trays as transportable surfaces to arrange miniature tablescapes on or use them to serve guests.

- **Throws:** Soft, comfy throws are perfect to have in every holiday color or theme. They fold nicely away and can transform a room into a holiday look just by draping them over the arms of a chair or sofa.

- **Mirrors:** Place mirrors under candles to reflect more light, use larger mirrors as trays to set up a pretty tablescape, or use as a serving platter for setting up fruits or vegetables on a buffet. Mirrors double everything!

A Holiday Decorator's Toolbox

Carry the following in your toolbox for easy installation of all types of decorations:

- Clothespins
- Low-temperature glue gun/glue sticks
- Candle lighter
- Extension cords
- Up lights and spotlights
- Duct tape (several colors)
- Hammer
- Nails
- Picture-hanging hardware
- Thumbtacks
- Transparent tape
- Office stapler
- Staple gun
- 25-foot measuring tape
- Level
- Chalk line
- Chalk
- Water soluble marker
- Permanent marker
- Monofilament
- Scissors
- Wire cutters
- Paddle wire
- Electrical tape

Checklist for Groovy Holidays

In need of a quick plan for a great holiday? Follow this easy planner, and you'll have a swinging holiday in no time. Yeah, baby, yeah!

- ❏ Size up your space.
- ❏ Determine how much time you have.
- ❏ Figure out how much you want to create or make yourself.
- ❏ Set a budget.
- ❏ Make a plan.
- ❏ Be realistic.
- ❏ Enlist help when needed.
- ❏ List any special needs of your guests.
- ❏ Check your supply inventory.
- ❏ Go shopping for items needed.
- ❏ Get organized.
- ❏ Gather decorating toolkit.
- ❏ Decorate.
- ❏ Have fun.
- ❏ Prepare for the next holiday!

Wiley, the Wiley Publishing logo, For Dummies, the Dummies Man logo, the For Dummies Bestselling Book Series logo and all related trade dress are trademarks or registered trademarks of Wiley Publishing, Inc. All other trademarks are property of their respective owners.

For Dummies: Bestselling Book Series for Beginners

Holiday Decorating

FOR

DUMMIES®

Holiday
Decorating
FOR
DUMMIES®

by Kelley Taylor

WILEY

Wiley Publishing, Inc.

Holiday Decorating For Dummies®

Published by
Wiley Publishing, Inc.
111 River St.
Hoboken, NJ 07030
www.wiley.com

WILEY   is a trademark of Wiley Publishing, Inc.

About the Author

Kelley Taylor is a freelance craft and home decorating designer and founder of CreatingHomeDécor.com, a site for do-it-yourself decorating and craft enthusiasts. Her work has appeared in several books and publications, and she appears regularly on television shows demonstrating her quick-and-easy home décor projects. Her past work as a visual merchandiser, floral designer, craft editor, and holiday decorator gave much inspiration for this book. Now she knows why she wore so many hats. She and her husband Byron live in southern Connecticut with their son Lex.

Dedication

This book is dedicated to my husband, Byron, who continues to decorate my world with his beautiful, supporting, and loving spirit.

To my son, Lex: Your smile lights up my world. I'm so happy and amazed God blessed me with the miracle of you.

And in loving honor and memory of my sweet companions who passed during the process of this book. Gertie, Stogey, and Scout: The time I spent with you was never enough. You're missed dearly.

Acknowledgments

So many thanks, so little time. I'd like to extend a hearty thank you to the wonderful staff at Wiley, especially my project editor, Jennifer Connolly, whose knowledge, insight, direction, and incredible patience helped guide the book to make it what it is today. To my copy editor, Christina Guthrie, who can take this designer's broken text and work her grammatical wand to make it sing, and to Pam Warren, my long-time friend who just happens to be technical editor for this book. Thanks for making sure the ideas presented were explained clearly. I'm so glad we went through instruction-writing boot camp together so many years ago!

A special thanks also goes to my acquisitions editor, Tracy Boggier, and to the graphics department for the wonderful illustrations. And I can't forget to extend gratitude to my agent, Jessica Faust, at BookEnds. You were divinely sent.

To all the visitors, subscribers, and contributors to my Web site, CreatingHomeDécor.com, thank you for your support and loyalty while I've taken a few months off to finish this book. I hope you all feel it was worth it.

Thanks to my family, friends, and advisors — through this process you've been a source of strength. And to Blake Edwards — my best friend for about 20 years — thank you for leading my personal cheering section.

An appreciation beyond comprehension goes to my husband, Byron. You are my soulmate, friend, confidant, and rock. Without you my life would not be possible — you have my undying gratitude. And to my sweet little boy, Lex, may you always know that you make every single day a holiday for me. I love you both with all of my heart.

Most of all, thanks goes to God. Without His divine design, there would be no cause to celebrate and decorate these splendid occasions we call holidays. This book was a gift from Him — I hope I've done it justice. If so, to God be the glory.

Publisher's Acknowledgments

We're proud of this book; please send us your comments through our Dummies online registration form located at www.dummies.com/register/.

Some of the people who helped bring this book to market include the following:

Acquisitions, Editorial, and Media Development

Project Editor: Jennifer Connolly

Acquisitions Editor: Tracy Boggier

Senior Copy Editor: Christina Guthrie

Copy Editor: Greg Pearson

Acquisitions Coordinator: Holly Grimes

Technical Editor: Pam Warren

Editorial Manager: Christine Meloy Beck

Editorial Assistants: Melissa Bennett, Elizabeth Rea

Cover Photos: EyeWire/Getty Images, www.gettyimages.com

Cartoons: Rich Tennant, www.the5thwave.com

Production

Project Coordinator: Kristie Rees

Layout and Graphics: Jennifer Click, Kelly Emkow, Joyce Haughey, Jacque Schneider, Mary Gillot Virgin

Proofreaders: TECHBOOKS Production Services, Brian H. Walls

Indexer: TECHBOOKS Production Services

Publishing and Editorial for Consumer Dummies

   Diane Graves Steele, Vice President and Publisher, Consumer Dummies

   Joyce Pepple, Acquisitions Director, Consumer Dummies

   Kristin A. Cocks, Product Development Director, Consumer Dummies

   Michael Spring, Vice President and Publisher, Travel

   Brice Gosnell, Publishing Director, Travel

   Suzanne Jannetta, Editorial Director, Travel

Publishing for Technology Dummies

   Andy Cummings, Vice President and Publisher, Dummies Technology/General User

Composition Services

   Gerry Fahey, Vice President of Production Services

   Debbie Stailey, Director of Composition Services

Contents at a Glance

Table of Contents

Introduction

· ·

*H*oliday decorating can be elegant, whimsical, minimal, or over the top; holidays can hold significant meaning and tradition, or exist mainly for a rip-roaring good time. Either way, during each holiday throughout the year, people gather, celebrate, entertain, and, of course, decorate, which can be a challenge to your time, budget, and space.

Many books have been published on the subject of decorating, crafting, or decorating each holiday specifically, but I wanted to write a reference guide that you can easily and quickly use to decorate the major holidays — a guide containing simple decorating, craft and holiday ideas, techniques, and tricks that resist any obstacle of time, money, and space.

And that's what you've got right here.

Although I would've loved to, I couldn't include an expansive, all-inclusive, let-you-know-everything-there-is-to-know about each holiday in this volume (who could move the darn thing it would be so thick?). But what I have given you are the basic fundamentals for designing your holidays, your way.

Holiday decorating is for anyone and everyone who loves to celebrate very special occasions. And a holiday isn't limited to the ones listed in this book! An anniversary, a special birthday, a warm welcome home — all these are holidays that we cherish and want to celebrate. So this book shows you how to plan, budget, and decorate any of the special occasions in your life, no matter what your budget can afford, what skill set you may have, or what living arrangements may be bestowed upon you now. And the best part is you can just skip to the sections that interest you.

Decorating for the many holidays throughout the year is rewarding. It allows you to stretch your creative muscles often and shake up your décor a bit. Armed with this book, you can find numerous ways of using what you've already got and start accurately planning for your next holiday or special occasion confidently.

About This Book

This book is for you if:

- ✔ You have no idea where to start and just need some ideas to get you going.
- ✔ You've already got a huge collection of your own holiday stash and need to get organized before pilfering and plundering.
- ✔ You need an all-in-one reference in order to decorate most of the major holidays.

Part decorating guide, part stylist guide, and part craft instruction book, *Holiday Decorating For Dummies* helps you access the knowledge you need to create beautiful homes and great gatherings that anyone would feel welcome in.

Even if you don't fall into any of the groups I mentioned, this book gives you clear explanations of how beautiful yet practical holiday decorating is done. You don't have to worry about suggestions of over-the-top decorating here — that I'll leave to you. I present only basic ideas that are easy to grasp (and do) and give you the insights and idea starters to help you become your own best decorator.

You find planning tools, decorating ideas, decorating tricks, crafting basics, care and cleaning tips, storage solutions, and more. All you have to do is pick what you're interested in and go. Dive in!

Conventions Used in This Book

When I refer to holiday decorating, I use it in the broadest terms imaginable. Normally, when people talk about holiday decorating, the Christmas season comes to mind. In this book, when I discuss holiday decorating, I include all holidays in general and how to decorate for any or all of them.

Holiday decorating is an easy topic to explain, although there will be times when I use the terms *visual merchandising* and *styling* to complete a look. These are simply conventions I use to describe the attractive arrangement of items in a designated area. Visual merchandisers — people who make displays in department stores make merchandise look more appealing — are pros at making unique arrangements that make you stop and take notice. Stylists — people who are hired by ad agencies, celebrities, magazines, and photographers — make things look beautiful for the lens of a camera. They usually design, protect, sculpt, and carve out a brand image for their clients. They primp and prop homes for beautiful photographic shots.

So when I talk about how you can style and visually merchandise your home by making beautiful holiday vignettes, you can know that it's just a fancy schmancy way of saying, "Make it look purty."

A couple other conventions:

- ✔ When I introduce a new term, the word is *italicized.*
- ✔ Keywords in bulleted lists are **bolded.**
- ✔ Web sites and e-mail addresses appear in `monofont` to help them stand out.

Foolish Assumptions

I assume that you know what a holiday is and that you know this book doesn't contain entertaining ideas or recipes for holiday cooking, or concepts on home decorating. For those subjects, I suggest that you pick up a copy of *Christmas Cooking For Dummies,* by Dede Wilson, or *Home Decorating For Dummies,* by Patricia Hart McMillan and Katharine Kaye McMillan (Wiley).

I assume that you have very few crafting skills, so the instructions I give are very basic techniques that you can adapt as you need them. Although the instructions may be basic, each project is suitable for any crafting skill level, so don't shy away from trying any project I include in this book.

How This Book Is Organized

This book is organized in parts to help you find what you need a little more easily. Each part covers an aspect of holiday decorating, so you can just go to the section that applies to you or your situation. Here's a rundown of what you'll find.

Part 1: Becoming a Holiday Decorator Extraordinaire

Whether your desire is to have the best decorated house on your block, or you need quick tips on how to set a buffet, you find the decorating basics you need in this first part of the book.

I've gone to great lengths to show you from the get-go that even though you may have to overcome various challenges, you can easily get on your way to decorating whatever holiday you choose with style, fun, and panache. Because holidays seem to be a bit overwhelming in general, I spend quite a bit of time getting you focused on the hows and whys of decorating. But I also show you how to find ideas from things around you every day, and how to pull a whole look together by using an inspiration piece. You'll have fun collecting decorating skills from which you can build a firm foundation.

Part II: The Practical Stuff: Money, Space, and More

In Part II, I show you how to get yourself, your money, and your time organized, so that you have more realistic expectations when it comes to holiday decorating.

This part shows you how to make a decorating notebook complete with project plans and design space-planners for every room in your home, and it gives you a good start at getting it all together — not just for the holidays, but period.

You also find out how to care for and clean the treasures you have, and you find neat little tricks on how to store unique items that are exclusive to holiday decorating (like how to keep those darn lights from tangling!).

Part III: Getting to the Heart of the Holidays

In each holiday chapter, I start with a planning and organizing section, giving you simple reminders of what else you may need to plan around or count on during each given holiday season. Make notes in the margins around this section of anything you have personally planned that time of year, so you can organize everything accordingly.

To begin the decorating process, I give you an inspiration piece list that breaks out common items normally associated with each particular holiday. I also list color palettes, and I give you some ideas for using botanicals and fabrics when shopping for each holiday.

Along with the inspiration piece list, you find sections for just about any decorating challenge you may think you have. For instance, if you're low on time, go immediately to the "Decorating in a Flash" section where you find ideas for quick-and-easy decorating. It's a valuable resource for those of you who are on the go.

If you just don't want to spend a lot of money decorating for a holiday, the "More Splash for Less Cash" section helps you find cost-effective ways of decorating. "Jazzing Up Smaller Spaces" illustrates wonderful ideas for inflecting just a small holiday touch to those small spaces we all have. This section's also good for those who live in cramped or temporary quarters because most of the ideas are geared for space-saving solutions and temporary installations that go vertical instead of taking up floor space. Heck, I guess that's good for anyone to know.

Perhaps every holiday I've ever celebrated always involved my family or friends. That's why I loved giving ideas on how you can involve your family (or friends) in decorating for the holidays at the end of each chapter. Most crafts and creative projects are great for kids of all ages, meaning that you can enjoy roping in grandparents and friends in a good, creative mess that then turns into decorations.

Part IV: Crafting for the Holidays

Being the crafty do-it-yourselfer that I am, I couldn't pass up the opportunity to give you a valuable section of general craft techniques that you may find helpful in completing your holiday décor.

Many of the techniques I explain are very, very basic, so even small children can do them with supervision. Some of the crafts I include are paper crafts, crafts involving metal and wire, crafts with flowers and botanicals, embossing, painting, etching, and sewing. (Actually, you don't *have* to sew to make a few of the fabric accessories — I give no-sew instructions for most, so if you can glue and iron, you can complete the projects.)

Remember that you don't have to craft anything in this book to decorate. But isn't it nice to know that you have everything in one place if you decide you want to? Have fun. Spend a little creative time making something by hand, by heart.

Part V: The Part of Tens

No *For Dummies* book would be complete without a Part of Tens. In this part, I give you a couple of lists that are easy tips for holiday decorating that can be quickly accessed through a "top ten" format. Keep these tips in mind when decorating for the holidays.

Icons Used in This Book

As you glance through this book, you find a few icons that draw attention to specific types of information you may find helpful to note. Here are the icons I use in this book and what they mean:

The tip icon points you to little tidbits of information that you may find helpful when completing projects, planning, or decorating in general. It may also guide you to a few more creative ideas or variations you can try to adapt from any of the decorating projects or ideas I give you.

This icon points to information I want to remind you of. (Sorry if I preach too much.)

Be sure to pay attention to this icon. I only use it to alert you to something that may be hazardous to you, your family, or your friends.

I use this icon (found mostly in the craft chapters) to give you creative ideas that help take your crafts to the next level — think of it as a way to adapt your crafts to look more like what the pros may do.

Where to Go from Here

This book is laid out so that you can pick it up at any point, in any place, and find the information that you need to know. If you already have a good, basic knowledge of how you like to decorate, or you have a huge amount of holiday décor just waiting to be placed, you probably want to tackle the first part of the book that tells you how to lay out, style, make vignettes, and decorate in general. If you haven't even begun to think about decorating for a holiday, still try to read the first of the book. It may help you define what kind of holiday decorating you want to do and get you on your way.

If you love to make things, you may try going straight to the holiday chapters and make notes of the items you want to try to make. Then you can flip to the craft instructions to whip up your own holiday creations.

At any point, you can always come right back to the table of contents to find what you need quickly.

So, without further ado, let the holidays — and the decorating — begin!

Part I
Becoming a Holiday Decorator Extraordinaire

The 5th Wave
By Rich Tennant

ⒸRICHTENNANT

"Of course I'm proud to be married to a policeman.
I just don't want to decorate every holiday with
orange traffic cones and crime scene tape."

In this part . . .

Holiday decorating is a blend of playing the parts of set designer, prop stylist, interior designer, visual merchandiser, and homeowner. You didn't know that you were so skilled, did you? Don't ever let decorating intimidate you! In this part, I give you holiday decorating basics along with the tricks and tools to plan, dream, and decorate for holidays with stunning style.

Chapter 1

Setting the Stage for Holiday Decorating

*Y*ou may be feeling intimidated about decorating for the holidays, or you may be ready to dive right in. No matter what level of decorator you may be, I give you some tricks that you may not already know, I give you ways to conquer the decorating-fear bug, and I give you tips that can turn you into a quick-change artist — for any holiday — if that's what you want to do.

If you worry about time, money, and skills, fahgetabahtit. Read on! You can find some real world ideas that aren't so unachievable that you'll throw up your hands in frustration. But don't get the wrong idea. Just because I present simple ideas doesn't mean that they're plain and blah. Elegance is simple! Many of my so-called simple ideas are tricks that set designers, magazine stylists, and interior designers use all the time to transform the plain into extraordinary — and you can do it, too!

You're getting ready to embark on quite a fun ride as you glance through this chapter. After going through some basic concepts and getting past some obstacles and common myths about holiday decorating, you'll be ready to dress up your home stage with some holiday décor.

Defining Decorating for the Holidays

Even if your home's style hasn't changed since 1976, with a few simple strokes, your home is refreshed, revamped, and revitalized at the holidays. Unlike regular decorating where you have to pain over what color to paint the walls, what upholstery you should pick, and what furniture style will last a few years, each specific holiday makes it easy. You have a theme, a color palette to choose from, and merchandise and motifs usually mass manufactured, so you can purchase and decorate when you're ready.

Now before I go on, I want to clarify what holiday decorating is, and isn't.

Year-round decorating

Holiday decorating is not just Christmas decorating. (For some reason, that's automatically where people's minds go.) Holiday decorating is year-round. It celebrates many special occasions and important events. It's seasonal. It has many styles. It's constantly changing. It's performed outside, inside, and upside down. You make things, you hang things, and you store things; it constantly evolves. But it does *not* have to be intimidating — it's fun!

Temporary decorating

Even though holiday decorating happens year-round, holiday decorating is also temporary. When I say temporary, I mean that nothing is set up, strung up, hung up, or put up that doesn't come down. Really, that's the beauty of it. Even if you make a complete mess of things, it's only temporary!

Realizing that holiday decorating is temporary, though, takes a certain kind of mindset. In a normal decorating situation, if I choose to add a porcelain vase to my décor, I know exactly where it will live.

In holiday decorating, your décor has to be a bit durable, will take up storage space out of season, will take certain packaging restrictions, and that's just the beginning. Your holiday decorations have to withstand a certain amount of wear and tear within a short amount of time. They may be subjected to abnormal use as well, like, say, at a party.

So, temporary decorating is both a blessing and, sometimes, a curse. You don't have to worry too much with it at this point; the main thing is, you'll want to assess your storage space and look at the sections in each holiday chapter titled "Jazzing Up Smaller Spaces" for space-saving decorating ideas.

Clearing Decorating Obstacles

What do you feel is standing in your way of decorating for the holidays? Is it time, budget, space, or skill — or all the above? Let me just put some of these preconceived notions to rest. You *can* decorate. Really, you can!

Out of time

Feeling like you don't have enough hours in your day to get everything done? It's a common problem. So many things have to be done that it's hard to squeeze in holiday decorating, I know. But don't worry: I include several quick tips and ideas in each holiday chapter. Look for the "Decorating in a Flash" sections, in particular, for specific ideas. And, of course, you can always tell folks that you're a minimalist at heart if you run completely out of time.

Out of money

Finding the ol' pocketbook a little light these days? You needn't ever sacrifice necessities to decorate for the holidays (besides, I wouldn't want you to). I help you find ways of decorating frugally in each holiday chapter. Many of the ideas in these sections show you how to repurpose, reuse, revamp, and restyle many of the same items over and over.

I firmly believe that you should set a budget no matter what — whether you have all the money in the world or are on a strict ramen noodle diet.

By setting a budget, you can readily figure out how much you'll be spending every season, so that it can feed into your normal budgeted household expenses. You'll also be able to calculate, after putting everything down on paper, whether the huge after-season sale items are really worth it or not.

You can find out more about how to set a holiday decorating budget (including having an emergency fund) and stick to it in Chapter 5.

Out of space

If you barely have enough room to hold your personal belongings, you may find it hard to justify acquiring many seasons' worth of holiday decorating supplies.

A simple solution (because you want to decorate, right?) is to read the sections in each holiday chapter that are specifically geared toward small-space decorating.

These sections aren't meant for tiny apartment dwellers only. Doesn't everyone have a tiny bathroom, sitting area, or some other space that has to be dealt with? Find some inspiration to decorate smaller spaces. Bonus? The ideas take little time, effort, or cash!

Out of your mind

Not everyone can have the talent of a poet, artist, or interior designer. Guess what? You don't have to. So don't go crazy thinking that only professionals or incredibly "crafty" people can decorate for the holidays — decorating for the holidays is for everyone.

Holiday decorating is easy if you take it in small, manageable chunks. As I show you in this book, you don't have to have an extraordinary amount of talent to come off looking pretty amazing when decorating for the holidays.

Even if you can't make frozen bread dough rise (oh wait, that's just me), you can figure out how to use just a few props and look at things with a fresh eye — no talent necessary. It's really a simple formula. So stop thinking you have to be the next Picasso to have a well-decorated home for the holidays.

Debunking Decorating Myths

Okay, so you know you have the time, money, space, and talent to decorate, but you still aren't convinced that you can come up with some great looking décor. Perhaps you're stuck believing in one of the many decorating myths I discuss in this section.

Aiming for perfection

First of all, let's get real. Nobody's perfect. Even the most famous models gracing the covers of magazines (that includes houses, too) get professional help to look the way they do. Not all of us can have stylists on staff to decorate our houses for a photo shoot or keep it looking like it belongs on the cover of our favorite decorating magazine. However, I do provide tips and tricks in this book that can help you get it looking as if someone did.

Now, I'm not saying that you shouldn't strive for perfection, or actually achieve it once in a while. I'm merely saying that you shouldn't get so wrapped up in achieving and maintaining perfection that you lose focus of why you decorate in the first place — to create warm, inviting interiors that welcome family and friends.

Kids tromp in snow and mud, pets leave their hair on items, friends prop their feet on coffee tables, and spouses can leave dried-up cereal bowls on kitchen counters. That's just life.

Decorating, especially at the holidays, is to be lived around and in and all over. That's why we have holidays, to join together and celebrate. One of the underlying themes you find in this book is that, although you can decorate perfectly, if your guests don't feel comfortable, you've defeated the very purpose of your decorating.

Again, form follows function. Try to make comfort part of your idea of perfection instead of everything in it's place staying in it's place. And if you're blessed enough to already know this, can you please tell my husband? He hates my dried-up cereal bowls.

Believing you can do it all

Every holiday — if you celebrate it — can get really hectic. You may want to throw a party, attend parades, purchase gifts, and still have time to live a normal life with its crazy demands.

Thinking that you can do it all is a great and noble belief, but is it a reality? If you're hardheaded like me, you refuse to believe that it can't be done. But allow yourself a little slack when it comes to the decorating part.

If you just put up a few decorations, as opposed to decking the whole house, I doubt that anyone will say, "Gosh, I can't believe they didn't have the bathroom decorated!"

Start with a decorating goal in mind and work up from there. In Chapter 6, I give you a planning tool to help you realistically set your plans in motion. In addition, each holiday chapter contains sections that give you little things to do when you're short on time and/or money. And if you really want to go all out, next year's looking a bit better all the time, isn't it?

Creating everything from scratch

Whoa! Whoever said that you had to *make* everything from scratch is out of his or her mind! Take it from me, the one who touts creating your home décor (www.CreatingHomeDecor.com — shameless plug), I believe that you can make just about anything yourself if you want to, including from-scratch recipes, but sometimes, it just ain't feasible — or frugal for that matter!

So although I give you ideas and instructions for making things in this book, don't take it as the only way to get a custom-designed look. If you like the idea, go out and look for an item that's similar. Not everyone is crafty, nor does everyone want to be. If you buy your garland and wreaths instead of crafting them because you don't have a forest growing in your backyard, and purchase your eggs to dye at Easter instead of raising them in your own chicken coop, you're no less qualified to decorate your house beautifully.

Many times, I buy things premade, such as gingerbread houses, because I just simply ran out of time, and I couldn't possibly do a job that's half as good! It doesn't make your decorating any less important, beautiful, or meaningful. The mere act of decorating for a holiday is meaningful in itself.

With imported merchandise and new technologies driving the cost of many manufactured items down, you can easily find many decorating items cheaper than if you bought all the raw goods and made them yourself. Of course, there are always exceptions to the case.

I do believe that there's something intrinsically satisfying about making things yourself, especially if it's a hobby or personal interest. You find many instructions for making things yourself in this book, and you may actually want to try some of them — if only to say that you've done it once.

But never, no never, think that you have to make everything yourself or that someone else is more talented or skilled in holiday decorating because he or she can. You may have a better eye at putting things together or arranging items on a mantel instead of pricking yourself on the wire tying up millions of bows.

Decide what you want to make yourself by evaluating your own personal interests, what you feel you're good at, and how much play time you have. You may, in fact, decide that making things is not the route to go, or you may come off with a completely handmade holiday. And if you do, I want to see how you made your own Christmas lights.

Keeping up with the Joneses

Remember that some of the biggest blessings come when you do what's best for you, not when you discover that you've finally outdone your neighbors. Trying to keep up with competitive neighbors, friends, or, yes, even family is a self-defeating behavior that saps the life out of a holiday. You'll get so wrapped up in trying to purchase more, throw a better party, and buy bigger stuff that you'll quickly drain your bank account and your spirit of the season.

Place your hand on this book right now and pledge to me that you will put your time and energy on focusing what's best for you. (And don't you dare say that beating the competition is best for you!)

Concentrate on the meaning of the season, take the high road, and avoid competition in decorating your home for the holidays. You'll feel better about what you do and don't do at the holidays if you do it just for you and your family.

Finding the Pleasure Principle

The idea of decorating for a holiday shouldn't shower you with tension, leaving you wondering what in the world you're going to do and how you're going to find the time to do it. You should *enjoy* holiday decorating, and the ideas in this section can help you make sure that you do.

Keeping the fun in the holidays

It seems silly to say "Remember to have fun!" during the holidays, but the reality of stress-filled seasons is prevalent in almost every household. There are places to go, people to see, presents to buy, things to arrange — and that's on top of all the regular hustle and bustle you probably already have going on in your life.

Sometimes, when I mention holiday decorating to a group of people, they grimace, sigh, and I can just see the energy draining out of them right before my eyes. I know: Holiday decorating can be time consuming and energy draining. Some people even procrastinate or forego holiday decorating altogether because of the hassle they're anticipating.

I'm not giving a lecture here on Fun 101. But perhaps the following suggestions can sway the way you envision decorating:

- ✔ Don't take on all the labor of decorating by yourself. Involve the family. I'm *not* saying to bark out the orders while they submissively obey; instead, creatively think of ways to incorporate or have fun with your family or a friend while still accomplishing your decorating tasks.

- ✔ Pencil in an afternoon or day to take the whole family to pick out pumpkins or a Christmas tree. Help a child make his or her own kinara or menorah. Use the sections in each holiday chapter titled "Involving the Whole Family" as idea starters for coming up with other fun ways to decorate. As you glance through each chapter, make notes in the margins of any other decorating ideas you think may be appropriate to enlist help or have someone tag along for company.

- ✔ Hold tree-trimming parties, invite close friends over to decorate for Purim, and find as many ways as you can to infuse joy into every occasion.

If you've tried all these tips, and you still find your decorating to be a burden, pare down what you're trying to do. Life's too short not to have a bit of fun while you work.

Remembering why you're decorating

At some point in time, most everyone forgets the reason for any season. Although you don't have to pore over history books at every President's Day, remembering why you celebrate each holiday is important.

Holidays mean different things to different people. Find your inspiration through the stories and history that have been passed down and keep them tucked away in your heart while coming up with your decorating plans. I've found that when my clients firmly understand that the reason we all decorate is to celebrate, it suddenly takes on more meaning.

It's also important to decorate not just for yourself, but also for others. Years ago, I was in charge of compiling a series of Christmas books in which I was immersed in Santas, reindeer, Christmas trees, Nativity scenes, and every other thing you can imagine that had to do with Christmas. I was so sick of the whole topic that I couldn't decorate my own home at Christmas for years until my little boy came along. And then I rediscovered the joy of decorating to see the delight in *his* eyes. He was seeing all this for the very first time!

List all the reasons you celebrate, so when you get a little down or overwhelmed, you can accurately adjust your feelings about what you're doing.

Taking your audience into consideration

I follow the theory that form follows function. When I consult with clients to discuss the different ideas they have, I also note whether they have children in the house, allergies, pets, special routines, how they use rooms, and so on. I know how they use their spaces, so I get a good idea of what I need to stay away from.

For example, I would most certainly never suggest black velvet anything for someone who owns a white, long-haired cat. Neither would I place poisonous plants, expensive breakable items, or vintage rugs where a toddler can harm himself or the décor by my carelessness.

When you're decorating for a holiday, think of every person who may come through your door. Make sure that you plan around your audience.

For instance, if you have grandchildren, nieces, or nephews, what may be fine for a very grown-up environment may not be practical when they come to visit. You have two options:

- ✔ Adjust your decorating to accommodate them, caring for their safety and keeping your sanity.
- ✔ Allow extra time at the holidays to say, "No, no! Don't touch that!" and be constantly tense instead of enjoying your holiday gathering.

Perhaps striking a happy medium is a good option for you — having an incredibly decorated pad while not having anything breakable is certainly possible. Simply list what you need to exclude, just in case, and you should be fine.

Keeping the basics in mind

Holiday decorating becomes easy when you keep these basics in mind:

- ✔ No worries — your theme and color palette are chosen for you for the holidays.
- ✔ Make the things you want, and buy the rest.
- ✔ Skip to the parts that mean the most to you.
- ✔ Do only what you have the time, money, and space to do — the rest will follow.
- ✔ Blend religious holiday decorating in your home when called for.

✔ Defy the need to aim for perfection (even though you know that you could be perfect if you wanted to).

✔ Keep this book handy for reference. (You didn't think I was going to leave that out, did you?)

Sharing Cultures and Religion during Holidays

Many people you know or welcome into your home may have different religious beliefs or celebrate holidays other than the ones you celebrate. Don't tiptoe around diversity. Celebrate it.

Holidays are the cause of much angst, I'm afraid, even without having differences of religion. If you have a blended household or will be welcoming guests of many faiths into your home, remember two things:

✔ You don't have to shove your religious holiday down their throats.

✔ You don't have to neglect your holiday, either.

Try implementing a few of these ideas that complement blending several holidays and cultures:

✔ Choose a neutral decorating scheme that's based on seasonal decorating (meaning summer, winter, fall, or spring) rather than decorating for any particular holiday.

✔ Stay away from adding any particular color that's associated with a certain holiday color scheme. Focus on making an elegant and tastefully decorated home where anyone would feel welcome.

✔ Use lots of candles in neutral colors and keep the tabletops as neutral as any other day you may gather together for dinner.

✔ Decorate the house with seasonal swags, garlands, and centerpieces.

✔ If gifts are to be exchanged, place them on a gift table, instead of under a tree, and get together on a day other than the specific day any particular holiday is celebrated.

People of different religious backgrounds and cultures appreciate their holidays being included in the decorating mix. Most don't mind whether or not you practice their beliefs. Instead, they like the acknowledgement of cultural diversity or the fact that equal weight is given to each specific holiday instead of focusing on one.

To bone up on holidays that you're not familiar with, visit a library, read this book, and find out more about your friends' and family's various beliefs, or ask them yourself what means the most to them. They might appreciate the fact that you took the time to seek their input and give you fabulous ways of including their symbolic holidays into your own holiday decorating.

You have countless options for decorating for a holiday without having to go theme central. Keep your audience in mind and seek creative ways to decorate. Hopefully, you can find much of the help you need right here in this book.

Finding More Holidays

The United States is a melting pot of cultures, traditions, and religions. On top of that, we have special interests and hobbies that also bind us together in celebrations. Many of these events and occasions include decorating. Here's how you can find out where to go to find more information and gather ideas for decorating your event.

Observing religious holidays

If you worship or celebrate specific religions or practices, your congregation can apprise you of dates you should be aware of for special events or celebrations. Look for classes to find out more about specific religious holidays offered by your place of worship. They can give you detailed information about the correct way to celebrate — and decorate — any holiday associated with religious practices. They can also guide you to sources where you can find merchandise to help you celebrate or decorate with meaningful items for a particular holiday.

Finding cultural or traditional holidays

If you're part of an ethnic or cultural group or want to start decorating and celebrating cultural events that are part of your heritage, find a resource center near you that has historical accounts or books containing more information about celebrations or holidays from your heritage or home country. You can find many sources on the Internet by doing a keyword search in your favorite search engine. Refer to the section in this chapter on looking online to find out more about what you can find and how to find it.

Often, online searches lead you to local or regional resource centers. These places are set up around the country to help connect people with their roots. The staff can provide information, text, references, and more — often free of charge — to help you start planning your celebrations.

Visiting your library

Visit your local library to gain access to more holiday decorating resources. Study the encyclopedias and other reference resources to find more information and history on certain holidays. Besides finding out about specific religious holidays, you can easily find more holiday-specific recipe books, decorating books, and magazines. You can find out what the Pilgrims really ate for dinner and discover that — can you believe it — Thanksgiving really wasn't an official national holiday until President Abraham Lincoln appointed a national day of thanksgiving in 1863.

Ask your reference librarian for *Chase's Calendar of Events*. This book is full of special days, weeks, months, holidays, historical anniversaries, fairs, and festivals for holiday or special-interest junkies. Laid out in an easy day-by-day, month-by-month format, you can quickly find something to celebrate or research for more decorating ideas. Usually, contact names, addresses, Web sites, or phone numbers are included in each listing, so you can find out more information about each event. *Chase's* is revised annually, with the new editions coming out in the fall for the following year. It really is an invaluable resource for the holiday-decorating inclined. You'll be able to find something to celebrate and decorate each and every day, if you want to!

Looking online

The Worldwide Holiday & Festival Site (www.holidayfestival.com) has an extensive database of events broken down by country, religion, and other specific categories. It's relatively easy to navigate and gives you great tools for exploring other cultures and traditions.

Likewise, a wealth of other special-interest sites provide great information on holidays in general. Simply type in the name of a holiday or a special-interest keyword or phrase into your favorite search engine. You'll find many sites you can visit to get specific holiday information with calendars to go along with them.

Chapter 2

Decorating Basics

. . . .

. . . .

I've always heard that a magician never reveals his secrets. Well, you're in luck — I'm not a magician.

In the course of your holiday decorating adventures, you'll need to hang something, rearrange furniture or furnishings, and place new items out for display. Often, in a normal decorating situation, a home's décor evolves over time. With holiday decorating, you have to snatch things in and out before the darn holiday has come and gone!

You don't have to produce showstopper holiday décor, but being a skilled quick-change artist is something that certainly comes in handy at the holidays. In this chapter, you discover some holiday decorating basics as well as how to wave your wand to create holiday magic quickly and easily. Along with the instant formulas for making tablescapes and vignettes, you find a compiled list of decorating wizardry.

Accessorizing Basics for the Holidays

Accessories are finishing touches to your wardrobe and to your home's décor. When decorating for the holidays, you depend heavily on accessories because you don't want to give your décor a complete overhaul every holiday. Accessories are to your home what jewelry, scarves, and hats are to your wardrobe. They set the mood and tone.

Check out *Home Decorating For Dummies,* by Patricia Hart McMillan and Katharine Kaye McMillan (Wiley), for more information on how to decorate your home for year-round style; check out this section for some basic tips on accessorizing for the holidays.

Choosing holiday styles and colors

You need to evaluate how your home is decorated year-round before you plan on accessorizing for the holidays, so that your holiday décor blends well with your home décor, giving each room a cohesive look.

Follow these tips to ensure that your holiday décor looks great in your home:

- ✔ If your home furnishings are neutral in color and simple in pattern, holiday prints, colors, and patterns (as well as your everyday accessories) will pop against the neutral background instead of compete with it.

- ✔ If your home furnishings are dripping with eye-popping colors or patterns, try reversing the above technique. Purchase holiday items in neutral colors when possible and feasible. Many major holidays can incorporate metallics, greens, whites, and off-whites in their color schematics. Natural materials are always considered neutrals and can be wonderful to use in active or busy interior décor.

- ✔ Purchase or create holiday décor that matches the style of your room — for example, if you have a more traditional look, opt for traditional holiday décor. If your room doesn't have a style at all, plan ahead and buy holiday decorations that match what you eventually want the room to be someday. Such a wide selection of holiday merchandise is available that you're not limited to one specific style anymore for any holiday.

Each room in your home can be decorated differently. As long as the décor fits the mood of the room it goes in, you don't have to carry the same theme or style throughout your entire home if you choose not to.

You may not come across exact matches in style, but at least you'll be aware of what you need to look for when purchasing your holiday decorations. Make sure to peruse catalogs as well for your holiday decorating supplies. Sometimes, you find a bigger or better selection than at your local retail stores.

- ✔ Holiday decorating is wonderful because color schematics are mostly predetermined! Have you ever seen a Halloween without orange and black, or a Valentine's Day without red? Most holiday-themed merchandise has elements of traditional holiday colors, so you don't have to worry much about color.

Choosing what you want to flatter

Accessorizing means to accentuate. If you add gorgeous strands of pearls to your neck, the eye is drawn there automatically. If you wear tons of rings, your hands get noticed. If you wear big bangle earrings, your face and ears draw attention.

When you accessorize what you wear, you're choosing features about yourself that you want to draw attention to. In decorating, you do the same, only it's called *choosing a focal point.*

In your home, you arrange your furniture around a focal point. These are the main areas you'll want to festoon and style at the holidays. I can't stress this point enough: *Only add accents to areas where you want to draw attention.* That means that you don't ever have to worry about getting a centerpiece to go on top of the television.

Great areas to focus on in your home are

- Fireplace mantels
- Dining and kitchen tables
- Buffets or sideboards
- Staircases
- A large furniture or accent piece, such as a sofa, armoire, mirror, or painting
- Unique light fixtures, such as sconces or chandeliers
- A beautiful window
- Doorways

Use these areas to create and style unique vignettes (see the section "Making Vignettes Appear before Your Very Eyes" later in this chapter for more details).

Getting the right fit

Proportion, scale, and balance are important to bring about a balanced look, and the last thing you want to do is buy the perfect holiday accessory only to find out that it just doesn't look right because it's too wide, too tall, or even too small for that "perfect place." Many showrooms have tall ceilings and expansive space that can fool the eye into thinking that furnishings or decorations will fit in and around your home when they really don't.

Literal weight versus visual weight in holiday decorating

Traditionally, you always begin arranging a room's furnishings according to its *visual* weight or size. In other words, an oversized leather chair may weigh more physically, but a floor-to-ceiling tapestry carries more weight visually by its sheer size.

After placing your major home furnishings in a room, begin arranging your holiday decorations according to visual weight. For example, at Christmas, you begin by placing the tree (the heaviest or biggest decoration in the room). After that, perhaps drape your garland (lighter), string lights (even lighter), and then hang ornaments (lightest). If you have a large Christmas village display, you'd probably set it up before draping garland because when the two items are arranged together, the village carries more weight visually than garland and generally has to be worked around.

To make sure that you find the perfect fit for that perfect accessory, before you go shopping, arm yourself with the following tips:

- ✔ **Take accurate measurements of the rooms and spaces that you want to decorate (see Chapter 6 for more information).** Take the measurements with you when you shop and check the measurements of things you want to buy. If you don't have a measuring tape with you (don't you keep one in your pocket?), ask a sales associate to measure large items for you. For other items, check tags and boxes for accurate measurements. Sketch your item on graph paper, as explained in Chapter 6, to see if it fits. If you have a hard time squeezing it in, skip it. You can decorate with other items that won't take up so much space.

- ✔ **Purchase yard decorations that don't stand taller than your roofline.** I've seen some great houses look pitifully small because the owner put a giant inflatable snowman on the front porch that stood taller than the home. (It made it look like a little elf's house.)

- ✔ **Buy decorations that balance a room, so that the eye is drawn around the room evenly; purchase decorations that accent focal points.** For instance, you may have a huge picture window in your living room and a fireplace on the opposite wall. As you know, a fireplace only goes so high. To bring balance to the room, you may want to purchase a wreath to hang above the fireplace that visually extends the height of the fireplace up almost to where the windows on the opposite side of the room go. That way, the focal point of the room — the fireplace — isn't ignored.

✔ **Visually weigh the pieces you have in a room, checking height lines as you go, before you buy a new accessory.** You don't have to go making everything symmetrical, just try to purchase somewhat equally proportioned furnishings to offset any imbalance you may have in your room.

Keeping it simple

Remember the old saying that less is more? Well, I come back to this saying over and over throughout this book because it's so important. Make sure that you don't jam pack your room so full of holiday accessories that your eye can't feast on the simplicity of the room or the season. Accessories are meant to complement, not to detract from your home's décor. No doubt, if you keep the simplicity rule in mind, you'll have the best-dressed house on your block.

Paying attention to details

Attention to detail is essential when decorating for the holidays. You'll be adding several elements to your décor that may take a little extra attention. For instance:

✔ Making sure that cords are secure to prevent tripping, or hiding them so that they don't stand out

✔ Trying to add holiday touches without overwhelming the eye

✔ Adding more decorations while trying to integrate them with your décor

When decorating for the holidays, you're essentially staging your home visually. You want to make your home comfortable and attractive, so the rest of this chapter is dedicated to making you a stylist for your own home's photo shoot for a magazine cover. Well, at least picture yourself as a stylist. Before long, you'll be making tablescapes and arranging vignette's quicker than you can say, "Abracadabra"!

Creating a Bag of Tricks

I keep a little place in my attic studio reserved for decorative items that I use to style different areas of my home for different seasons, occasions, or holidays. I admit that it's a hodgepodge of items collected, handed down, found on the side of the road, and bought brand new. My husband calls it mounds of junk; I call it my "stylist stash." Whatever the name, it's my own personal bag of tricks! If I need a filler item to flesh out a look for a tablescape or vignette, I can always rely on my collection to pull it off.

Everyone needs a stash of tricks to pull from to amaze others. Read on for more information on what to include in your stash as well as some tips on how to organize it so that you can decorate in a flash.

Making your list and checking it twice

Have you ever needed a quick touch-up right before you have guests over? Or do you wonder what details put the finishing touches on a room? This list of items is what I refer to when I need to go from drab to fab in minutes. Start looking at the following ordinary items in a whole new light:

- **Fruit:** Almost every luscious photo in a home and garden magazine is accessorized with a big bowl of fruit or vegetables. Have a supply of quality faux fruit in your stash. Hopefully, you'll have enough fresh fruit in the house to display quickly, but if your cupboards are bare, you'll have some great-looking fruits or vegetables to toss out in a glass compote or hearty basket. It's a great way to add a lived-in look at the last minute.

- **Flowers and foliage:** Flowers and foliage represent life, so adding them into a room freshens and invigorates otherwise stale décor. Everyone notices fresh flowers, so use them as centerpieces and highlight accents. Plants or foliage fades into the background, so use them as fill-in pieces or as add-ins to an already accessorized area that still needs something "more."

   Invest in quality silk flowers to reduce maintenance and have on hand anytime. Don't buy clusters of cheap-looking silk flowers that are unusual colors; buy authentic-looking flowers that stay true to nature.

- **Books:** Books are worth gold when decorating nooks and crannies, cozy and inviting spots, and bare areas that need accessorizing. You can find great sets of bound books at tag sales and thrift stores if you don't already have your own collection. Standing some on their ends while stacking some flat adds height and dimension to an end table. Set a lamp or arrangement on top of some for a more whimsical look.

- **Candles:** Lighting is key in decorating. Candles act as quick and portable light sources wherever you need highlighted accents, and they automatically add touches of warmth to any room. Whether you have votives, tealights, pillars, tapers, or those big oversized jars of scented wax, candles add a touch of simplistic elegance to a room. Arrange in clusters and stagger heights if possible.

✔ **Fabrics and other linens:** Think of fabric as an element: a throw, table-cloth, pillow, cushion, slipcover, tapestry, window treatment, and so on. Do you have any fabric remnants that can be used as a quick decorating touch? For buffets, I love to bring out fabrics that fit the mood to deco-rate the buffet table — old quilts for a Sunday down-home get-together or shimmering satins for cocktails and hors d'oeuvres.

✔ **Ribbons:** Ribbon is a perfect accent to add to the Christmas tree and to wreaths, lamps, or ornaments. Swirl them around tablescapes and vil-lages, make bows for chairs, and use ribbons anywhere else you can imagine. Make sure to get a few extra spools in neutral colors or colors that match your home décor, so that you can use ribbon through the year for last-minute decorating.

✔ **Vases or bowls:** I stock many different kinds of glassware and pottery in all shapes and sizes. You never know when someone may surprise you with a bouquet of flowers (I can dream, can't I?). Use vases or bowls to hold everything from ornaments to fruit, flowers to branches, or leave them alone to strike an artistic pose. You'll quickly love what you can do with these little items in your stylist stash.

✔ **Accent pillows:** Soften hard lines of sofas, chairs, or other seating areas with accent pillows. Pick a few different shapes and sizes to change out or re-cover for the holiday season. To change them up in a hurry, try finding pillow slipcovers to go with each season or holiday. If you have trouble finding them, make your own. Flip to Chapter 19 for instructions.

✔ **Baskets:** Baskets are wonderful textural items that come in any artistic shape, color, or size. Use baskets for storage to house stacks of maga-zines, your knitting, or for holding masses of pine cones during fall and winter months. They also come in handy for entertaining. Use them to hold napkin-wrapped silverware, line them with a cloth and toss hot dinner rolls in them, or use them to hold waterproof containers full of flowers or plants.

✔ **Trays:** Trays are wonderful and useful items to start collecting or keep on hand. I use trays as surfaces to arrange miniature tablescapes (for more on tablescapes, see the "Making Tablescapes" section later in this chapter). This way, I can move the tablescape from room to room as needed or desired. I can set it up in my workroom, making my mess in there, and then transport it to my vignette whenever I want.

✔ **Throws:** If you think that throws are only for decorating during cold weather seasons, think again. Throws come in all sorts of fabrics — from the nubbiest chenilles to the nicest woven cottons and quilts — and they add texture and layers to a room's environment. Sure, they look great when tossed over chairs or on sofas in the winter, but they're also great to have on a bed or by an office chair. Besides, you never know who's going to be cold, even during the summer months. Keep an assortment in your stash (or make some, using my instructions in Chapter 19) to "throw" out on occasion.

- ✔ **Picture frames:** I love to collect picture frames. They not only hold my loved ones' photos, but they can also frame a special holiday greeting card, artwork my little boy did for me, or a pressed rose from a special Valentine's Day.

- ✔ **Mirrors:** Mirrors reflect light and are great for optical illusions. Use large mirrors or small mirrors. Cluster them on the wall to make your home appear lighter, brighter, or larger. In holiday decorating, you can double the candlelight you have by simply placing a mirror underneath lit candles. When setting up buffets, try using mirrors as platters to arrange fruit, hors d'oeuvres, pastries, and more, making a small sampling seem more expansive.

A decorator's toolbox

Here are some of my favorite things to have on hand in my toolbox. I carry these items with me to most installations, taking pieces in and out as needed. Having these tools handy means that you don't have to make any last-minute trips to the store for supplies. You might also make a separate holiday toolbox containing specialty tools or gadgets that are holiday specific, such as plastic hooks to hang holiday lighting or suction cups to hang wreaths or garlands.

- ✔ Clothes pins
- ✔ Velcro
- ✔ Low-temperature glue gun/glue sticks
- ✔ Candle lighter
- ✔ Extension cords
- ✔ Up lights and spotlights
- ✔ Duct tape
- ✔ Hammer
- ✔ Nails
- ✔ Picture-hanging hardware
- ✔ Thumbtacks
- ✔ Transparent tape
- ✔ Office stapler

- ✔ Staple gun
- ✔ Food coloring
- ✔ 25-foot measuring tape
- ✔ Level
- ✔ Chalk line
- ✔ Chalk
- ✔ Water-soluble marker
- ✔ Permanent marker
- ✔ Monofilament
- ✔ Scissors
- ✔ Wire cutters
- ✔ Paddle wire
- ✔ Electrical tape

Organizing your holiday stash

Now that you have a list of items you can style with, you can start rummaging through your home, taking note of what you have. Straighten and style as you go, or grab a big box and start collecting any items you no longer want to display but can see decorating with at another point in time.

You may want to start claiming space in your home to start your own stylist stash. You can use an extra closet or even purchase plastic bins for under-the-bed storage. Many of the items I list can pack away quite well, so any small space you have will do. If your collection starts to grow, you can always weed out items that have seen better days or no longer fit your style.

If you have the incredible expanding collection, try to keep like items stored together. This way, you'll be able to access everything more easily.

Whether you start your own stylist stash or not, you're armed with the elements you need to begin arranging fantastic tablescapes and vignettes with ease and style. And that ain't no hocus-pocus.

Making Tablescapes

Tablescapes are arrangements of items gathered in a grouping on top of a table. They're sometimes called *tabletop arrangements*. In each holiday chapter, I give you an inspiration list from which you can choose plenty of items to make a tablescape to fit your time, budget, and space, but typically, you can use anything as a prop for a great miniarrangement. Refer to my stylish stash list in this chapter if you just need a quick reminder of the things you can use.

A tablescape can include a centerpiece, or it can simply contain an arrangement of your favorite items. Tablescapes refer to the way things are laid out, like in a landscape painting. And they're not just for dinner anymore. They're wonderful to arrange on coffee tables, end tables, or any other occasional piece that lends itself to holiday decorating — even mantels or shelves.

Normally, you might have a simple tablescape already arranged on an occasional table. You may have arranged a tall candle set aside a small floral arrangement and a stack of thick coffee-table books. To adapt your everyday décor for the holidays, you can

 ✔ Add a small holiday-themed collection on top of the stacked books.

 ✔ Replace the stack of books with a stack of holiday-specific ones. Be sure that you don't place anything on top of them, so guests are encouraged to leaf through them leisurely.

✔ Replace your normal floral arrangement with a seasonal one.

✔ Change out the color of your candles.

✔ Add a holiday-themed item at the base of your candles, such as an ornament, some greenery, or another token representing the holiday.

✔ Remove your regular tablescape items and replace them entirely with snow villages or other holiday collections you may have.

Don't forget to take the opportunity at the holidays to dress up other tabletops that don't normally get duded up. Simple holiday items grouped together are an easy way to add holiday sparkle to any surface.

If you want to make your own tablescape, I have just the right formula. Simply gather and arrange the following items, or a combination of them, on no more than ⅓ of your table surface space to make an instant tablescape:

✔ **Light source** (lamp or candles — sometimes both).

✔ **Hard line accent** (photo frame, book, a collectible item).

✔ **Botanical element** (flower, bowl of fruit, plant or other item).

✔ **Fabric item** (a table topper, runner, ribbon, a tapestry remnant, a napkin.)

✔ **For the holidays:** Add only *one* holiday item to a premade tablescape, or make one or more of the previously listed objects holiday merchandise.

Making your own tablescapes is easy if you keep these few things in mind:

✔ **Gather interesting items of different textures together.** Good items to have are books, decorative plates displayed on stands, bowls filled with fruit or other decorative items, vases, flowers, candles, decorative orbs, and other home décor accessories.

✔ **Arrange items in staggering heights.** Stack a few books and use them underneath items to raise them if needed. If you have a lamp on a table, use that as your tallest height, and work with other smaller items to fill in your tablescape.

✔ **Take up no more than ⅓ of your table with a tablescape unless you don't intend to use the table for anything else but display.** You want your tablescape to stay intact, so leave room for people to set down drinks or the TV remote without bumping into your lovely arrangement.

✔ **Use your surfaces wisely.** If you set up a gorgeous tablescape on your coffee table but no one has a place to put their dishes, cups, or other items for which that coffee table was intended, you've defeated the purpose of decorating. Decorating is meant to enhance — not to hassle.

If you want to place a tablescape on a surface you may need to use unexpectedly, such as an ottoman, try arranging it on a decorative tray so that you can move or shift the display without having to take it down or rearrange it.

Making Vignettes Appear before Your Very Eyes

Vignettes, not meant for stage alone, are pleasing arrangements of furnishings or decorations that are picture perfect. And when I say picture perfect, I mean it literally when you're beginning to figure out how to style vignettes in your own home.

A vignette can be made anywhere — an entry hall, a wall, a sitting area. Outdoors, you can arrange vignettes on your front porch, lawn, or sidewalk. You may be used to seeing wonderfully visually merchandised windows in a department store, or an arranged setting of furniture and accessories in a furniture store — those are vignettes.

When you start to think about how to style vignettes in your home, you'll want to pay even closer attention to how the pros light and arrange these merchandised areas.

You see, your eye works much the same as a camera. You can only take in so much at a time. Besides mothers (who seem to have eyes in the backs of their heads), I don't know many who can see 360 degrees at one time. Okay, even though I'm a mother, I still haven't managed to be able to see everything at once. And neither can your guests. That's why knowing how to style a vignette makes sense for holiday decorating. It gathers decorative items together in one conducive scene to bring your attention and focus to it.

Don't think vignette's have to be larger than life either! Have you ever seen a small nativity scene on an expansive church lawn? Do you even see the church at first? Your eye strains to see the detail. And your vignettes can do the same.

Making vignettes is easy if you keep these things in mind:

✔ **Have a backdrop such as a wall, a house, or a landscape from which to build depth.** Arrange items to draw the viewer into your scene. Most likely, your vignette will have a tablescape of some sort except when you decorate outside for certain holidays. Tablescapes next to tombstones at Halloween doesn't exactly work does it?

✔ **Let the vignette tell a story.** For example, a front porch with two rocking chairs on each side of a small table with a large glass pitcher of lemonade and two glasses says, "Relax and take comfort here." Add an American flag waving in the breeze hung from the column and red, white, and blue bunting draped on the porch rail, and you have a picture of what America is like on the Fourth of July. And isn't it comforting?

Your vignettes at holidays like Yom Kippur should make you feel reflective and subdued. They should be entrenched in tradition. At holidays like Halloween, your vignettes should take on the scariest and spookiest feel. That's the beauty of holiday decorating with vignettes. You can achieve all these "feelings" simply by changing out the décor.

You can find many inspiration pieces, decorating ideas, and vignette-inspiring ideas in each holiday chapter. Simply choose an area to decorate and then decide where you want something holiday-ish to go. Use the tips in Chapter 6 to outline your room specs. Lay out items and furnishings you want to include in your vignette.

As you style your vignette, grab a large empty picture frame and hold it up to view your "set." You've seen those directors on TV that hold up their thumbs and first fingers to make a box and peer through it with one eye. They're getting an idea of how a scene will look through a camera's eye. You can do this, too! If nothing else, punch the bottom and top out of a cardboard box and look through it just to check your work. It's amazing how you can really edit a vignette by minimizing all distractions.

When you've styled what you think is a perfect vignette, grab a camera and look through the viewfinder. What do you see? Cameras have a way of taking out all dimension, flattening the look. If you still like what you see, congratulations. Success! If not, take a moment to gather a few more items, take a few more out, hide the cords, rearrange, or primp the setting as you like. Remember that it doesn't really have to be perfect, it should only convey the main message that you want to send holiday warmth and cheer (and that goes for any holiday!).

Vignettes do not stand alone. They're still a part of your home's overall appeal. Take that camera and move from your vignette to view the other parts of your room. See if you can make easy transitions from your vignette to your other decor.

Here's my instant formula for making holiday vignettes:

✔ **Focal point:** Is your eye automatically drawn to something you've decided to single out?

- **Tablescape:** Make sure that you have at least one tablescape in your vignette if you're arranging interiors. Exterior tablescape vignettes are fine, too, but for some holidays, you may not need one.

- **Vertical element:** A Christmas tree, hanging wreath, banner, tall item on tablescape, or other item to draw the eye up is always necessary.

- **Cluster of holiday items:** Instead of scattering a few items to cover a large area, group them close together to engage continuity.

- **Continuity to surroundings:** Does your vignette flow well from one room to the next? Does it match the room's feel? Does it make you have a particular "feeling" when you look at it? Stand back and evaluate.

- **Camera or photo frame test:** Remember to check your work by looking through a camera or eyeing your vignette design through an empty photo frame. Edit your vignette as necessary.

- **Lighting:** If you need to, use up lights, candles, or lamps to light up interior vignettes to draw attention to them; use spotlights, floodlights, luminarias, or porch lights to accent exterior vignettes. If you decorate with items that provide illumination themselves, you don't need to go to additional lighting measures.

Quick Fixes for Decorating Dilemmas

Having to decorate on the fly is a reality of holiday decorating. So use these tips when you need to make your own decorating magic.

Making items taller

Use books, boxes, pans flipped over, or pedestals to make items appear taller or to give them height. Use any item that's sturdy and can withstand the weight that you place on it. Make sure that the pedestal is wider than the base of the item placed on it. To hide boxes, pans, or other not-so-decorative items, drape table linens or large pieces of fabric over them and puddle the excess at the bottom.

Displaying collections

Group collections together instead of spreading them out around the house. Take the term literally: *A collection of items isn't a collection unless gathered in one place*. Line up glassware, gather seashells in a bowl, hang specialty ornaments together on one tiny tree instead of dispersing them among all the other inexpensive ornaments. Hang collectible plates together. Display greeting cards in one area of a room.

Collections make more sense when arranged together, and they provide interesting focal points that may otherwise be lost if separated. Find a niche where your collection will fit and then arrange to your heart's desire.

Adding texture

A well-designed home includes a variety of textures and surfaces. It's not hard to achieve. Think in terms of opposites. If you have a smooth surface, find a rough texture to place on it. If you have a soft surface, balance it with a hard lined item next to it (thus the couch and coffee table combo). If the couch is smooth leather, add chenille, tapestry, or velvet pillows in the winter. See? Just think in opposites.

Layers also add texture and dimension. If you refer to the tablescape section, you notice that a simple vase is beautiful sitting on a table, but add a lamp, a plant, some books, and a photo frame and it suddenly becomes a rich layered look. Either way, the vase still holds its beauty, but to add texture and dimension, just layer a few more items.

Patterns can also add visual texture to your surroundings. Your eye does give value and weight to decorative items and notices textural differences. A solid-colored comforter gets dressed up when accompanied by many pillows in separate prints or patterns.

Arranging and hanging pictures or banners

You may have a blank wall reserved for hanging decorative items, such as pictures, art, or banners. If you have reservations or face hanging things on your wall with much trepidation, don't worry. Here are two easy solutions to getting it right before you ever have to make a hole in the wall.

Place on the floor

Arrange your frames, decorative wall hangings, and other items on the floor to get a good sense of how they'll look on the wall. Then you can go about hanging one at a time, moving each piece from the floor to the wall.

Trace and tape

My favorite way of arranging items to be hung on a wall takes a bit more time and effort, but it seems to have the best effect.

Take plain newsprint and lay your decorative item on it. (Tape several sheets together if the newsprint isn't large enough.) Trace the outline of the item onto the newsprint, label it so you'll know which item it represents, cut it out, and tape it to your wall with painter's tape. You can remove, arrange, and rearrange until you get it right. Then go about hanging your items one at a time to replace all your traced drawings.

Adding color

Add color to your interiors by bringing in holiday colors as accents. Choose one or a collection of colors you want to use for any given holiday. Use my inspiration list at the beginning of each holiday chapter to give you some ideas of colors that you can use. Purchase accent items such as pillows, throws, table linens, flowers, or holiday merchandise in your chosen colors.

I have a collection of pretty and inexpensive clear glass bottles I bought at an import store. I fill them to the same level with water and add a few drops of food coloring to match the holiday theme or mood. Sometimes, I line them up in a sunny windowsill so that the sun can stream through them. At night, I line them up on a shelf or mantel and place tealight candles behind them to illuminate the color around the room. It's a very simple way to add a little holiday color without going crazy, and I can change it as often as I like, with any season.

Hanging decorations while protecting interiors

Office supplies are your best friends. An office stapler unfolded can staple paper items to your wall, transparent tape can secure lightweight items to walls and windows, bent paperclips are perfect S-shaped hooks to replace ornament hangers, and thumbtacks can hold numerous hanging objects such as wreaths, garland, and banners. None of these items make large holes or require a tool to secure decorations.

Before you go hammering large holes in your interior spaces for the holidays, try using some of these office supplies to be your own MacGyver.

Hiding ugly carpeting or floors

Outdated or worn floors are a common decorating dilemma. Until you can replace them, an easy solution is to place an area rug over them. If rugs aren't your game, try bringing the eye up, giving your guests something else to focus on. Decorate at eye level and keep decorations off or away from the floor. If floor decorating can't be helped (like presents placed under a tree), try to keep decorations to a minimum.

Masking a messy kitchen

At some point in time, during some sort of holiday, you may entertain in your home. In my home, everyone seems to gravitate to the kitchen whether I want them to or not. It's the hub of activity — warming, cooking, washing. I spend most of my time in there, so it's no wonder that if anyone wants to speak to me, he or she has to follow me to the kitchen. To say that my kitchen's a pretty sight is another thing.

Don't sweat it if your kitchen starts looking messy. If anyone criticizes, you can swiftly take his or her plate away till they straighten up, or you can use these quick tips that I've found helpful:

- Purchase some large plastic tubs to stack dirty dishes in and set them out of eyesight if possible.

- Install a temporary curtain to separate the staging area from eyesight. Maybe this is where you can hide those dirty dishes until you can get to them!

- Drape a table to the floor. If you won't be using a kitchen table for seating guests, you can stash all sorts of items underneath a table that's been draped with a tablecloth that touches the floor. If you can spare the space, rent or borrow a collapsible folding table and drape it. Not only can you use the extra tabletop or counter space, you can store all sorts of stuff underneath it. Use my instructions in Chapter 19 for making a tablecloth to fit your particular table if you can't find one premade.

Chapter 3

Discovering Tabletop Decorating Basics

In This Chapter

▶ Setting up centerpieces

▶ Arranging casual and formal table settings

▶ Folding napkins creatively

Set tables are often decorative showstoppers in their own right. If you've ever been to one of those fancy homes that are open to the public for tours, you've probably noticed that they keep the table set. Rarely does one of those homes have a bare dining table with perhaps a simple floral arrangement. Photos of dining rooms in a magazines or books are also always decked out to the nines — likewise, your table, no matter how big or small, should be set magnificently for the holidays.

Because most holidays are centered around gathering friends and family to the table, figuring out how to decorate your dining areas festively is an important part of decorating for the holidays. After reading this chapter, you'll know how to pick the right centerpiece, set the right place setting — formal or casual — and fold napkins like an origami expert.

Finding Your Center

Centerpieces are not reserved for flowers only. Many items, such as an arrangement of fruit, a candelabra, a gathering or grouping of ornaments, an empty vase that's artistic in it's design, or a clever arrangement of food, can become the centerpiece of a table.

First, check out the holiday chapters to get specific centerpiece ideas. Many holidays, especially religious holidays, have particular instructions rooted in tradition for placement and content.

After you've gathered some specific ideas for your centerpiece, you may need to decide on some basics, such as where to place centerpieces (and don't say, "In the center!" — I mean which tables, smarty pants), heights of the centerpieces, as well as the number of centerpieces. I provide you with those answers in the following sections.

What tables are worthy of centerpieces?

Besides the obvious dinner table, I like to have an arrangement of some sort on every surface that serves guests. An entry table with a guest book, a bar where drinks are served, and a buffet table are just a few examples of where centerpieces are appropriate or can be placed.

One small arrangement is enough for these tables. Though small, these centerpieces pull a room together and soften blank areas when they're not in use.

If you want to go it alone on these smaller arrangements and create your own centerpieces, check out Chapter 21 for some floral arrangement ideas.

Handling centerpiece height

Deciding how short or tall an arrangement should be depends on what kind of holiday entertaining you plan to do and where the centerpiece will go.

Dinner tables

Deciding on the height of your dinner table centerpiece is simple — just keep this one rule in mind: *People want to see each other*. Keep the top of centerpiece below eye level if it sets directly on the table. If you want a tall centerpiece, raise the base of it above eye level, so that people can look at one another underneath it.

You can't go wrong with smaller, low-profile arrangements on dining tables. They don't interfere with guests mingling while standing up or sitting down, and they draw attention down to beautiful table settings.

If you decide that you want to try out a taller centerpiece, check out the following tips to ensure that your centerpieces are at the right height:

✔ Sit down at your table in advance to get a measurement of what you consider eye level for most of your guests. Take this measurement to your florist and tell him or her what your minimum requirements are for where the bottom of the arrangement should be.

✔ Place an arrangement that may block eye contact on a tall, thin pedestal to bring the base of the arrangement above eye level, or rearrange the flowers in a very tall vase.

✔ Choose tall candlesticks or short votives rather than placing flickering candles in an eye-level area. You don't want to blind yourself while chatting it up with guests!

Buffets

For buffets, you focus on the food and the table itself rather than on other people, so you want a centerpiece that demands eye contact, not one that avoids it like on dining tables.

So a towering arrangement elevated above the spread and at eye level works wonders because

✔ It makes an incredible statement, bringing the eye automatically from anywhere in the room directly to the location of the food.

✔ It gives your buffet height as opposed to a picnic-style layout where everything is the same level.

✔ It remains high above the steam trays, so the flowers don't wilt as easily around hot hors d'oeuvres and will never come in contact with the food (well, unless it just falls!).

Number and size of centerpieces

How many centerpieces you need depends on the size and number of tables you're using.

As a general rule, for smaller tables (seating two to four people), one medium-sized centerpiece, approximately 18 inches in diameter, will do. You don't want to crowd a table with an oversized centerpiece arrangement that doesn't allow for any shifting in stemware or place settings.

For larger tables (seating six or more people), I usually go by the *one-for-every-six rule,* making the arrangement itself just a bit larger or fuller (20 to 24 inches and up). A table that seats six can fit one medium- to large-sized centerpiece (18 to 24 inches) without crowding the table, as shown in Figure 3-1.

For larger table centerpieces, you can insert filler material, such as candlesticks, on either side of it. Or you can place an odd number grouping of votives or other small objects in between.

The same holds true for large banquet seating where you have very long tables or tables that are connected end to end. You should place a centerpiece in the middle of every six place settings, not counting chairs at the heads of tables (see Figure 3-2). Centerpieces need to be medium- to large-sized ones (20 to 24 inches or more), but again, any dead space in between can easily be filled with votives or other small items. You do want to be careful not to go overboard, though. You still need to leave room for butter dishes, salt and pepper shakers, gravy boats, and so on. Just keep that in mind.

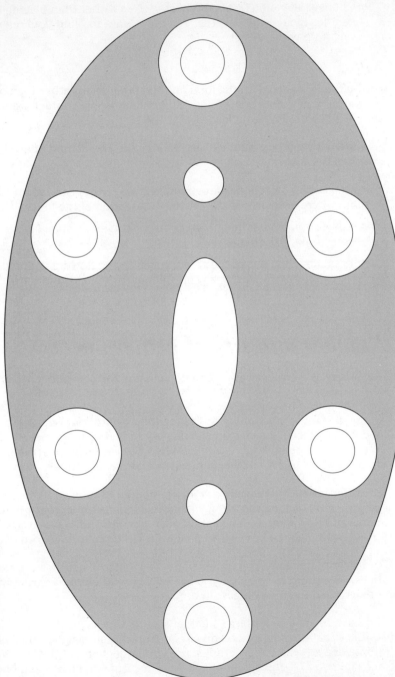

Figure 3-1:
Centerpiece
placement
for a table of
six guests.

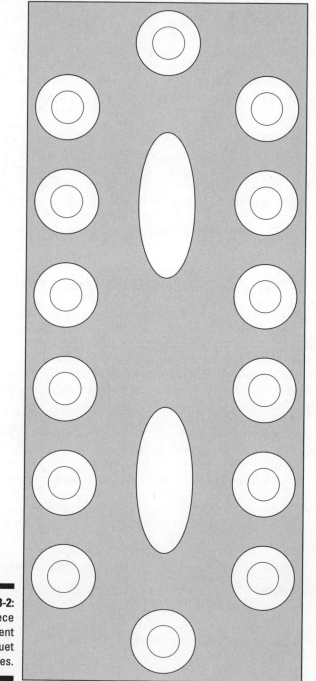

Figure 3-2:
Centerpiece
placement
for banquet
tables.

Table Setting Basics

You may choose, for certain holidays, to set your table up and keep it set up through the holiday season. I give you some basic table setting layouts here, but go back to Chapter 2 to find out how to design beautiful tablescapes. There, I show you how to incorporate many different items to make a beautiful table complete.

All decorative purposes aside, you want to keep your table settings simple for dinner parties: Keep utensils, glassware, and dinnerware down to a minimum — unless, of course, you just love washing all those dishes. Don't set out a plethora of utensils unless your guests will actually use them during the course of the meal. Setting out lobster forks when you're serving turkey will just confuse everyone. You don't need the additional clutter or confusion, and guests need to feel comfortable that they're using the right forks.

Casual dining: No pretension, just food!

Most holidays shared between family and friends are perfect for dining casually yet stylishly. Casual table settings allow people to feel at home and are perfect for less formally decorated holidays, such as St. Patrick's Day, Halloween, and, sometimes, Hanukkah. Although you can always go all out for any holiday, a casual table offers guests an opportunity to graze at the buffet, filling their plates as often as they like, or scrape every last drop of delicious soup from bowls.

To show you an example of a casual table setting, I assume that you want to serve a salad, soup, bread, a main course, and a beverage. If you serve coffee and dessert, you can place these items on the table right before serving them. Following Figure 3-3, a casual table setting comes together simply:

- Place dinner plates approximately 2 inches from the table's edge and center them squarely in front of each chair.

- Put soup bowls on top of the dinner plates.

- Salad plates go above the forks to the left side of the dinner plate.

- Position bread plates slightly above the salad plate closer to the dessert fork.

- Silverware should be laid out in the order that guests will use it: Work your way from the outside in. Forks belong on the left of the dinner plate; knives and spoons go to the right. Sharp knife edges should always face the dinner plate. Butter knives should be laid flat on the bread plate with the cutting edge, again, facing in the direction of the dinner plate. Dessert forks or spoons can be placed horizontally at the top of the dinner plate.

✔ Place water glasses above the dinner knife. Optional red and white wine-glasses or champagne flutes are staggered around the water glass.

✔ Napkins go to the left of the plate, inside a drinking glass, or in the center of the plate.

✔ Place cards (perfectly optional) work best placed above the dessert utensil, centered with the plate.

Feeling formal

If you're hosting a Passover Seder or an Easter brunch, you may opt for a more formal table setting. Valentine's Day is also a great opportunity to whip out the fine wedding china and crystal to make a dinner at home special.

Figure 3-3:
Here's a lovely but informal place setting.

2"

For a full-blown formal dinner party, you can refer to Figure 3-4 to add more detail to your place settings as needed: The following list corresponds to the numbers in the illustration.

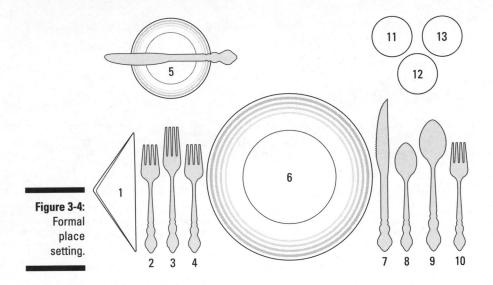

Figure 3-4:
Formal
place
setting.

1. Napkin

2. Salad fork

3. Dinner fork

4. Dessert fork

5. Bread and butter plate, with butter knife

6. Dinner plate

7. Dinner knife

8. Teaspoon

9. Soup spoon

10. Cocktail fork

11. Water glass

12. Red wine glass

13. White wine glass

All sorts of utensils are laid out here, but don't add them to your table unless you intend to use them with a course you are serving.

Protecting your precious upholstery

Scared to death that your upholstery may get slammed by a stray glass of Christmas red wine? Planning on a pretty wild Purim? You have plenty of decorative options to protect your chairs from the occasional mishap that may come with holiday entertaining at home.

If your upholstery is worth protecting and you entertain a lot (or plan to), check into these easy fabric options that can be thrown in the wash with no discomfort or guilt of host/hostess or guest. It will make you and your guest more at ease so that you can relax and enjoy the holiday, serve whatever you want, and never have to worry about the expensive furniture again.

Slipcovers

Make your own or purchase inexpensive pre-made slipcovers for your dining room chairs. The selection in fabrics can't be beat. Not only do they come in a vast array of colors to match any holiday, you can usually find them in neutrals and textures that go with any occasion. The pricier slipcovers found at boutiques, some department stores, and specialty shops come in gorgeous cotton and synthetic sheers, patterns, and prints, allowing the gorgeous architectural detail of your chairs show through.

Chairseat slipcovers are a great option for those who just want chair seat upholstery protected. But because chair seats come in all shapes and sizes, you may have to have them custom made or try your hand at making your own. Many patterns are available on the market today.

Chairseat slipcovers are my favorite for changing out the look of my dining room for every season and holiday and are more cost-effective than traditional chair slipcovers because they use less fabric. They're easier to wash and store, again, because of the smaller size, and they make terrific additions to your holiday décor.

Chair runner

Perhaps the easiest way to protect your dining room chairs is with a simple elongated rectangle of fabric. A chair runner allows you to protect most of your upholstery because it runs down the center of your chair, floor-to-floor, and is cinched at the waist of your chair (where the back meets the seat) with a gorgeous ribbon, fabric tie, corded tassel, or other belt made of creative materials. I've used a length of beaded trim to hold the chair runner in place and attached a small bouquet of fresh flowers to the back of the tie. Try adding themed holiday touches to the ties of your slipcovers or table runners. Your choices are pretty much unlimited when it comes to fabrics and materials to cinch up the runner. Purchase or make them with sheers or daring fabrics. Get creative with chair runners. They're a beautiful way of protecting your upholstered dining chairs easily while making a dramatic statement. For instructions on how to make a simple chair runner, go to Chapter 19.

Protecting your fabrics

Most premade slipcovers seem to have a good protective coating already infused into the fabric to bead up water, helping to clean up spills. If you make your own or want additional protection for your slipcovers, buy an aerosol can of fabric protector, usually found at supermarkets or discount stores. If applied according to the manufacturer's directions, this invisible layer helps resist dirt, oil, and water-based spots. You can also find carpet protector if you want to help save that antique Oriental rug. Just remember to test the product in a small area before applying to the whole piece.

Napkin Folding Made Easy

Just as a beautiful bow can set off a floral arrangement, a crisply starched napkin, or weighty paper dinner napkin, folded in interesting shapes brings art to the table and can accentuate a decorated holiday table with style.

You can do many of these quick, easy napkin folds in this section in just a few minutes. After you get the hang of it, you may find that these napkin folds are easy enough to do anytime — not just at the holidays!

If you want to expand on your skills a bit more, try some of the specialty folds at the end of this chapter. They're perfect for theming your table to each specific holiday.

For care and cleaning of your napkins and other table linens, don't forget to check out Chapter 7 for more details.

Basic napkin fold

Placed under silverware or arranged neatly atop a plate, a basic napkin fold is a safe way of always getting it right.

Fold a napkin in half, then in half again to make a square. Fold the napkin again and press the folds. As an alternative, fold two sides of the napkin square into the center and press. Flip the napkin over so that you display crisp and clean edges.

If you have monogrammed linens, beaded edging, or specialty napkins, a basic napkin fold is probably really all you need. But if you want to try out other options, here are just a few of my favorites.

Fan-fold options

Using a simple accordion-style pleating technique, you can do a few napkin folds that work really well with napkin rings. Place these napkins in the center of your plate at each place setting.

Fan

This simple fold is a classic (see Figure 3-5).

Fold your napkin in half. Beginning at one short end, start folding the napkin in an accordion style, making folds approximately every inch.

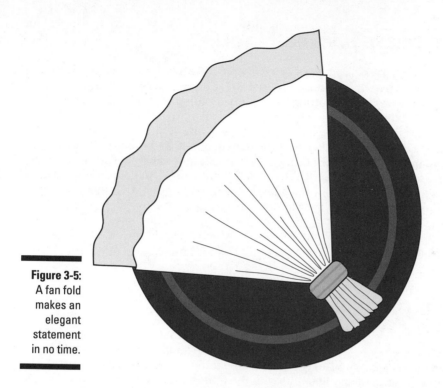

Figure 3-5:
A fan fold makes an elegant statement in no time.

Insert one folded end into a napkin ring. Push the napkin ring up no further than ⅓ from the bottom. Fan out the top pleats.

Double fan

This fan-folded napkin provides a fuller fan than the previous napkin fold. It looks especially good tucked into an empty water glass or wineglass if the napkin is starched very well.

To begin, start accordion pleating an unfolded napkin, making folds approximately every inch. Fold the pleated napkin in half and thread the folded end into a napkin ring or tuck it into a water glass. Fan out the top pleats.

Fanned Bow

A fanned bow allows special holiday napkin rings to become the centerpieces of your place settings.

To make a fanned bow, fold the top and bottom edges to the middle of the napkin. Beginning at one short end, start folding the napkin in an accordion style, making folds approximately every inch.

Insert one folded end into a napkin ring and push the napkin ring up to the middle of the folded napkin. Fan out pleats on each side.

Decorative pocket

Decorative pockets (see Figure 3-6) can hold silverware, flowers, place cards, or any other treat that you want to tuck in. You can place it in the center of each plate at each place setting, or if it'll be holding utensils, you can place it to the left of the plate.

To make a decorative pocket, fold the napkin in half and then fold it in half again to make a square (or start with a folded paper napkin). Turn the napkin to make a diamond shape with the folded point closest to you. Separate the free edges and begin folding each layer down to the point. Continue folding down layers, leaving last layer up.

Tuck the sides of the napkin to the back. Insert your silverware or other desired item.

Buffet parcel

Try this pretty wrapping technique for when you want to accent your table with special ribbon. To do this fold, fold the napkin in half and then fold it in half again to make a square (or start with a folded paper napkin). Turn the napkin to make a diamond shape with the folded point away from you. Center the silverware on the napkin close together.

Figure 3-6:
A decorative pocket fold is pretty as well as functional.

Fold the side points in to touch the edges of the silverware, making small triangles. Overlap edges over the cutlery and tie a ribbon around the center of the parcel.

Holiday-specific napkin folds

Certain holidays lend themselves to getting creative with napkin folding techniques. In this section, you find other options for making napkins a truly themed decorative accent. Impress your friends. Try a few.

Heart

At Valentine's Day, this heart fold is a great alternative to make your holiday table special (see Figure 3-7).

Start by folding a napkin in half. Fold it again lengthwise, making one long rectangle. Hold your finger at the bottom center of the napkin and fold each side up, making a point (see Figure 3-8). Fold triangles under at each top corner of the napkin to make a heart.

Insert a rosebud in the center fold for a sweet variation. You can also use the reverse side of the heart fold to tuck in valentine cards, utensils, or any other sentimental item.

Figure 3-7:
Heart
napkin fold.

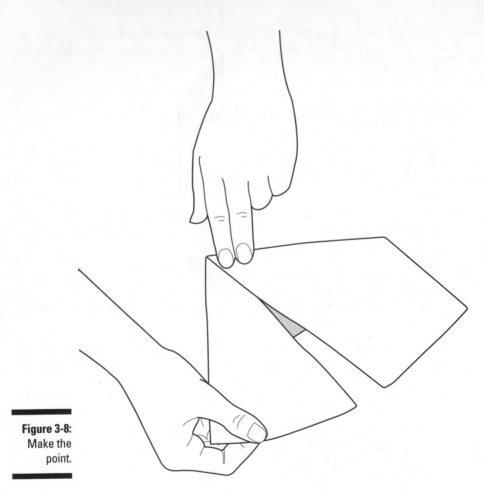

Figure 3-8:
Make the
point.

Four-leaf clover

Although I call the fold in Figure 3-9 a four-leaf clover (when created with a green napkin for St. Patrick's Day), you can use this particular fold for any holiday. Its center lends itself to holding treasures such as chocolate gelts for Hanukkah, sprigs of evergreen at Christmas, or a small basket with a beautifully decorated egg nestled in it at Easter.

To begin, fold each corner of the napkin into the center. Repeat again by folding the newly made corners into the center (see Figure 3-10). Press or crease folds into place.

Holding the folds together in the center, flip the napkin over Pressing a finger firmly in the middle of the napkin to hold folds in place, reach under the napkin and begin pulling all the points out (shown in Figure 3-11) until complete.

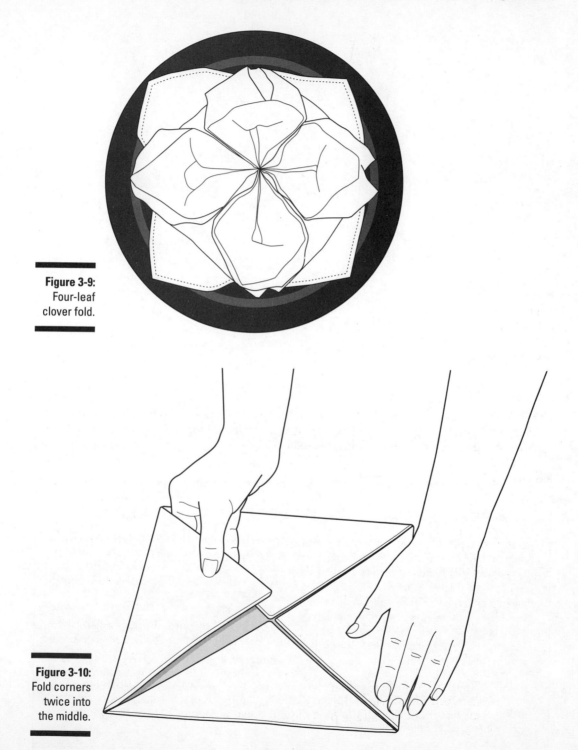

Figure 3-9:
Four-leaf
clover fold.

Figure 3-10:
Fold corners
twice into
the middle.

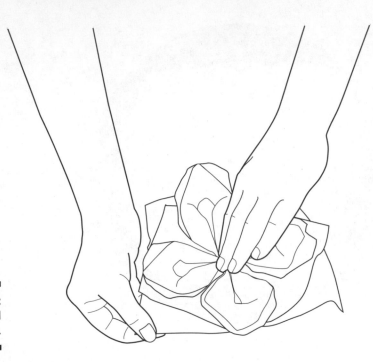

Figure 3-11:
Pull out all
the points.

GI cap

For any patriotic holiday, this little napkin fold is sure to be a hit if you can
keep it off the kids' heads. This fold, shown in Figure 3-12, is best for heavily
starched napkins, or paper napkins.

No folding, no laundry: Fanning paper napkins

On occasion, you may want to just whip out the
paper napkins and forget about laundering your
cloth ones. This technique, made popular by
busy bartenders everywhere, makes grabbing
only one beverage or dinner napkin quick and
easy. It's equally as easy to do and a great way
to display your paper napkins instead of just
plunking out a stack from the plastic wrap they
came in. Try it — it's easy!

1. Remove a stack of napkins (3 inches high
   or less) from the package. Fan one edge of
   the napkins (as you would a deck of cards)
   to separate the edges, keeping them from

sticking together. Place the stack on a solid
surface, such as a table.

2. Turn a glass on it's side and place it on top of
   the stack of napkins. Press the glass firmly
   on the stack and start spinning it clockwise
   on the napkins. Continue spinning until the
   stack has swirled to your liking.

Work in small stacks. You can always place several small stacks together to make larger ones,
so that you don't have to replenish them often.
Use two different holiday colors and layer them
for a really cool look.

Figure 3-12:
GI cap fold.

To begin, fold a napkin in half with the fold at the top and the edges toward you. Fold each side in to the center.

At the top of one side, pull apart one of the folds to press into a triangle shape (see Figure 3-13). Fold the outside edge of the napkin to the back. Repeat with other side (see Figure 3-14).

Fold the bottom flap up to the bottom of the triangles, and then again at the fold, and press or crease into place (see Figure 3-15). Flip the napkin over and repeat for the other side.

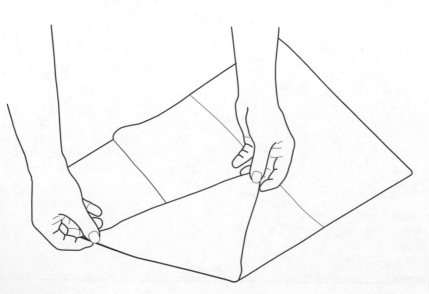

Figure 3-13:
Pull apart
and press
into a
triangle.

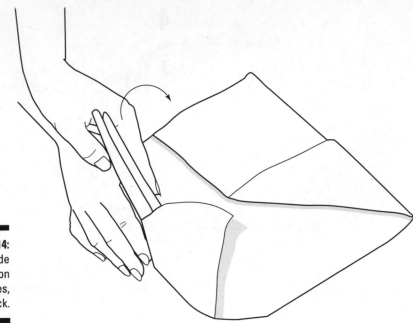

Figure 3-14:
Fold outside
edges, on
both sides,
to the back.

Pull apart the sides of the cap and place on the center of a plate.

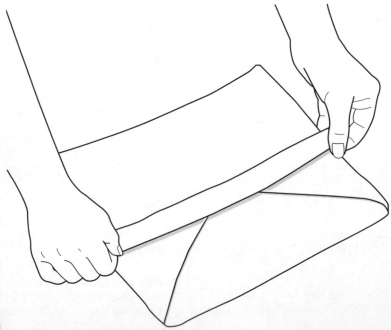

Figure 3-15:
Fold bottom
edges up
twice and
press into
place.

Chapter 4

Finding Ideas and Inspiration

• •

In This Chapter

▶ Locating sources for ideas and inspiration

▶ Analyzing inspiration pieces for decorating

▶ Looking at things in a with a whole new perspective (or, in a whole new light)

• •

Chuck the notion that you have to be a creative genius to come up with ideas for the holidays! Although everyone is creative in some way, anyone can use a little bit of inspiration when feeling stuck in a rut or at a loss for where to start gathering ideas.

You can take inspiration from ideas all around you to find the right look for your home or to update what you already have. In this chapter, I show you some great places to discover that much-needed inspiration and give you some ideas to achieve your holiday decorating goals.

Finding Your Inspiration

You don't need to sit and wait for an epiphany of divine inspiration — we're just talking about decorating, for heaven's sake! Finding inspiration for your holiday decorating is as easy as watching TV, flipping through magazines and books, and yes (my favorite) shopping at retail stores. These resources that I can access every day give tons of ideas and inspiration for coming up with clever holiday vignettes. Want to know how to turn one of your favorite pastimes into an aha moment? Read on. This section gives you ideas on how to turn the ho-hum into holiday inspiration!

Taking tips from the tube

Prime time, daytime, cable, and even public access television shows have great ideas that can be adapted to suit your decorating style. PBS (Public Broadcasting Stations) airs various craft and design shows. Morning talk and news shows on the major networks do great style and craft segments. And your local television stations sometimes air local slants and sources on decorating for the holidays. But don't limit yourself to shows that are specifically about crafts and decorating. You can find some of the best ideas in regular prime time, daytime, and cable television programs.

Tape your favorite shows, so that you can scan them later for ideas. You can fast-forward through segments, play back things that you want to see demonstrated again, and keep up with special holiday programming, referring back to your taped shows when needed.

So check your local listings for days and times, sit back, relax, and take notes! You're about to discover your next great idea. Who knew watching the ol' boob tube would come in handy?

Picking up on the prime time extravaganza

Because television producers spend lots of money hiring the very best set designers to define their shows' looks, great decorating ideas abound in nearly every prime time program. Take some time to watch your favorite shows, which are excellent sources for swiping decorating ideas.

Take your decorating cues by checking out the color of the walls, sofa, accessories, and treatments behind those fabulous actors. Make notes to yourself if you like the layout, the colors, the way something was arranged, or the accessories used on the set, and then implement some of those ideas in your own home.

Although you can watch any show to gain great ideas, check out the shows in the following list to discover a wide variety of decorating styles that you can incorporate into your own home.

- ✔ *The West Wing* (NBC): During the holiday season, this simulated White House is decorated for Christmas. The style is traditional, elegant, lush and (sorry, no pun intended) politically correct. Grab your inspiration here if you need ideas for decorating architecturally beautiful elements done to perfection.

- ✔ *Friends* (NBC): This show always features Monica's fabulous apartment decorated in casual style. It's always comfortable, simple, and chic. The *Friends* set is a perfect example of hip and trendy style with touches of traditional elements like crocheted afghans or quilts flopped over the sofas.

  The show even addresses the blending of Jewish and Christian holidays. If you have a blend of cultures, styles, and eclectic tastes, *Friends* is a great show for gathering ideas to decorate sensationally.

- ✔ *Everybody loves Raymond* (CBS): This program shows family decorating at its best. You may see construction paper hearts taped to the windows for Valentine's Day or homemade gingerbread houses at Christmastime. The house is moderate in size, warm, and lived in. This show makes no pretentious gestures when it comes to the holidays. It's a great place to see examples of holiday craft ideas for kids and how you can blend them in with your decorating.

✔ *Frasier* (NBC): If you pride yourself on being a modern minimalist, tune in to this popular program. From the beginning, this show has set a style pattern of being sleek, stylish, and contemporary — well, excluding the dad's broken-down recliner, of course. The designers make very subtle changes in furnishings that never distract the viewer, and holiday decorating (again, besides the few that the dad makes) is done tastefully and in an upscale fashion.

The shows listed in this section are certainly filled with inspiration, but you aren't limited to just prime time TV. Keep reading to discover the drama that makes daytime television another great decorating idea resource.

Soaking up soap sensations

Lucky for us, every soap opera character lives in a mansion or perfectly styled home — making soap operas a great resource for decorating ideas. Pay attention to the set designs the next time you watch a soap. They have the most elaborate sets, which reflect seasonal changes, and their holiday decorating is over-the-top. So watch some soap operas for inspiration (yeah, that's it, you're watching strictly for *inspiration* — you're not hooked or anything), and make notes of what catches your eye. Besides, you can catch up on what's happened in the last few seasons — it's research after all!

Connecting to cable how-to programming

Cable networks specialize in giving viewers a magazine format in 30-minute and hour-long shows. They bring in guests, do demonstrations, and show before-and-after shots. You can always discover something new when watching these programs.

Home and Garden Television (HGTV) has an exhaustive list of shows worth watching to get ideas; some of my favorites are *Sensible Chic, Design on a Dime,* and *Decorating Cents*. But don't forget about other networks, such as The Discovery Channel *(The Christopher Lowell Show),* The Learning Channel *(Trading Spaces, While You Were Out, Designing For The Sexes),* DIY network, Oxygen, and the Style network to name a few, which all provide how-to programming for holiday decorating.

These particular networks air shows on everything from decorating to cooking. During the holidays, you can expect most of the shows to have at least one episode that focuses on holiday-specific how-to ideas. As with all television programming, check your local listings for times and channels.

Most of these shows have accompanying Web sites. Some sites give really good instructions; some don't, but it's always good to check. Plus, you can see their season lineup and topics at the click of a mouse. Some Internet sites send you reminders for when to watch! Talk about serving up some programming! Later in this chapter, you can read more about surfing the Web.

Perusing magazines and books

Glancing through magazines and books is a great way to find ideas. With all the decorating, women's, lifestyle, special-interest, and style magazines on the market, you have plenty of pages to add to your decorating notebook or idea files (flip to Chapter 6 to find out how to put one of these together). In addition, you can get ideas from catalogs, craft books, leaflets, newspapers — basically, anything in print.

Just because you have dozens of different publications to choose from doesn't mean that you have to spend a fortune on them! Go to your local library. Look at current *and* back issues. Depending on your library's policies, they may have several years of back issues, and in one sitting, you can get enough ideas to last you through many seasons. You can also spend a leisurely afternoon sipping a cup of coffee curled up in chair at your favorite bookstore. Only buy the magazines and books that really appeal to you and that add value to your home library. Browse through the rest for free.

Taking regular trips to the library, supermarket, and bookstore to check out books and magazines is a great way of expanding your knowledge base. Look for holiday books, holiday magazines, and holiday items displayed together. And don't forget to shop these special displays right before or after the holidays. Many times, retailers discount holiday items deeply, so you can buy your inspirations for a song.

Gather all your ideas into one file, preferably your decorating notebook (find out more about decorating notebooks in Chapter 6). If you own the magazine, you can rip the pages out to bind in your notebook. If you're just looking through it, either make a copy or sketch out the design idea and make detailed notes, so that you can refer to them later. Make sure to note where you got the idea and on what page number you found it — you may want to refresh your memory later.

The following list gives you some ideas on finding the best publication resources for decorating success:

✔ **Find decorating magazines that are different from your usual style.** When you're looking at the rows of magazines, how do you know which ones to pick? Chances are good that you already have some favorites, but don't start there. If you're looking for ideas and inspiration — meaning that you're really trying to get out of a rut — try magazines that you normally pass up. Look carefully at each photo and product page. Although a magazine may not be your particular style, you may discover a unique way of displaying items, a color that you never thought of trying, or the use of a product that you never knew existed. You already know that your standard favorites give you plenty of ideas; now, open your mind for different inspiration to strike.

✔ **Select special-interest magazines.** Special-interest publications (SIP's) are magazines that contain information on one specific topic; they may be published one or many times a year. Usually, SIPs are from magazine publishers that collect ideas and inspiration for individual holidays, techniques (like stamping, faux finishing, stenciling, and so on), or rooms (bed, bath, kitchen, and so on). Often, a quick trip to the check-out stand at a supermarket can get you an armload of inspiration from these special publications.

✔ **Use stylebooks for ideas to tweak your current décor.** If you have a particular style of decorating, say French country, southwestern, or garden style, you probably already have a good idea of what will work or compete with your established décor. Tweaking styles for the holidays means incorporating what you have with what you want. Stylebooks can help you get ideas.

Combine elements found in any decorating stylebook with holiday elements. For example, tuck sprigs of dried lavender into a holiday wreath to give it a wonderful French country flair. Drape chili-pepper garland around banisters at Christmastime, or display statues of howling wolves at Halloween if southwestern flair is your thing.

✔ **Thumb through holiday-specific books.** You can find many books on specific holidays. If you prefer one holiday over another or you want to celebrate a holiday not covered in this book, head to your library or bookstore to find some books that cover your specific holiday.

Surfing the Web

Hey, I *run* an Internet site (www.creatinghomedecor.com). Do you think that I'm going to forget to include checking the Web for great ideas and inspiration?

In addition to all the great ideas that you find everywhere else, don't forget the abundance of resources on the Internet, which just happen to be available all the time — for free! So when you're up at four in the morning from your neighbors annoying Christmas lights flashing in your window, you can find out how to fight fire with fire, or at least find out how to make a light blocking window shade.

Most magazines, books, and television shows have an online presence that dishes up fresh content from wiring a lamp to fixing a fence. In addition, they give sources, excerpt from their print pages (if applicable), and compile seasonal information in one place. These sites are wonderful sources of inspiration.

And don't forget that you can also find a wealth of homemade sites produced by enthusiasts of just about any topic. They care, as I do, about pulling together great information from lots of sources on their particular topic of interest.

To find Web sites, plug in your holiday keywords to your favorite search engine, such as Yahoo! or Google, to come up with pages upon pages of sites to view.

Be sure to enter *specific* search terms, such as "how to make a clay dreidel" or "how to make New Year crackers," into search engines instead of "dreidel" or "crackers". That way, the search engine can give you shorter lists of sites that are more specific to the information that you're looking for.

Cruising retail stores

Retail stores change out merchandise seasonally, so they're a natural choice for gathering ideas for the holidays. Not only do stores know how to decorate, they also know how to create props, style, and, if they're really good, sell merchandise by the way they display it. Most stores try to display only the items they have available for sale. So if you see something in a store's front window that you really like, chances are good that you can buy it on the spot.

Visual merchandisers (the people who make the great storefront displays) work with tiny spaces and challenges everywhere. They have to make sure that their displays are secure, don't pose hazards, and are properly lit. (Gee, and I thought I had it bad when I didn't have an outlet for my Christmas lights!) Take some ideas from these decorating masters, and you'll be able to create an attractive, safe, and maybe even kidproof, holiday display.

Visual merchandisers often make *vignettes* (little 3-D decorative snapshots of life). They can take a normal item and frame it so that your eye is drawn to its sparkle, or to another design element like shape or color. When you find a good vignette in a retail store or window, stop and sketch it in your mind or on paper. You've probably seen hundreds of vignettes in stores in your life, so think about why this particular one has caught your eye.

Make notes to yourself. Do you like the layout, the colors, the way something was arranged in staggered heights, or maybe how filled out the area was? Did you like the basic furnishings, or was it the accessories that you adored? How did the vignette make you feel?

Put these notes about your favorite vignettes in your decorating notebook (see Chapter 6 for more information on decorating notebooks; see Chapter 2 for more info on making vignettes). You may not use them this season or where you are now, but you can certainly draw inspiration from them in the future or aspire to them when decorating in general.

Using Inspiration Pieces

Every interior designer or decorator I've ever seen on TV or in a magazine always seems to refer to an "inspiration piece" when he or she shows off beautifully done rooms. What is an *inspiration piece*? Simply put, it's any item that inspires you for choosing colors, theme, or style for your decorated room.

My inspiration pieces have ranged from an antique iron bed that my grandmother salvaged from her barn to a piece of pottery I found at my local garden shop. I saw an episode of *Trading Spaces* (it's on The Learning Channel [TLC] if you're one of the handful of remaining people who's never seen the show) where one of the designers used a scrabble board to design a man's basement game room. She drew inspiration from the colors of the squares to do accent pillows and accessorize, and she used the square shapes as inspiration to mask off the floor into a tiled grid pattern.

Analyzing your inspiration piece

Suppose that you decide to use white tulips as your inspiration. To analyze how white tulips can inspire your room, take out a piece of paper and a pencil and break it down like this:

Colors

List colors that you can use, such as a soft white (derived from the petals), soft to bright yellow (from the stamen or anthers), black (from the pistils or filaments), rich green (from the stem), light green with touches of yellow (from the leaves).

Using this initial list, I'd choose one of the colors, such as the light green or yellows, for decorative items to hang on the walls, reserving white for perhaps the furniture pieces or accent trim. I'd use black for accessory pieces, such as throw pillows, iron architectural accents, lampshades, vases, and other subtle decorative items.

Complementary colors

Don't stop your possible color list with the hues defined from the inspiration piece alone. List all colors that have a relationship to the item. With tulips, any color of tulips, flowers, and fauna can blend beautifully in this decor. Likewise, if you used a cup of coffee as your inspiration piece, you'd also list cream, sugar, cinnamon, cocoa, and other relational object colors as complementary colors. Remember that nothing stands alone. If you keep this in mind, you'll never be afraid of choosing colors again!

Patterns

Because a tulip doesn't really have a pattern per se, you can use any pattern in the colors listed above. Examples of patterns include checks, stripes, damask, polka dots, floral, scenes, and so on. Look at your inspiration piece for shapes and patterns repeated. Add those elements to your list.

Textures

The petals of a tulip are silky and somewhat waxy to the touch. The pistil represents clean hard lines, and the furry pollen-bearing stamen gives the flower texture. Using this analogy, possible textures you can use in decorating include silk, chintz, soft leather, sisal, bamboo or wood, chenille, velvets, and so on.

Related objects

List objects related to tulips, such as grasses, baskets, ribbon, vases, water, earth (as in the color), sky, iron, and picket fences. Remember that nothing stands alone. Everything touches something else.

Developing your style and theme

After you go through the relationship process with your inspiration piece, you can get a firm grasp on what style and theme starts developing, depending on your likes and dislikes. By using the white tulip for inspiration, you can go with several decorating styles. A classic upscale decorating theme can be achieved by using damasks and silks, clean lines, and rich woods. Or, you can go garden-style with all sorts of architectural garden elements, or you can go Zen-like, using all the elements of the earth. And still, a casual and eclectic style can be achieved by throwing bits and pieces of any listed item into a room; they all go together because they all relate.

Also, by going through this process, you may find that a particular "inspiration piece" doesn't work for the area you intended, but it can work out perfectly for another room in your home.

So really, you can use *anything* that you love, find, or desire and bring your next decorating project to an "inspired" level. Throughout each holiday chapter in Part III, I give you a list of items that you can use as inspiration pieces. From there, you can decorate with bits and pieces of things that speak to you. Find your inspiration!

Assessing What You Already Have

Whether you want to change items that you already own or desperately need some budget-conscious ways to begin defining your holiday style, you can start by repurposing, reusing, recycling, and restyling — four closely related ways of using what you already have, yet still different techniques! Let me explain.

Repurposing

Repurposing means to use an item that's normally used for one thing (like a throw or painter's drop cloth made of cotton canvas) and change it into something else for another function, like turning it into pillows or a slipcover. Repurposing items can mean simply looking at new retail items in a different light. A cool egg cup can hold a single ball ornament, making a unique place card (simply write the person's name in a metallic paint pen on the ornament's surface). A copper kettle can become a fireplace accent by holding mounds of scented pinecones that are ready to be tossed into the fire. Think about *transforming* items from their usual purpose into something else. Repurposing is one of the most creative ways of turning new and previously owned items into works of art.

Reusing

Reusing items can save you big bucks when decorating for the holidays. Items that are reusable for decorating, such as menorahs, wreaths, bows, and twinkle lights, can save you money. The idea here is to invest once and then use many times for many holidays.

White lights, for example, are heavily used at Christmas. But couldn't you warm up a romantic Valentine's Day night by stringing some up on a balcony or porch for a chilly, snuggly nightcap? Or think about reusing them for a sparkling Fourth of July get-together. Use them on fences, rope off festivity parameters that may be hard to see in the dark, or wind them around tree limbs for lighting your evening from above. You can take individual items from one holiday into the next in many ways if you just plan in advance.

Recycling

I'm a huge fan of recycling. When I lived in Manhattan, it was a common occurrence to see furniture, rugs, lamps, and accessories thrown in a pile in front of apartments. It was also common to see well-dressed urbanites sifting through heaps and carting them home to recycle them into their own homes. Talking about dumpster diving going chic!

Recycling, for this book's purposes, means taking an item that's meant for the trash and turning it into a decorative item. For example, wire clean, empty jars (vintage or hodgepodge) together with aluminum wire, making them into sparkling tealight holders. A roadside chair, with the caning busted out of the seat, turns into a Thanksgiving decorating treasure by placing a large potted mum inside the opening for a welcoming autumnal feel at Thanksgiving.

Yes, you have to be somewhat crafty, and you can't be afraid of cleaning things. Most of all, you have to be daring enough to dive into a pile of rubble to get to that section of picket fencing in order to recycle it into a Halloween vignette.

Trash to treasure. It can be a beautiful thing.

Restyling

Restyling makes ready-made items better. Take a slipcover and embellish it! Have an old wreath? Take out faded flowers or ornaments and add new items or a fresh bow. What about old ornaments? Paint, stencil, stamp, write on, glue on, stick on — well, you get it. Embellish your heart out. Restyling takes items to a new, personalized level. You can breathe new life into an item by updating it or giving it a whole new look. Restyling is perfect for you if you're the type of person who never accepts things as they are and says, "But wait till I get my hands on it!"

Flex your creative muscles by repurposing, restyling, recycling, or reusing. Look at things with an eye for what's possible instead of frowning on heaps of stale stuff. By changing the way you look at things, you can find inspiration and ideas all around you.

Part II
The Practical Stuff: Money, Space, and More

The 5th Wave   By Rich Tennant

"It's always hard to know with Denise whether she's decorating for a 4th of July party or having a yard sale."

In this part . . .

During the holidays, you may find yourself trying to juggle your schedule, budget, and space for decorating! In this part, you find ideas and tools for getting organized. You begin gathering all your ideas together, creating your own decorating notebook, and charting your path through the hectic holidays with ease. And to help you take care of your holiday items, you find a complete guide on cleaning and storing decorations, so that they last for many years to come.

Chapter 5

Budgeting Your Time, Money, and Space

. . . .

In This Chapter

▶ Using your time wisely

▶ Finding creative solutions to setbacks

▶ Working your budget right

. . . .

*P*erhaps you really, really want to decorate for the holidays but have no idea how you'll fit it into your already hectic schedule and tight budget. You have a vet bill to pay, which cuts severely into your holiday decorating funds. You work long hours and have plenty of prior engagements lined up, which cuts severely into your holiday decorating time. Or perhaps you want to decorate, and money and time present no problems, but you live in an apartment that has decorating restrictions or roommates to contend with.

Whatever your lifestyle and whatever your situation, you may have to face one or more challenges — jobs, budgets, locations, situations, motivation, needs — when making your holiday decorating decisions.

In order to overcome those challenges, you must stay flexible. Flexibility allows you to work with any time, budget, or space issue. What you see as challenging may, in fact, be just another opportunity. Become a master of rolling with the punches, and you can work around anything. As someone who's decorated a shopping mall for Christmas, I can attest to that!

Taking Advantage of Time

If you're like me, you never feel as if you have enough time to do the things you have to do, much less the things you *want* to do, and holiday decorating falls into that "want to do" category. So, unless you have a Jeeves who can carry out your decorating plans for you, you have to budget your time wisely to get your decorating done. The following tips, as well as the project forms I discuss in Chapter 6, can help you take advantage of the time you have to complete your holiday decorating.

Filling out a project form means that you've already estimated how long decorating tasks will take. So take advantage of short stints of time to accomplish those small tasks.

In just five minutes, you can

- ✔ Make new project pages for your decorating notebook
- ✔ Test all the lights for your holiday display
- ✔ Hang a premade wreath on your door
- ✔ Gather and light candles for mood lighting
- ✔ Fold napkins, using my napkin-folding techniques in Chapter 3

In ten minutes, you can

- ✔ Gather all your decorating supplies together in a basket
- ✔ Fluff all the bows on chairs, wreaths, mantels, or anything else that displays one
- ✔ Iron and place table linens for the kitchen and dining room tables
- ✔ Make a list of any items you need to buy

In 30 minutes, you can

- ✔ Pull all your holiday-specific decorations out and place them in the right areas to be decorated
- ✔ Add a few holiday colors to your home in various places and spaces

And that's just a small sampling of what you can do. Casual floral arrangements are easily arranged in a short amount of time (see Chapter 21) as well as adding a few throws or changing out seasonal slipcovers for pillows or chairs.

Switch out candles, trim wicks, dust or polish your holiday decorating items. Rearranging and decorating for the holidays doesn't have to take a lot of time.

Also, try double dipping into your time budget. For example, you can create lovely things for your home while spending time with your family. While preparing dinner, you can be overseeing shamrock pressing that your kids are doing for St. Patty's Day décor. For a little one-on-one time, you can prepare an afternoon of doing nothing but decorating Easter eggs with your children. For other ideas of decorating you can do with your family, you can refer to the "Involving the Whole Family" sections in each holiday chapter. You'll be able to squeeze in great holiday decorating while enjoying some quality family time.

Don't be overwhelmed. Even if you can't plan a whole day or a weekend to decorate for a particular holiday, you can always refer to the sections in the holiday chapters called "Decorating in a Flash." I include ideas that you can implement on a whim just in case the spouse calls and says, "Uh, my mother is coming over for dinner tonight." No, the ideas aren't extravagant, but they're quick, easy, and impressive. And chances are you'll be able to pick up what you need at the grocery store along with the groceries or take-out food from the deli that you'll transfer into your own serving dishes (sneaky, but effective!).

Monitoring Your Money

Regardless of how much decorating you want to do, holiday decorating doesn't have to be a financial burden. Just check out this section for ways to make the most of your decorating budget.

If you find yourself running a little low on cash or just don't want to spend a whole lot on a particular holiday, check out the "More Splash For Less Cash" sections in each holiday chapter. I give you some great ideas for making things yourself, as well as reusing or repurposing items. I also suggest inexpensive alternatives or things you can buy that just don't cost much. Just because your budget may be tight doesn't mean that your home has to look that way.

Controlling impulse buying

Keep impulse purchases under control.

When challenged with the impulse to buy, write down the item, the store where you saw it, the price, and the dimensions and walk away. Try sketching it out on your planning pages and see where it can fit in. If it just doesn't work in your decorating layout, you haven't spent any of your budget on it, and you'll be doing fine. If you decide that you just can't live without it, call the store and have them put it on hold for you. You can run back and get it.

If you're on vacation, at an auction, or the item is a one of a kind, you may want to go ahead and purchase it. Just evaluate if you can fit the item into your decorating scheme — or in the garage, whichever comes first. Be sure to ask whether you'll be able to return the item, if necessary, and hang on to your receipt. Hopefully, you won't need it, but in case you do, you're set.

Shopping closeouts

You can find great bargains at closeout stores, but you have to keep the following in mind to avoid overspending:

- ✔ Arm yourself with a list of items you want and need *before* you go. If you follow my guide on making a decorating notebook in Chapter 6, you may want to bring it along, too — along with steel-toed shoes and elbow pads.

- ✔ Check items to make sure that they're still in working or usable condition.

- ✔ Look for measurements to make sure that your purchase is the right size, or length, and buy only according to what you need.

- ✔ Never — no matter how good of a deal it is — buy something that you think is neat but have no idea where you can put it.

Finding stores that are easy on the pocketbook

Another way you can save in general on all your holiday decorating items is by shopping at mass-merchandise stores.

Retail giants like K-Mart, Wal-Mart, and Target are perfect for finding beautiful holiday items for less. Plus, while you're there, you can pick up many other items for your holiday feasting and gift giving!

Many of these stores carry items designed by big names in the design world that sell for way less than department or specialty stores. Because of mass production and mass buying power, you can get designer accessories and holiday items in trendy colors or classic themes.

Don't discount shopping at these stores! They can save you a lot of money each holiday.

Sizing Up Your Space: From Mobile Homes to Mansions

With a little creativity — and a whole lot of adjusting — I managed to decorate my little apartment in Manhattan years ago for Christmas. Did that mean it was decorated well enough for Martha Stewart to visit, much less be impressed? No way! (I doubt that she'd be impressed with the "gourmet" hallway kitchen in the first place.) But the simple fact is you can decorate beautifully, with any size space, if you just open up your mind to the possibilities.

Evaluating your space

Check out what space you have and what you'll need it for. The size of the space you plan on decorating is important when deciding how many decorations to have, but it has no bearing on how you celebrate. You can be just as elaborate dressing up a small window as you can in a two-story entryway. (Check out each holiday chapter for ideas on decorating smaller spaces.)

Although the size of your space shouldn't impact your style, you should keep scale and proportion in mind. The bigger your space, the bigger you can go. A small display of a Christmas village or single jack-o'-lantern would get lost in that two-story entryway, but floor to ceiling decorations or decorations suspended from the ceiling would make a fabulous statement.

On the other hand, you can let normal or smaller sized items shine in smaller spaces. You don't have to go miniature, but you can pare down how many items you have in a smaller space and still display great holiday style. For example, you can display a smaller grouping of three pillar candles in staggered heights rather than a massive grouping.

Paring down without giving anything up

My preferred way of decorating is to use things sparingly. You may have a lot of space, or you may not. You may have a lot of decorations that have accumulated over the years, or you may just be starting out. Regardless of your situation, you won't sacrifice style by whittling down your grandiose ideas of decorating. Just check out the following ideas:

✔ **A little goes a long way.** If one yard ornament is pretty, then a slew of them must be even better, right? Wrong. Sometimes, just a few items will do.

This holds true for lighting in general, too. If you choose to light the exterior of your home, start slowly. You can always add later if you feel that it's just not enough. Refer to Chapter 17 for tips on how much is too much regarding outdoor holiday décor. They provide you with a good checkpoint to know whether your decorating has gone over the top.

✔ **Choose the very best.** Pick out something very special to be the centerpiece for your holiday. For example, choose a quality-constructed flag or bunting with sturdy stitching and UV-protected fabric (so the colors won't fade) for the Fourth of July instead of purchasing several less-than-first-quality items just because you want to display a lot of them around your home. Invest in a nice menorah that's beautiful to behold all by itself. Even ornaments and candles have variances in quality. Choose just a few simple, high-quality holiday items to display, and they'll make a better statement than quantity ever could.

Decorating vertically: Making the most of your space

If you're challenged with decorating either a small space or a space filled with furniture and thus lacking floor space, consider using the walls of your home as holiday decorating spaces. Reserve that limited floor space for getting around.

Banners, artwork, wreaths, candles — even some Christmas trees specially made for small spaces — can be hung on the wall. Windows and ceilings are game, too. I once walked into a holiday open house where paper snowflakes — the type you made as kids — dangled from the ceiling, and the effect was simply stunning. Hardly any other decorations were needed at all.

Some of the prettiest decorating is done at eye level where you can see it as you walk around the house. You don't have to have a lot of table space or floor space to do some amazing things at the holidays. Just look at walls and ceilings as your decorating canvas and refer to my creative solutions in Chapter 2 for hanging things temporarily. You'll be on your way to decorating vertically for the holidays.

Knowing your limits

If you live in an apartment, town house, garden home, dorm room, condominium, or co-op, you're sharing walls with people who may not have your particular tastes or celebrate the same holidays.

Check with your community association or housing management staff to get the regulations for decorating the exterior of your home. When you close on a property, you may receive a phone book-sized manual of guidelines for what's allowed and not allowed on your property (especially if you have a neighborhood association), but if you rent, you may be unclear as to what you can or can't do. Check first so that you don't spend time or money on stuff that

you just have to take down. (You do your blood pressure a favor as well!)

Next, check for rules and regulations for interior (and exterior) decorating. If you own your place, you really don't have to worry about this, but if you're living in a rented or temporary housing situation, you want to be sure what the rules are for mounting, taping, or hanging decorations. You don't want to risk losing a deposit or being charged for additional holes in walls when you can implement plenty of alternative decorating ideas and suggestions for the holidays. At the very least, check out my tips for temporary decorating in Chapter 2.

Chapter 6

Getting Organized

In This Chapter

▶ Getting yourself — and your supplies — organized

▶ Putting together a decorating notebook

Decorating in general is usually a gradual process that takes time and evolves as you go along. A piece here, a piece there, a find picked up on the side of the road. . . . Okay, *holiday* decorating ain't that way. You have a time frame, a deadline — a beginning and end. The date's been set, and you have no power to change it. You must find a way to work schedules, events, and errands into this hectic schedule. And, oh yeah! Wait a minute. You've also got to decorate!

Planning, preparation, and organization are keys to your future success in decorating beautifully (and without stress) for the holidays. So roll up your sleeves, grab a pen and some paper, and get started. This chapter gets you organized, so that decorating accounts for the least amount of hassle on your holiday list.

Creating A Decorating Notebook

A *decorating notebook* contains everything that you need to know to plan for your holiday decorating. Not only can you reference the layout of any room in your house, but you can also check out specific holiday decorating notes, clips, product information, calendars, project lists, and more right in your binder. Additionally, using a decorating notebook for holiday planning allows you to keep track of what you have and what you still need to make or buy.

A decorating notebook can be made from a blank book, three-ring binder, scrapbook, or any other bound notebook in which pages can be added and deleted as necessary. Whatever you use, your notebook should be able to hold swatches, paint chips, photos, clippings, notes, receipts, measurements, layouts, diagrams, and sketches of ideas that you want to try, as well as anything else you may need.

Read on for suggestions to create a decorating notebook that will keep your ideas and plans organized beautifully.

Dividing and conquering

Make a section in your notebook for each room or area of your house that you may want to decorate for the holidays. Don't forget to include common-space areas as well, such as foyers, hallways, or landings. Porches and decks are also great sections to add to your notebook — they can be decorated, too.

Taking pictures

The best way to plan your decorating is to have visual references to the areas you want to decorate. Grab a camera and a couple rolls of film, or pick up a disposable camera, and shoot away. Turn on every light in the house and keep your camera in flash mode for the best pictures. You'd be surprised how dark a room looks on film when, in reality, it's really well lit.

Normally, taking photos is best in the morning or evening. But for do-it-yourself interior shots done in a flash, try taking your photos during midday when the sun is directly on top of your house. This way, you won't have to worry so much about sunlight flooding through a window ruining a snapped shot. Avoid taking pictures directly into the sun.

After you've had your photos developed, separate them into each room category and mount them on archival-safe paper found at any photo supply or craft store. Slip the pages into plastic sleeves and bind them into your decorating notebook. These photos are great reference tools to have on hand when deciding on artwork or other décor. You never have to rely on just your memory when sitting down for a decorating planning session on a lunch break.

Measuring away

Take measurements of every area that's categorized in your notebook. Roughly sketch out a room as if you're looking at it from above and jot down room measurements. Check out the section later in this chapter, "Measuring and Laying Out a Room," for more information.

Adding information

Next, you'll want to add in blank pages or notebook paper in each section for sketching out ideas, writing down items/item numbers from catalogs or stores, and so on. Place a calendar, project forms, shopping lists, and invitation lists in your binder, divided into holiday categories. (For tips on how to customize some of these forms and lists, keep reading.) Also add swatches of fabric, photos of inspiration pieces, or other reference items of interest that you want to incorporate into each room for the holidays.

I find that by adding a multitude of clear plastic sheet protectors in sections of the binder, I never have to worry about where to put my loose items.

Planning for Holidays Year-Round

You best bet is to start your planning for *all* the holidays you want to decorate for in one sitting. This way, you know themes, colors, styles, and layouts well in advance, so you can shop, plan, and decorate better and more easily throughout the year. Plan as much as a year in advance for the bigger decorating holidays, so that you have plenty of time to prepare decorations that may take a while to make or to finalize any special arrangements.

Now, now, don't get overwhelmed. I don't mean that you have to plan every one down to the last detail — well, at least not at first. In this section, I give you the tools to get your planning started, so that you're organized for each holiday you plan on decorating.

Crying uncle: A word about assigning tasks

Although the bulk of the holiday decorating tasks may fall on you, remember — you *can* ask for help.

Holiday decorating is fun — and it can be fun for the whole family! When you plan and prepare your holiday decorating, keep in mind that you might like to have a little company while you're spending a few hours making everything nice to enjoy. And wouldn't you also like to have a little help if you're hanging off the side of your house stringing lights?

Plan and organize your holiday decorating days around people who can help you if needed. Ask nicely — give treats to those who help. Proper preparation by making lists and projects sheets makes it even easier for you to hand over tasks if you find yourself running out of time or energy.

As with anything, you'll find that by planning well in advance, you're less stressed and better able to get the big picture of what counts and what doesn't really matter at all.

Using a perpetual planning calendar

The first thing you should do when planning your holiday decorating for the year is photocopy a perpetual planning calendar for each month, making note of which holidays you want to start planning on decorating. You can usually make a perpetual calendar on your computer, or you can buy one at an office supply store.

Mark the following on your perpetual planning calendar:

✔ The dates of holidays you plan to decorate for

✔ The timeframe you have in which to decorate for each holiday

✔ Other special dates you want to decorate for, such as birthdays, anniversaries, or family reunions

✔ Schedules of anticipated time off from work or planned vacations

Organizing the details for a stress-free holiday

I'm a huge believer in making lists. Taking the time to write down a list of things that need to be arranged, bought, crafted, or completed frees my mind from having to keep track of everything. Added bonus? If anyone asks what can be done, I can shove a list in the person's hand and delegate tasks immediately. (For more about delegating tasks, see the sidebar, "Crying uncle: A word about assigning tasks.")

I give you the info here to put together an invitation card list as well as a shopping list — lists you can make that I think are helpful for stress-free holidays.

Invitation or card chart

Keeping an invitation or card chart with your holiday decorating notebook comes in handy. Preparing for holiday events and decorating around your audience is much easier if you know who your guests will be. Simply type up your own chart, using or revising my categories that follow, and add it to your decorating notebook to use for each holiday. The chart I make for every occasion includes columns for each person's

- ✔ **Name.** Put each guest's name in this column as it should appear on his or her invitation.

- ✔ **Address.** Include the guest's complete mailing address in this column.

- ✔ **Phone.** Put each guest's home phone number here, so that you may easily contact guests for changes in plans or last-minute emergencies.

- ✔ **E-mail.** Use this column to include personal e-mail addresses in case you need to contact guests for updates, send corrections to invitations, or send electronic invitations for casual parties or celebrations.

- ✔ **Date sent invitation/card.** Keep track of when you sent out invitations in this column.

- ✔ **Response.** When your guests respond, you can put their yes or no answers here in this column, along with the number of guests to expect.

- ✔ **Notes/special provisions.** In this column, list any particular that you need to remember for a guest, such as whether the guest has to leave by a certain time, needs childcare, wants to bring additional guests, is a vegan, is allergic to something, has other dietary constraints (hello menu planning!), or whatever.

If you tend to send cards to the same people every year or for several occasions, make a master list and photocopy it several times to insert in every holiday decorating section of your planning notebook. Having this list makes it so much easier to keep track of address changes or additions, or to keep up with who owes you a dinner!

Shopping lists

Make your shopping list after you've listed all the materials you need to complete a project *and* have double-checked your cupboards for supplies or ingredients that you already have on hand. (See "Creating project forms" for more information on how to formulate your materials list in order to create your shopping list.)

Holidays are sometimes hectic. Spending the five extra minutes to double-check whether you actually have the items needed may save you as much as 30 minutes or more by not having to run last-minute shopping trips for items that you thought you had.

Creating project forms

A great element to add to a decorating notebook is a *project form,* which keeps all your decorating information together by holiday or project. Project forms can be used to plan to plan holidays, events, decorating and craft projects, and even menu items you want to undertake for each holiday or event. The project form basically asks questions that you need to answer as you plan your project — you simply gather ideas and information to fill out the form.

You can make your own blank version by using any or all the categories I provide in the following list. You can use a computer or write one out by hand, whatever you prefer. I suggest creating a blank form on your computer and then making several copies to fill out as needed.

Project forms should contain, at a glance, elements that are present in every major project:

- ✔ **Date the project was started.** Place the date that you started your project (decorating, event, or otherwise), so you know when your initial plans were made.

- ✔ **Name of project.** Label the project form with a name of your event, decorating, or craft project. For example, in your Christmas Project Planning section of your decorating notebook, you can have project forms labeled "Outdoor Decorating," "Office Christmas Party," "Trim the Tree Party," "Christmas Luminaria Craft Project," and so on.

- ✔ **Description.** Write a one sentence or one paragraph description of what your project is. Using the "Outdoor Decorating" name of project example, your description might read, "Decorate the sidewalk, front porch, trees, and house, using a snowman theme." Your project form will give you places to include details later.

- ✔ **Target date for completion.** Use this date for when you want your decorating, event, or craft project to be completed. For example, you may want to have a holiday craft project completed well in advance before beginning to decorate your home. This date will give you a target to hit.

- ✔ **Total estimated time you think it will take.** Use this section to guesstimate how much time you think it will take you to complete your task list. Fill this blank in when you've gone through and listed every task you think will be required to get your project done. Include time for phone calls, shopping, and so on. Add up all the time in minutes or hours, and you'll know how much "time" to budget to get this task done.

- ✔ **Budget.** Whether you have all the money in the world or squeeze every bit you can from your budget, you'll want to set limits on how much to spend on your holiday decorating. My advice to you is to set your budget with a little cushion in it, so that if you need a fresh bouquet of flowers to set at your table, you won't ever feel guilty about going way over budget. Last-minute spruce ups happen. Set your budget lower than you're willing to go — meanwhile still sticking to it! But keep an emergency fund for running out to get more candles in a hurry. Your nephew just used yours for bowling pins.

✔ **Tasks.** List everything in the world you can think of that you may need to do for your project, such as look up recipes, look up how-to instructions, enlist someone's help, mail order an item to complete it, and so on. List them line by line (no matter how small the task may seem), and don't leave anything out.

✔ **Due dates.** Review your task list, line by line, and list due dates for completion of each task. Estimate how much time it will take you to do each step.

Check out Figure 6-1 for a filled-out example of the first part of a project form.

Holiday Project Form

Name of project:	Making Christmas Garland
Description:	Use leftover pine boughs
Date form was started:	10/1
Date for project to be completed:	12/1
Budget:	$20
Task:	Cut/trim branches in backyard.
To be done by (check off when complete):	11/29
Task:	Gather supplies and gloves.
To be done by (check off when complete):	11/29
Task:	Start binding branches.
To be done by (check off when complete):	11/30
Task:	Drape
To by done by (check off when complete):	12/1
Notes or sketches:	Swag approx 8 inches. 36 inches for every tie.
	Tie every 4 spindles on 5th.

Figure 6-1: The first part of a project form.

Your project form may also include the following elements:

- **Materials lists.** Make your materials lists, first noting every supply, tool, garnish, special dish, and so on that you need to use for your recipe, craft, or decorating project. You should make this list after you've sat down and written out specific, detailed plans for your holiday. Go around your house taking inventory and checking it off your materials list and then make shopping lists based on what you don't already have handy in the house.

- **People.** List the names of any people who'll be involved in this project, from the caterer to the florist or friend. Use this section to list contact information or at least people you want to get involved in your project. (And don't forget that spouses can be used for hanging lights!) Having this info reminds you to check about their schedules and so on.

- **Places.** If you'll be planning a holiday event somewhere other than your home, you can list that information here. Also use this section to list directions to special shops for holiday buying (related to the project) or places where you may be taking a class that's related to your project.

- **Timelines.** To accomplish your holiday decorating goals, you need to establish timelines. Use the following pointers to create timelines for each task you list on your project form:

  - Check out your list of tasks and estimate how long you think each task is going to take.

  - Using your time estimate for each task, work your way back to the current date or the day you need to or want to start your preparations in order to have the project finished on time. Make sure that you account for work schedules, play schedules, and that much-needed sleep.

- **Expenses.** Keep track of how much you actually spend. Record expenses related to completing this project in this section. Add amounts as you go to try to stay within your budget.

Check out Figure 6-2 for a filled-out example of the second part of a project form.

Project forms can help you with planning any project, not just holiday decorating. So make more than you think you'll ever need. It's surprising how, when you think that you've thought of everything, something pops up at the last minute. Your best bet is to make a new project form for each new big project you want to undertake. By keeping a few extras on hand, you won't have to make trips to copy shop so often.

Holiday Project Form *(continued)*

Materials/Tools Needed:	
• floral paddle wire	
• pruning shears	
• scissors	
• floral tape	
Money:	
Item:	floral paddle wire
Est. Cost:	$5
Actual Cost:	$7
Item:	floral tape
Est. Cost:	$8.00
Actual Cost:	$7.50
Total:	$14.50
Amount over/under budget:	-$5.50
Task Timelines:	
Date:	11/29
Description:	gathering gloves and supplies
Hours:	2
Date:	11/29
Description:	branch cutting
Hours:	1.5

Figure 6-2:
The second part of a project form.

Planning for "what if"

The best way to plan for an event properly is to face the dreaded "what ifs" and meet them head on. Plan back-ups, what to do if the dinner rolls burn, and all sorts of other holiday mishaps. Sure, you may think that you're totally over-preparing, and you may not do a thing about all the scenarios you work out in your head, *but* you will always have the calming peace that you've actively mentally prepared. And don't be surprised if you buy extra rolls for dinner and have a fresh package of batteries for the camera at arms length after working through this process.

Measuring and Laying Out a Room

Keeping diagrams of your room layouts in your decorating notebook helps you plan your holiday decorating so much better. Although most holiday decorations can be placed on a table or hung on a wall, in certain instances, you may want to rearrange a room for a special holiday get-together, string garland around the room (now how much will you need?), or find a place to prop that wonderful antique sled you found at a flea market.

If you keep accurate measurements and diagrams of your spaces, you can know in an instant whether the Christmas tree you want will actually fit through the door or the crypt you want to create for Halloween will fit in your front room.

I suggest that you not only measure your room, but also measure and make templates for all your furniture. This way, you can arrange and rearrange furniture on paper rather than having to lug things around a room just to see if they look nice.

Simply buy some graph paper, measure your rooms, and sketch out each room and its measurements on the graph paper. Don't forget to include doors and windows! You can purchase templates for you furniture and use them to move about your drawn-out room to rearrange furniture easily.

Organizing your holiday supplies

With so many holidays, decorations can easily get out of control. Make these tips your mantra for before-and-after organizing and storage bliss.

✔ **Prepare in advance.** Make lists and project forms, and check to make sure that tools are working well before you actually need them. Know what you've got before buying storage containers; otherwise, you'll have empty storage container clutter to deal with. Not good.

✔ **Buy extras.** Extra batteries for cameras, light bulbs, glue sticks, staples, tape, and other basic supplies that don't take up much room are great to have on hand.

✔ **Keep everything together.** Place all your decorations for like holidays together before and after use. Use a decorative basket (I like using a lidded picnic basket) as a storage box for small supplies. This type of container makes carrying hammers, nails, glue guns, and staplers easier, and it won't stick out like a sore thumb if you leave it out in a room.

✔ **Wrap as you go.** Bring storage containers out first when you're ready to pack up this season's decorations. Place containers by their respective contents. Disassemble and wrap items up as you go and get them in their proper containers.

Also check out Chapter 7, which is all about cleaning and caring for your holiday decorations.

Measure the walls above any baseboards or chair rail moldings — they prevent accurate measurements.

When laying out your room, draw symbols indicating where heating and air conditioning vents, electrical outlets, or radiators are located so that you'll know how to formulate a decorating plan around them. Indicate which switches turn on ceiling fans, lights, or electrical outlets by using a dashed line. You should also indicate ceiling, door, and window heights.

Don't worry if your layout isn't drawn perfectly. You're not making these drawings to show off drafting skills — you just want to have a good reference point when planning for decorating. If you really want to spend more time on this task, try visiting your local library and check out interior design or architectural resources that may be available.

Chapter 7

Keeping and Caring for Your Holiday Stash

In This Chapter

▶ Stocking up on supplies

▶ Discovering the best ways to clean and care for your decorations

*I*ndoor and outdoor holiday decorations are made of a whole slew of different materials — plastic, glass, wire, fresh, fake. Keeping track of what decorations you own is hard enough; now, you've got to figure out the best way
to keep them fresh while only pulling them out once a year.

In this chapter, you find out how to store your décor and maintain some of
these items. The upkeep of your investment is worth the time and effort to do
it right.

Caring for Your Indoor and Outdoor Decorations

Holiday decorations take a little more work only because they aren't used
every day. Your home décor gets pampered daily, weekly, or monthly; meanwhile, your seasonal decorating supplies take an extra beating from the once-
a-year pulling out and shoving back in shuffle that comes with the territory.

Special considerations for your seasonal décor are crucial to making the
items last year after year. Here are my best tips for keeping and caring for
your holiday stash.

Storing your stash

Careful storage of your materials ensures that when the time comes to decorate, you're ready, your items are in good condition, and your decorating goes quickly.

If you're starting out for the first time, or you want to get better organized, follow these tips:

- **Label everything.** Whether you use a labeling system, print out labels from your computer, or simply write on the box or bag, you must take the time to accurately label packed contents.

- **Stack and store boxes with labeled areas facing out.** Facing the labels out helps you to easily identify what you need to grab — it also helps ensure that you get the correct box when sending someone else up to the attic for a particular item.

- **Save the original box that an item came in.** This tip is especially important when the item is oddly shaped or unusually large. If you have several smaller items in their original boxes, simply store them together in a plastic bin to keep them all together.

- **Keep these items on hand:**
  - **Tissue paper:** Keep plain white tissue paper on hand for wrapping around fragile items or wadding up pieces to cushion and surround decorations.

  - **Corrugated boxes:** Sturdy corrugated boxes are great for storing loose, noncrushable items. Try to get multiples of one standard size of box to make stacking and storage even easier.

  - **Rigid plastic bins:** For breakable items or items you want to protect from any possible leaks in storage areas, rigid plastic bins are the best. You can purchase these items in clear plastic (my favorite so that I can see what I'm pulling out) or color-code your bins seasonally just like you would file folders. Either way, make sure that you protect them from extreme cold and heat because they can become brittle or melt all over your décor. Besides that caution, these items are worth their weight in gold for storage solutions that last.

  - **Plastic bags:** Trash bags, clean grocery sacks, and resealable baggies in different sizes are great to have handy when packing up the goods. I use them for just about everything. They're perfect for storing lightweight, nonbreakable items.

- **Packing peanuts:** To pack ornaments or other fragile items, have packing peanuts on hand. If you can't stand how they fly around the room when you're unpacking (ever gotten one stuck to your hand that you just couldn't shake off?), try placing small amounts in clean plastic grocery bags and tie them at the top. You can use these little bundles to nestle your treasures in.

- **Bubble wrap:** Wrapping bubble wrap around individual items is always a good idea when storing fragile decorations. Cushion sturdy items with bubble wrap, so that finishes don't rub together during transport and storage.

- **Packing tape:** Use packing tape to secure bubble wrap, tissue paper, or other items together. Tape box tops shut, so that in case they topple, contents won't come tumbling out, and no one gets chewed out — oh yeah, or hurt.

- **Permanent markers:** Have broad-tipped permanent markers to label storage boxes and bags. Permanent markers will pretty much write on anything — then again, they'll write on anything. Keep them out of reach of children.

I tend to stay away from using newspaper as storage material filler. Newspaper sometimes encourages nasty nesting with critters you just don't want around. Use tissue paper, if needed, instead.

Doing the small space shuffle

When you live in a small space, storing everyday necessities is a challenge, much less seasonal decorating supplies. But you can do it with a little planning and preparation.

Thinking small

Regardless of space, sometimes all you need to make a holiday statement is a small accent piece or small collection of related items grouped together. Pairing a live floral centerpiece with stunning tableware can be enough to create pure holiday style. Because you don't need to have a lot to get the point across, you don't need to purchase a lot of extra décor designed just for the holidays. When you choose to go sparingly with holiday decor, you really help yourself avoid unnecessary storage and clutter.

Take your own vase or container to your florist, so that you don't end up with something else you can't store, or make your own arrangement. I give you instructions in Chapter 21.

Pulling the ol' switcheroo

Buy items that can take on different looks for different holidays by simply switching out accent pieces. For example, adding different colored ribbons to reflect holiday colors or swapping out seasonal icons or items can change up a simple wreath. Fabric items that are reversible serve double duty for more than one season. One vase can take on any look depending on what you put in it. Switching out items for standard home décor pieces works great for well-invested purchases.

Folding things flat

When you start selecting holiday décor purchases, consider items that store flat or take up little space. Accent pillows can easily be transformed with pillow covers, which, thankfully, fold flat for storage or can be stored on the pillows themselves. Layer up to four different colors of pillow covers, peeling off and relayering them season after season. Table runners, placemats, and other fabric items that store flat are perfect for switching out seasonally.

Holiday Item Care and Cleaning Guide

When you're dealing with dozens of decorating items for dozens of holidays, you've got quite a collection of materials that have different cleaning recommendations and storage solutions. This section gives you instructions for caring for and cleaning more than two dozen items.

Always check manufacturers' suggestions on labels and packaging for specific care and cleaning directions. Keep instruction manuals and special tools or hardware together in plastic resealable bags and file them.

Although I firmly believe in taking care of items and reusing them over and over again, I want to caution you: Before you pack those items away, decide whether the items are going to make it another season. Blooms fade, and things do get damaged. If you find an item that has really seen better days, evaluate it. Can you do something else with it, or do you really want to take up valuable storage space only to toss it eventually? You'll save yourself a lot of time and energy (and space!) if you go through the process now before cleaning and packing it away.

For many more ways to care for and clean other items for the holidays, or just for cleaning tips in general, I found a Web site that gives a wealth of tips free for you to access. Mrs. Clean Jeans (www.mrscleanjeans.com) has collected a decade of cleaning tips that are worth checking out if . . . well, if you like to clean.

Another site worth visiting is How To Clean Anything.com (`www.howtocleananything.com`), which gives tips on how to clean and care for autos, home interiors, and home exteriors. And if you don't want to do it yourself, you can always search the database of cleaning professionals.

Candles

A light dusting is all you really need to clean a candle occasionally (an old pair of nylon hosiery works better than anything for this task), but if you need to do a deeper cleaning, use a cotton ball soaked in rubbing alcohol to swipe dirty and oily residue off the surfaces of an unlit candle. Use a cotton swab dipped in alcohol to get in and around detailed areas or around the wick.

Store your candles away from heat sources — if possible, in a freezer. Freezing your candles makes them burn cleaner, longer, and reduces or eliminates dripping.

To help your candles burn evenly, which allows them to last longer, follow this tip: Measure your candle from the edge to the wick (find the radius, in other words), and then only burn your candle for as many hours as the radius has inches. For example, suppose the radius of your candle is 2 inches. Burn that candle for only two hours at a time, and your candle will burn more evenly.

Clay

If you have an assortment of clay ornamental pieces, simply dust them regularly and carefully place them in bubble wrap for storing. Because clay can break or chip, and is sometimes water soluble, storing these items in a non-crushable, watertight plastic bin is best.

Doorways and doors

Accenting doors and doorways with garlands, wreaths, or banners is a beautiful way to make a first impression. For metal doors, use a wreath hanger that slips over doors, so that you don't have to drive nails into it. For wooden doors, you can screw in a tiny cup hook to leave in your door at all times. Screw the hook in high above eye level — you can always adjust the height of your hanging wreath or banner by tying it to clear monofilament (fishing line) and adjusting the height by adjusting the length of line. Hang the monofilament on the cup hook.

Faux botanicals

For the holidays, faux is often the way to go. The quality of faux flowers, leaves, wreaths, garland, plants, and other botanicals has greatly improved over the past few years. Sometimes, you have to actually touch them to know whether or not they're real.

Faux botanicals are especially wonderful because they help protect the environment, can be stored year after year, and never need watering, plucking or upkeep like the real things. They're also usually more cost-effective because you invest only once and reuse over and over again.

Clean and keep your faux botanicals, using the tips in the following subsections.

Silk/synthetic botanicals

Most silk flowers (which, oddly enough, are mostly derived from nylon material) are easy to clean with a simple dusting or gentle tapping to remove a light layer of accumulated dust. However, for more heavy cleanings, throw them in a sink or tub and shower them with lukewarm water. Use a soft cleaning brush as necessary.

For synthetic garland, using a vacuum attachment is good enough. Because garland is usually wired, I advise against rinsing it with water because the water may cause the wire to rust.

Paper botanicals

Dust florals or botanicals lightly with a feather duster, or vacuum with an attachment that's usually used for dusting.

Plastic botanicals

Wipe plastic botanicals with a damp soft cloth and, if needed, rinse with a shower of water.

As with all items that are made of these materials, keep out of direct sunlight and away from heat to prevent bleaching or melting.

Gingerbread houses and other edible/ nonedible food decorations

Want a challenge? How about trying to clean food that's been left out for days?

Gingerbread houses are cute to look at — and can be a terror to keep clean. Display gingerbread houses on a flat surface that's away from foot traffic. These little beauties are great for using as centerpieces. Just make sure that you keep them out of the reach of children who would love to break off a piece to munch on.

To clean any nonedible food item, basically blow the dust away or swipe the surface with a clean paper towel. Do not use a duster! Yuck. Dust particles from other cleanings could be transferred to your pretty gingerbread house, making it more of a cleaning disaster than it originally began.

Glass

Wash glass serving pieces in the dishwasher when possible. A dishwasher is less harmful than hand washing because it reduces the chances of chipping or breaking while handling these items in soapy water. Dry with a lint-free hand towel to reduce water spots.

Dust and clean glass surfaces often with a glass cleaner or use straight vinegar for a grease-cutting agent. Squeegee windows for the best effect, but if you need a good streak-free shine without the squeegee, crumple up newspapers and use those instead of paper towels. Works like a charm!

To store glass accents or glassware, wrap each piece in layers of white tissue paper and bubble wrap and store in a sturdy box or bin.

Lighting

For twinkle lights, replace all burned-out bulbs before taking them down and storing. To keep lights as untangled as possible, wind strings of lights around a round empty container such as a large clean coffee can. Wrap a rubber band or string around the top of the can and tuck the cord ends under it to secure in place. You can store hanging clips, extra bulbs, and other related items inside the can till needed.

For outdoor and indoor lighting, take care to check all lamps and lighting equipment for proper wattage and type of bulb needed. You can usually find the manufacturer's recommendations on a sticker at the neck of the lamp (where you screw in the bulb), on the cord, or included in an instruction sheet accompanying your lighting purchase. Never exceed the recommended amount of wattage when it comes to lighting. You could short out a fuse, run the risk of starting a fire, and ruin your lighting in general. Check, check, and double-check your lighting sources before replacing bulbs.

To store lighting equipment (besides strings of lights), remove the bulbs so that they don't break off or rust inside your lamp sockets.

If you do happen to break off a bulb and you can't get the bulb base out of it's socket, unplug your lamp or turn off the breaker feeding the electricity to the lighting source and (are you ready for this?) stick a raw potato in the socket till it "grabs" and unscrew the bulb base. I know it sounds crazy — but it works.

Metal

Different types of metal require different methods of cleaning and care. When you purchase a metal accessory, be sure to read boxes or labels on the merchandise. By law, the manufacturer is required to let you know what the item is made of. This way, you'll be sure to use the right cleaning and caring solution for your particular metal item. Additionally, many manufacturers suggest cleaning and caring solutions that you may want to make note of. Together with the information listed in this section, you'll be armed with the knowledge on how to care for most any metal item.

Special antiqued or distressed finishes

Today's home décor items have several metal-embossed accents or metal accent pieces attached. Most manufacturers have accounted for the fact that you'll want to clean these items regularly and have coated them well so that all you have to do is give them a once-over with a dusting cloth. However, many special finishes used nowadays to resemble older worn surfaces are a bit harder to clean. Just be careful when cleaning embossed or detailed surfaces. They can chip or come completely off.

Aluminum

For aluminum furniture, a silicone spray or a coat of car wax protects the surfaces from pitting and corrosion. Wrought iron can be sprayed with the silicone spray as well. Be sure to spray underneath furniture and completely coat decorative items front, back, bottom, and top to prevent rusting or pitting.

Galvanized metal

Galvanized metal is great for use during the holidays because it doesn't rust. The biggest problem you may have with these containers, though, is that they're rarely sealed properly — which means leakage all over the place.

Seal your dry galvanized metal container by caulking the inside seams with a clear silicone sealant, available in the plumbing section of any hardware or home improvement store. Allow the sealant to dry completely before filling the container with any kind of liquid or material. To clean it? Scrub away with just about anything — galvanized metal is almost indestructible.

Pewter

Pewter, made of an alloy of lead and tin, may become pitted or stained by acids and other chemicals in some foods, so wash it immediately after using it if you're using the item for food. Be careful not to dent or scratch it.

I've heard that rottenstone, a finer abrasive stone than pumice, boiled with linseed oil makes a mean paste for cleaning pewter, but I stick to a salt, vinegar, and flour concoction. Add 1 teaspoon of salt in 1 cup of white vinegar. Slowly add flour by the teaspoonful to make a toothpaste-like substance. Apply the paste to pewter and let it sit from 15 minutes to an hour. Rinse with clean, warm water and polish dry.

Today's pewter can be washed by hand in hot water with a mild detergent. Rinse and dry pewter thoroughly with a soft cloth. But go easy on the polishing — it's not meant to look like silver.

Silver

To clean silver items, rub a silver polish on them, using a clean, soft cloth. To clean between silverware tines, or to make sure that all the polish has been really removed, use a disposable soft floor-polishing cloth (like Swiffer) to slide and polish between tines.

Be careful not to use a silver polish on silver-plated items. It can eat away the surface. Instead, buy a polishing cloth specifically made for polishing and touching up silver-plated items. You can usually find them in fine department stores where silver-plated merchandise (including jewelry) is sold.

Brass, copper, and stainless steel

A cleaner such as Brasso, works well on copper, brass, and stainless steel. Follow the manufacturer's suggestions for cleaning.

As always, take care not to put your metal objects in harm's way where they can get bent or scratched. Make sure that you attach felt or rubber adhesive pads underneath metal objects to be placed on fine furnishings. Metal scratches!

Ornaments

Never dust an ornament while it is hanging. Gently clean ornaments by holding each one in your hand and dusting it with a soft polishing cloth.

It's always best to place ornaments back in their original packaging, so long as the packaging is still intact. If your packaging is damaged, store ornaments individually by wrapping each one in tissue paper then bubble wrap, if necessary. Store ornaments in a clearly labeled, noncrushable box or bin.

Outdoor furniture

Clean and condition wood, metal, wicker, plastic, or vinyl outdoor furniture for out-of-season storage.

Find out what kind of material your furniture is made of and refer to the cleaning solutions I've separated out in this section. For example, if you have aluminum furniture, spray it with a clear coat of silicone spray or polish it with car wax as I suggest in the metal section.

For cushion care, make sure that you protect your fabrics from touching any kind of chemical such as bleach or heavy-duty cleaners. Besides possibly ruining your fabric, the chemicals could harm the stitching, causing it to weaken. Also take care to keep suntan lotions away from fabrics — sometimes, their reaction with the sun causes fabric to stain. Just cover any fabric with a towel, and you shouldn't have to worry too much about it.

Most new cushions are treated, so that they are not damaged by summer weather and can be left outside all season. Fillings are usually polyester, which resists mildew and water. Although you should try to keep your cushions out of the rain, it they do happen to get soaked, simply remove them from their frames and stand them on one end. That should dry them quicker.

If you have vinyl cushions, you shouldn't have to worry about much — just make sure that the seams are stitched with polyester thread and are tufted with buttons to allow water to drain.

If you take care of your outdoor furniture during the season, a good cleaning before storing at the end of the season should be sufficient. Some manufacturers recommend deep-cleaning cushions at the end of the summer; check your manufacturer's recommendations to see if you should do so with your cushions.

Be sure that all your surfaces and especially your cushions are dry as a bone before stacking and storing them away for the winter. Place furniture in a well-protected area and drape with a water-resistant tarp. If stored in an enclosed area, a painter's cloth works well. Dust can, in fact, damage surfaces over time, and you'll want to protect them from as many of the elements as possible.

Outdoor nylon decorations

Fancy those inflatable, illuminated snowmen and Santas that are larger than life? Cleaning them before storing them away is fun — if you like dangling off tall ladders while trying to clean moving targets. Just follow these steps to clean your nylon giants:

1. **Fully inflate the figure during the day and wet the surface with a garden hose top to bottom.**

2. **Use a ladder to inspect the figure for any rips, loose stitching, and, yes, bird doodie.**

3. **Spray any stains with a solution of mild detergent and warm water, scrubbing the area with a soft-bristled nylon brush.**

4. **Rinse the item thoroughly with the hose, and allow the figure to air-dry completely (which shouldn't take too long).**

5. **Deflate, fold, and store the nylon figure in a watertight plastic bin.**

For nylon windsocks, banners, or other garden décor, follow the same cleaning tips in the previous list and remember to allow everything to dry completely before storing. Collapse windsocks and roll up banners for storing. Because these items are so lightweight, you can easily store them in plastic garbage bags and hang them in a storage area.

Painted surfaces on outdoor decorations

Gently clean any decoratively painted surface with a damp sponge in mild detergent. Touch up any areas you can with matching craft paint and then use a clear-coat acrylic spray. Allow the piece to dry completely before storing.

When storing, be sure to place bubble wrap or tissue around the item or between stacked items. The bubble wrap prevents chipping by keeping the painted surfaces from rubbing against each other.

Paper

From paper lanterns to paper snowflakes, dozens of holiday décor items are made from paper, both delicate and sturdy. Though you may not care to store crafted paper snowflakes or paper chains from year to year, you may have other paper items that you want to keep in good shape.

The best cleaning you can do for paper items is to dust them with a household duster. If the paper's coated, you can remove some splashes or spills with a dampened paper towel, drying the area immediately. For dimensional paper objects, vacuum them with a soft bristled nozzle attachment.

All paper decorations should be disassembled and stored flat. If possible, store them in plastic sheet protectors with an inserted piece of cardboard, cut down from spare boxes, for support. Store them in a watertight plastic bin and keep them in a dry area.

Photos

Taking photos at the holidays is a must. Spend the extra money to develop your film on quality photo paper and insert the pictures into archival-safe storage boxes until you're ready to mount them into a scrapbook or photo album.

Taking care of the negatives is just as important, in my opinion. If a photo is damaged or lost, or you want to enlarge a special photo, you'll never be at loss. Store your negatives in a cool, dark place inside the protectors they come in. Never touch a negative with your finger — your prints will remain forever.

When you're ready to mount your photos into an album, make sure that you use archival-safe, acid-free plastic sleeves and/or paper. A wide selection is available on the market today. A trip to a local scrapbook supply store will turn up more inspirational ideas for storing your photos than you'll know what to do with!

Keep photos away from direct sunlight and protect them against moisture or exposure to extreme heat sources. You'll treasure all the memories for years to come.

Plastic

Many indoor and outdoor decorations made of plastic are easily maintained by washing with warm, soapy water. For any molded or mildewed areas, thoroughly soak in a 1:4 liquid chlorine bleach to water solution and scrub with a sponge or nylon bristled brush. (Make sure to protect clothing and skin from splashes.) Wash the item again with warm, soapy water. Air-dry or towel-dry plastic items before storing.

Store smaller plastic items, such as plastic ornaments, in crush-proof bins and boxes; wrapping in tissue or bubble wrap is completely optional. For larger items, such as large figures for the yard, cover or wrap them up with a large drop cloth or old towel before storing upright or in a box. Try to keep plastic items from touching each other because the changes in temperature over seasons may increase the chance of them sticking to each other. Obviously, keep all plastic items away from direct heat sources — they'll melt!

Most plastic furniture can be washed with a solution of mild detergent (such as hand soap) and water. Because plastics scratch easily, never use scouring powders or other abrasives.

Recyclables used in decorating

Clean all water-resistant recycled containers thoroughly with a mild soap and dry them immediately after washing. Otherwise, you may end up with rusted containers.

Never reuse a container that's been used to store household chemicals for holding food or drink items. Residues may still remain.

Keep recyclables used for kids crafting in a noncrushable box or bin. Put all recycled items to the kid test: Never reuse materials that can cut or harm a child. If you keep this in mind, everyone will be safe when they reach into the craft bin.

Rugs, pillows, and throws for special occasions

Throughout this book, I suggest adding rugs, pillows, and throws to change up your holiday décor.

For occasional cleaning while on display, fluff pillows, vacuuming them when necessary. I find it best to insert them into a large garbage bag and gather the opening around a vacuum attachment. The vacuum sucks the dust — air and all — from the bag and after the nozzle is removed, you'll have fluffy clean pillows.

Shake out scatter rugs at least once a week, and throw them in the washing machine as needed. I've found that my rugs turn out beautifully washed in cold water and detergent on the gentle cycle. Never use the dryer; hang your rugs to dry instead.

If you have Oriental rugs, speak with a specialist on caring for your treasure. Call a local dealer for special cleaning instructions.

Before storing throws or any other woven item for a season, check the manufacturers' labels for care and washing instructions for your rugs, pillows, and throws. Mend any holes and remove loose threads and place in protective cases (try pillowcases in a pinch) to store for the season.

Serving pieces

Serving pieces, such as pottery or enamelware, need special care during the holidays. With heavy use, chipping can occur.

Care for your prized serving pieces the same way you would fine china or crystal — handle carefully, wash delicately, and dry and store in protective coverings. Although these items may weigh more and seem sturdier, they sometimes chip more easily than the daintiest stem of crystal.

Table linens

Because there are so many types of table linens made of many materials, I give you the old "check the label" advice for proper care and cleaning directions. However, I've found these tips to be most helpful in keeping your linens looking great for a long time.

For spills — especially wine or juice stains — soak the area with water or club soda and shake a mound of table salt over the stain. Let it sit for a while and then brush the salt away. Use a stain-treating spray, if needed, on the area and launder as soon as you can.

When preparing to iron table linens, gather up a spray bottle of water, starch (for natural fibered linens such as cotton or linen), and sizing (to use on synthetics or fabrics with blends). Set your iron to the correct setting according to what your linens are made of and place a clean sheet on the floor underneath your ironing board. The sheet keeps large clean tablecloths from touching a dirty floor while ironing — not that you have a dirty floor.

To iron linens, spritz water and starch or sizing, whichever works for your material, on the reverse side of your linen. Ironing on the back side prevents the possibility of a shine on the fabric. If you have round tablecloths, place the center of the round on the smallest end of your ironing board. Rotate and iron the tablecloth a piece of pizza at a time. Easy as pie, eh?

If you have embroidered details or stitching on your linens, place a clean white towel on your ironing board and place the embroidery face down on the towel. Spray the back of the stitching with water and iron the piece allowing the steam to "raise" the design. Starch if desired.

Don't worry about ironing or starching table linens before storing them. Just fold them up and iron before placing on your holiday table.

Wicker, rattan, and baskets

Wicker and rattan furniture are great elements to add indoors and out. Cleaning it is as simple as cleaning any other furniture — dusting and vacuuming when needed. Winterizing them and maintaining them is a little more difficult because they're made of natural fibers, which break down over time.

To keep your wicker from deteriorating quickly, keep it under a covered porch or use it indoors. Exposure to extreme elements — or lots and lots of rain — harms the fibers, causing them to break and the paint to chip.

If your wicker needs a deep cleaning, take it outdoors and spray it with a garden hose, using a soft nylon brush where necessary. Allow it to dry in full sun.

If you need to touch up the paint, gently scrape any loose chips and any remaining mold or mildew with a stiff nylon brush and spray paint with several coats of paint. Allow paint to dry in between coats. Don't forget to turn the piece over and paint the underside as well. These areas seldom see sun, so they're major sources for collecting cobwebs, dust, mold, and mildew. If you want extra protection for your wicker pieces, you may also seal the surface with a clear coating of polyurethane spray.

You can clean, keep, and touch up woven baskets by using these tips as well. You can also occasionally clean baskets with a good oil soap formulated for wood.

Wire

You'll be using wire on many things for holiday decorations, but that's not the kind of wire I'm talking about here.

Many items on the market today (and many things you can make) are made of wire. Napkin rings, lampshades, beaded garland, ornaments, even wire topiary forms and lighted yard displays are fashioned out of wire.

For outdoor wired forms, you don't have to do more than check it occasionally and clean it with warm, soapy water. For interior home accessories, most decorative wire items have a protective coating that resists fingerprints, tarnishing, and scratches. For everyday care and cleaning, gently clean the item with a good polishing cloth, taking care to keep wire décor from getting crushed or bent.

If a heavy-duty cleaning is needed for coated wire accessories, dip a cotton ball or swab in a 1:1 cleaning solution of rubbing alcohol and water. Rub the wire with the solution-soaked cotton ball, and then rub the wire clean with a dry cotton ball or cosmetic wipe.

Sterling silver wire or uncoated copper and brass wire can tarnish. In these cases, use a cotton swab dipped in a silver or metal polishing agent and swab areas that need sparkling up. Polish with a soft cloth and store in a soft cotton cloth in an airtight container.

For all other wire accessories, wrap them in tissue and store them in a non-crushable bin or box.

Wood

Protect and care for your wood surfaces by cleaning them with a mild oil soap and dusting as needed. Shine surfaces with an orange oil polish for a fresh, clean smell. Prevent scarring wood furniture from holiday decorations. Protect your surfaces by using felt pads on sharp metal items and table-cloths, place mats, and hot pads when serving food.

Wreaths and garlands

After lightly cleaning your wreath with a soft cloth, vacuum, or gentle-bristled brush, place it in a trash bag and tie the ends together. Place the wreath in a deep, sturdy box. If you can't find an appropriate container for your wreath, another option is to hang the wreath in a closet or other storage area in the bag. Of course, if it's real, toss it out after it sheds to nothing.

Part III
Getting to the Heart of the Holidays

The 5th Wave   By Rich Tennant

"Brian Foley, you know that's not what I meant when I told you to hang holly on the front door."

In this part . . .

This part is full of wonderful holidays to celebrate and decorate! Get planning and organizing tips, inspiration piece lists, and a ton of ideas for decorating spaces of all sizes, with any budget, for people on the go. Grab creative ideas on how to get the whole family involved in decorating, and plan your outdoor decorations for stunning views inside and out. It's all here — create and decorate!

Chapter 8

Designing a Romantic Valentine's Day

In This Chapter

▶ Decorating for fun, elegance, and the family

▶ Setting the stage for romance

I love Valentine's Day! From bed to bath, dining room to family room, Valentine's Day is an easy and fun holiday to show your sweet side. I provide you with plenty of ideas and inspiration for creating your best Valentine's Day look inside and out, no matter what your budget, style, or space. So, kick it up a notch this year and create an irresistible décor that you, your family, and even your friends can enjoy.

Finding Your Inspiration

Infusing your rooms with a bit more passion and excitement, elegance and romance, or fun or whimsy shows just how much you care. So even if you already decorate your home romantically, Valentine's Day requires you to turn up the heat a bit on your romantic quotient, no matter who you plan to have over for the big day.

To find your inspiration for this holiday, first determine your audience. You don't want to be stuck trying to entertain 5-year-olds at a Valentine's Day party if you've decorated your home with delicate lace and loads of lit candles and rose petals on the floor! So ask yourself the following questions:

✔ Will you be decorating for an elegant, romantic dinner for two?

✔ Will you be hosting a children's party?

✔ Will you be hosting a fun party for your friends?

After you determine your audience, keep them in mind and glance through the inspiration list I provide in Table 8-1. Keeping your audience in mind helps determine what's best to use for inspiration, so feel free to jot down your favorite items that come to you while reading through the list. Don't forget to keep your audience's favorite places or things in mind, too — decorating with their favorites is a sure way to please.

Table 8-1	Valentine's Day Inspiration Pieces		
Colors	*Fabrics*	*Botanicals*	*Accent Items*
Red	Satins	Roses	Silver bowls, julep cups, and accessories
White	Silks	Carnations	Candles
Pink	Sheers	Calla Lilies	Poetry
Silver	Cashmere	Ivy	Books
Gold	Lace	Potpourri	Lockets
Black	Felt		Tokens of affection
Brown	Faux fur		Favorite destinations
	Fleece		Chocolates

Favorite movies can inspire the best decorating ideas ever. Re-create the look of interiors, places, and themes from your all-time favorite romantic movie. But don't limit yourself to your own favorites, or even to romantic movies. Consider re-creating your loved one's favorite movie — a whimsical jungle theme can make any Tarzan fan beat his chest with desire!

Planning and Organizing Your Holiday Decorating

Start planning for your Valentine's Day decorating by deciding exactly where you want to decorate. I've seen offices, parks, restaurants, hotel rooms, sidewalks, beaches, and more decorated for Valentines Day. Apparently, when Cupid takes hold, boldness occurs. You can add dramatic touches anywhere. Open spaces and public spaces, along with your own home, are all game for decorating.

I know, no one wants to think about planning so far in advance for something that's supposed to be romantic and spontaneous. Unfortunately, though, you have to plan a bit if you intend to do something out of the ordinary in some place other than your own home.

If you're thinking of surprising someone by doing something extremely romantic that includes decorating spaces other than your own, you need to plan now and get proper clearances and approvals and to check laws to make sure that everything you're wanting to do never warrants a fine. I believe in love and romance, but I believe in proper precautions as well. For public spaces, check with your local government offices, like the parks and recreation departments for the area in question. And, of course, if you plan on bringing alcoholic beverages, check to see if alcohol is prohibited in that area. Check and double-check to make sure that no one rains on your parade and douses those romantic flames.

Now, other than those little words of caution, you also want to call ahead to florists, caterers, and restaurants and visit department stores and retail shops for last-minute gifts that also serve as decoration. Oh yeah — and read through the rest of this chapter for some wonderful decorating ideas!

Decorating in a Flash

All the planning in the world doesn't mean that you won't end up having to decorate in a hurry. So if you find yourself needing to spiff up your space in a flash, never fear — just check out my ideas that follow.

Visiting the retail store

The most obvious way of decorating for Valentine's Day in a jiffy is to visit your local retail store and check out the special merchandise displayed front and center for this holiday.

Pick up gifts, photo frames, lockets, chocolates, cards, and candles all in one place. Stores usually have like items placed together and give not only great gift ideas, but also great decorating ideas. You can usually get in and out of a store quickly with an armload of decorating items that you can arrange to make a wonderful romantic vignette or tablescape. With these items alone, you can set a whimsical table with many surprises. Place candles in the middle of a table, wrap a necklace around a napkin, use the Valentine's card for a place card at a table setting, stack chocolates on dessert plates, and place a photo frame with a picture of yourself smack dab in the middle of a plate. Who wouldn't want that, right? And if you're looking for more ideas on how to make a stylish tablescape or vignette, refer to Chapter 2.

Using candles

If you have virtually no time to do anything else, go to a store and buy all the candles, in all shapes and sizes, that you can afford. Candlelight is probably the easiest, most transportable decorating medium around. Use it to cast a soft, seductive glow on everything.

Use creative containers for candleholders from around your house, such as vintage saucers, plates, empty wine bottles for tapers — use your imagination. Anything nonflammable that can contain dripping wax and provide a level surface is fair game. Remember that pretty bowls and other containers can be filled with water to accommodate floating candles also.

When grouping your candles, don't worry whether or not all your candlesticks or candleholders match. Gather up any candleholders you can find — even the fancy ones — for lighting up your home. You can even use saucers, coasters, tiles, or plates to place under pillar candles.

Check out these ideas to create a candlelit Valentine's Day setting:

- **In the bathroom:** Planning a seductive soak in the tub? Group candleholders on your sink, around the tub (be careful here — long hair tossing about may fall into the candles!), and even on the floor. Then fill your sink with water so that you can place floating candles in it.

- **In the bedroom:** Similar to the bathroom, start placing candleholders on any flat surface in your bedroom — dressers, bedside tables, plant shelves . . . get the idea?

Always be careful when decorating with candles. Just refer to my candle safety tips in Chapter 25 to make sure that your passion is the only thing burnin' down the house.

Using what you have on hand

You don't have to go wild to spice things up — romantic decorating doesn't always come packaged in satin sheets and fire-red velvet pillows. No matter what your everyday decorating style may be, simple touches and a few additions to your normal décor can spark up the heat. Just check through all your cabinets for your prettiest or finest dishes and linens and use them to display the items in my ideas that follow:

- Add to your room a few more candles, flowers, champagne, and sexy foods that you can eat with your hands such as strawberries and chocolates.

- Fold crisp white napkins into heart shapes for a romantic dinner or picnic (see Chapter 3 for instructions).

- Deck out bed trays with your finest linens and crystal and nice silver bowls of fruit and plates of cheese.

More Splash for Less Cash

Valentine's decorating doesn't have to dip way into the budget. Just dip into your creative soul and let the romance flow.

Getting petals for pennies

Call florists and ask if they have boxes of scrap flower petals for sale. Often, florists break apart the heads of roses and other flowers that are half spent or that shipped broken, and they sell them for just a few dollars a box. Obviously, they may be low on these little gems around Valentine's Day, but it's worth checking.

Here are just a few ideas for what you do with these petals:

- Scatter them along pathways, indoors or out, to lead your sweetheart to a special, romantic location.

- Sprinkle some over your bed.

- Run a bath and put a couple handfuls into the bath water.

- Toss some petals on your dinner table in between place settings or along a table runner.

Just make sure that you don't scatter them in areas that may become stained when the petals are stepped on.

The chalk zone

The best, and one of the most romantic, decorating ideas I ever saw cost about $2 for a bunch of sidewalk chalk. Yep, sidewalk chalk.

A friend of mine works in a high-rise building. Her boyfriend, on a whim, a budget, and under pressure, wanted to make her day. And he did. He went to the nearest discount store, bought a couple of pieces of sidewalk chalk, and decorated the nearest sidewalk that he knew his girlfriend could see out her office window.

He wrote, "I LOVE YOU, LADY C." in letters about 3-feet-tall each. Sure, he was laughed at, and swooned at, while he did it, but after calling his girlfriend from his cell phone to tell her to look out the window to see his decorated sidewalk, he decided it had been worth the effort.

Decorating a sidewalk doesn't take any skill — just unabashed courage and a box of chalk. Who knew that decorating so romantically could cost only $2?

Having a picturesque picnic

One of the most wonderful yet effective romantic decorating ideas is quite simple to do. Toss a warm blanket on the floor — by a fireplace, if you have one — and make a picnic. Arrange a couple of pieces of fruit in baskets, add sparkling wineglasses from your cupboards, and crackers and cheeses from your pantry (or picked up at the deli). Coupled with a nice bottle of wine, your picnic makes a pretty vignette suitable for any fun or romantic occasion. Plus, you just picked up dinner!

Jazzing Up Smaller Spaces

Often, a simple tablescape in your chosen theme will do quite nicely for small-space decorating. You can choose from many options, depending on the style or effect that you want to achieve. Check out the following ideas to find out what works best for your space:

✔ For a touch of fun, place a door mirror down the center of your table to use as a table runner. Scatter little candy-shaped hearts with cute words on them down the middle. Nestle a few votive candles in jars filled at the bottom with red heart candies and place them on the mirror. For place cards, use your Valentine greeting cards instead. Prop them on water glasses or toss the envelope and stand them in the center of your place setting.

- ✔ For an elegant look, set your table with simple white linens accompanied by your best crystal and china. A few silver candlesticks, some soft music, and a beautiful bouquet are all that you need for a stunning tablescape.

- ✔ For an even more dramatic, elegant look, drape garlands of strung faux pearl beads or crystals to mirrors or chandeliers.

- ✔ For a cozy, more intimate feel, spark up your spaces for romance by using just a little hot color to make a large impact. Infuse a few red pillows, with some plush faux fur throws, and light the candles, baby!

- ✔ For a simple look, spruce up a small dining or occasional table with a nice bunch of fresh flowers. Purchase a ready-made bouquet from your florist, or make your own arrangement or wreath to hang on your door, using the instructions I give you in Chapter 21. Highlight a table arrangement by spotlighting it under a track light, or place a can light from below to make a dramatic up light.

Involving the Family

Having the whole family join in to decorate for Valentine's Day makes the day even sweeter and more special. A few construction paper hearts, some glue, glitter, and paper doilies can bring enough child's play to the kitchen table for good family time. Plus, you now have decoration for the windows if the kids want to jazz up their own spaces.

But you don't have to stop there. You have other ways to keep the kids decorating for days. Just adapt the pressed wax paper leaf craft in Chapter 21 for this holiday. Press a few rose petals between layers of wax paper, or take this opportunity to use all those broken crayons your children may have. Use a vegetable peeler and shave several pieces off multiple colors of crayons. Follow the direction for pressing leaves between wax paper to melt the crayon wax. You get a nice "stained glass" effect that you can cut into different shapes, such as hearts, cupids, or other drawn designs. You can use cookie cutters to trace patterns. The whole family can cut out and hang their own designs in windows or doorways.

Four things to do with your Valentine's Day roses

If you just got a beautiful bouquet of roses, chances are you hate to kiss those babies goodbye. Here are a few ideas to make them last a bit longer:

✔ **Prolong their beauty.** Grab a few of those little packets of floral preservative provided by florists to add to your bouquet's water if you can. But if you received the roses as a gift, chances are that's not an option. Provide nutrients to your cut roses to help them last a bit longer by making a solution of equal parts of lukewarm water and, get this, lemon-lime soda. The sugar and citric acid serve as the food; the carbonation helps the flower to take up the nutrients more efficiently. Add a few drops of liquid chlorine bleach to keep the water clean. It's a simple homemade recipe that works.

✔ **Preserve them.** Follow the instructions I give you in Chapter 21 for waxing, pressing, preserving, or air-drying your roses. These simple projects can make your gift of beauty last and last.

One of my dearest friends kept all the roses that her sweetheart had given her over the years by air-drying the petals. When they got married, she walked down the aisle on the dried petals instead of fresh ones, and at their reception, small bunches of dried petals were opened for throwing over the newly married bride and groom. Very symbolic. Very cool.

✔ **Make potpourri.** Make decorative potpourri out of your dried petals and greenery. Add your favorite scent of essential or aromatherapy oil to your dried rose petals and toss them in a bowl with a few dried herbs, seed pods, or other preserved botanicals. Don't worry if you don't want to make your own from scratch. You can simply add your newly dried rose petals to existing potpourri as a fresh pick-me-up touch.

✔ **Frame them.** Air-dry, preserve, or press your roses and then frame some as a keepsake. With today's selection of shadow box frames, readily available at craft and framing stores, you can arrange and display pieces of your bouquets easily and effortlessly for instant art.

Try displaying one single rose from your bouquet by cutting the bloom from the stem as close as possible. Hot glue it in the center of the shadow box frame. Hand letter the date and a sentiment or note on a strip of handmade paper and glue it in the shadow box frame under the rose. Preserve a lasting memory forever — and get a decorative accessory to pull out every Valentine's Day, too!

Chapter 9

Celebrating Everything Irish: St. Patrick's Day

In This Chapter

▶ Exploring Irish charm

▶ Finding luck with different decorating ideas

Y ou don't have to be of Irish descent to be enchanted with Irish culture, especially at St. Patrick's Day. The spirit of St. Patty's Day embraces the heartwarming message of the importance of home and family.

Long gone are the days when the only way you could celebrate and decorate for this holiday was with a "Kiss Me I'm Irish" T-shirt and a pint of green beer. Now, you can either embrace the traditional, fun way (insert T-shirt and beer) or opt for a more soothing, understated Celtic style. I separate ideas for each style under each heading, so you can skip to the ideas that most appeal to you. Either way, this chapter gives you plenty of ideas to start your St. Patrick's Day decorating.

Finding Your Inspiration

To help you define your focus, I've provided you with inspiration pieces for traditional décor and for Celtic décor. Table 9-1 lists the traditional stuff, and Table 9-2 lists the Celtic pieces. Perhaps you want to decorate an office party in rip-roaring Irish decorations but decorate your home with a more serene and naturalistic Celtic flair. Keep these different themes in mind when you're going through the inspiration lists. Make notes of anything else you can add or how you can adapt pieces from one list into the other.

Table 9-1	Traditional St. Patrick's Day Inspiration Pieces		
Colors	*Fabrics*	*Botanicals*	*Accent Items*
Kelly greens	Cottons	Shamrocks	Leprechauns
Black	Prints with St. Patrick's Day Themes		Pots o' gold (filled with gold coins)
White	Plaids		Flag of Ireland
Orange			Shamrocks
			Little People (or Fairies)
			Limericks

Table 9-2	Celtic Inspirations		
Colors	*Fabrics*	*Botanicals*	*Accent Items*
Greens — from mossy to light celadon	Irish linen	Moss	Charms
White/Ivory	Cotton	Shamrock plants	Celtic Crosses and Knots
Browns — light to dark	Accent fabrics in greens or other earth colors	Twigs, bark	Irish blessings
	Plaids	Bells of Ireland	Crystal
	Lace		Leather
			Family crests
			Claddagh symbol
			Stone or pebbles

Think "Emerald Isle" when decorating — natural colors, deep greens, perhaps a running fountain so that you can hear a gentle trickle of water in the background. Think soothing, peaceful, and lush. You'll come up with many ideas for decorating with this mindset. Ancient Ireland, with its castles, cottages, and moss-covered huts, are sources of inspiration when deciding how you want to decorate for this holiday.

Planning and Organizing Your Holiday Decorating

You need to decide where you want to decorate and in what style or theme. Although a Celtic theme may sound pretty, it may not be exactly what your guests had in mind when they arrive at your St. Patrick's Day party at your house. Make sure to choose a style of decorating that fits in best with your audience. If you're decorating a classroom, I doubt that moss or Irish linen decorations are appropriate; likewise, if you want an upscale, elegant look, you don't want to have plastic pots o' gold and pictures of leprechauns on your wall. Decide who you're decorating for (even if it's just for you) and what seems most appropriate. Then gather a pen and paper and start taking notes from your inspiration list and jot down any other ideas that may come to you.

Check your local calendar section in your newspaper for any special parades or events centered around St. Patrick's Day and enter them in your calendar. If you are planning a party, you may want to host a get-together after a parade, or choose a different date altogether. List all the decorating you want to do, and then read on! Plenty of Irish-inspired decorations await.

Decorating in a Flash

If you just found out that guests plan to come over for some Celtic celebrations, you may need to arrange some Irish décor in a hurry. Check out some of my ideas to get your creative juices flowing, so that you can add a little touch of the Emerald Isle around your home.

For quick touches throughout the house, try using

> ✔ **Simple items you may already own that can be customized quickly for St. Patrick's day decorating.** Pick up a gold paint pen or marker at a craft store and emblazon some of your favorite Celtic words or Irish blessings on candles, flower pots, votive holders, or on stones or pieces of slate. Even simple kitchen ceramic tiles from a hardware store can serve as coasters (and take-home gifts) with a blessing printed on each one.
>
> If your handwriting is like mine, you may want to opt for transferring images onto these items. Follow my instructions for transferring images to surfaces in Chapter 24.

- ✔ **Novelty items, purchased from a party supply store, that reflect traditional Irish décor and are geared for St. Patrick's Day.** Little black cauldrons can be filled with gold foiled chocolate coins. Paper goods with shamrocks and leprechauns printed on them can accent dessert tables. Little hats — paper or plastic — can sit at each place setting.

- ✔ **A galvanized metal tub, filled with ice for an instant "bar" where you can serve cold beverages at the end of your buffet.** For other quick buffet décor ideas, check out the following:

  - Group plenty of Irish coffee mugs together on a tray and place near your coffee service.

  - Mass groupings of glass or crystal in unusual shapes look great and serve a purpose. Use them for holding mints or sugar cubes for coffee or tea, or fill them with water and float candles in them.

  - Attach small gold charms, found at a craft store, with a little green ribbon to serving utensils for a little touch of Irish charm.

- ✔ **Your food as part of the decorating as well.** Irish food can be quite decorative; here are some ideas:

  - If you serve little crocks of potato soup or hearty Irish stew, serve cloverleaf-shaped rolls with it. They'll give your appetizer a little Irish charm. (You can often find these rolls in your supermarket's bakery around this time of year.)

  - A few drops of green food coloring tints all sorts of food items — well, if you're into eating and drinking green things!

  - Using one cookie cutter, you can cut your finger sandwiches into shamrock shapes, make custom cookies, have a pattern for cutting out paper decorations, and more.

  - Refer to Chapter 3 for unique table settings and napkin folds. Not only is the four-leaf clover napkin easy, but it also looks great at any place setting.

If you're looking for a more Celtic way of decorating in a hurry, visit a garden center. Purchase natural materials, such as spongy green mosses, shamrock plants, and smooth river stones, along with a few rustic planters. Hot glue pieces of moss to the decorative planters before repotting shamrock plants into them. River stones can be placed in the bottom of clear glass jars to hold small taper or votive candles to line your walkway. A flat of wheat grass works nicely for a low centerpiece on a dining table.

If you just keep "simple" in mind, you'll never be at a loss for how to add a little Irish charm to your décor. As a last resort, use the Irish blessings and Gaelic words I give you in the "Irish inspirations" sidebar to make more decorations in a flash.

Irish inspirations

Use some of these Irish blessings or Gaelic words to add to decorative items, such as candles, stones, or coasters. Include them in invitations, print and frame them to set on desks, or present to guests as take-home gifts. Add a few pressed clovers or a small charm to give them a finishing touch.

Blessings and prayers:

May the road rise
Up to meet you,
May the wind be
always at your back,
May the sun shine warm
Upon your face, the rains
Fall soft upon your fields
And until we meet again
May God hold you in the hollow of his hand.
—Irish Blessing

May there always be work for your hands to do;
May your purse always hold a coin or two;
May the sun always shine on your windowpane;
May a rainbow be certain to follow each rain;
May the hand of a friend always be near you;
May God fill your heart with gladness to cheer you.
—Irish Blessing

May the lilt of Irish laughter lighten every load,
May the mist of Irish magic shorten every road,
May you taste the sweetest pleasures
That fortune ere bestowed,
And may all your friends remember
All the favors you are owed.
—Irish Blessing

The joy of God be in thy face,
Joy to all who see thee,
The circle of God around thy neck,
Angels of God shielding thee,
Angels of God shielding thee.
—Celtic Prayer

Celtic words and their meanings:

- ✔ Cead mile failte: A hundred thousand welcomes

- ✔ Slainte: Cheers

- ✔ Sláinte chugat: Good health to you

- ✔ Go mbeannaí Dia duit: May God bless you

- ✔ Go n-éirí leat: All the best

- ✔ Oiche Mhaith: Good night

More Splash for Less Cash

Most of the ideas in this chapter cost you hardly any green. Still, here are a few more decorative things you can do that give you even more bang for the buck, investing in only one stamp.

With one Irish-inspired stamp (say a Celtic knot or Claddagh symbol) you can:

✔ Stamp paper invitations or place mats (see Chapter 23)

✔ Emboss velvet papers or green velvet accents (see Chapter 22)

✔ Stamp it into a lump of clay resembling a stone, so it looks like it's engraved

✔ Stamp the design onto linens, using it as your beading pattern (see Chapter 26)

✔ Stamp the design on a pillar candle for one simple accent

✔ Etch simple glass items by using the stamped design as a pattern (see Chapter 27)

See? One stamp can be your whole inspiration piece to make nifty accents to place around the house.

Symbols of Ireland

Along with the flag of Ireland, Irish blessings, the potato, and a host of other symbolic items you may conjure up associated with St. Patrick's Day, you may want to keep your eye out for these two elements found in a variety of merchandise and decorative items.

The Claddagh symbol, a wreath shaped emblem with two arms holding a heart in its hands, is almost as synonymous with Ireland as the shamrock. It's always been associated with a ring — no beginning and no end — and is prominent on the traditional wedding ring of the Irish. It remains a universal symbol of love, loyalty, friendship, and fidelity. Often, you can find it on home décor items such as doorknockers, picture frames, and crystal bells to name a few. With such variety, anything bearing the Claddagh emblem is great for adding to your decorations for St. Patrick's Day. If you've never seen a Claddagh symbol before, check out the following illustration.

A Celtic knot is a line drawing of several intertwined lines that represent no beginning and no end (see the following illustration). The Celts first used these intricate drawings as a way to fill in

blank space. That's right. This artwork started as pure style elements to fill in borders of manuscripts, sculptures, and jewelry. Generally, they didn't appear as isolated elements, although today, you can find several different shapes, designs, borders, and sizes of Celtic knots emblazoned on home décor items. The significance perhaps of the Celtic knot lies in the symbolism of interconnectedness — a great little thing to have around at St. Patrick's Day.

Jazzing Up Smaller Spaces

Just because you have a small space doesn't mean that it has to cramp your holiday decorating style! Just use some of my ideas below for your small spaces, or use them as inspiration for your own ideas:

- **Use pressed shamrocks, prints of Irish Blessings, or even greeting cards to customize your frames for this holiday.** Frame bits of embroidered linens or lace that you may find or have had passed down to you. If your family has a crest, frame a copy of that along with your other touches of Ireland.

- **If you're looking for something traditional to do to smaller spaces, try throwing out a bit of Kelly green throw pillows and add a touch of plaid in the mix.** Gift-wrap an existing pillow by folding a yard of plaid fabric around it and securing the flaps with an oversize kilt pin found in fabric stores. Hang a purchased banner that proclaims "Happy St. Patrick's Day!". You'll keep those Irish eyes smilin' with even the smallest touch.

✔ **As classic as the Emerald Isle itself, Waterford crystal and Wedgwood bone china are perfect ways of upscaling and paying tribute to this holiday.** Although you may or may not own pieces from these collections, display some of your more brilliant pieces of cut glass vases, stemware, or candy dishes. Bring out the good china and lavishly set place settings with accents of green, orange, and white — the colors of the Irish flag. Looking for an elegant touch of orange? Ask your florist to order you up some coral roses. They pop when a low arrangement is placed against a backdrop of mossy green table linens. You'll really love the look.

✔ **Purchase a few tapestry Irish blessing accent pillows for a little reminder of St. Patrick's Day on window seats or comfy chairs.** Or, a small smooth stone can represent the magical Blarney stone. Kissing it is optional (and, sometimes, unexplainable to passersby).

Involving the Whole Family

Having the family pitch in to decorate for St. Patrick's Day can be great fun. Here are a few ways your little leprechauns can get in on the action:

Display any artwork brought home from school with a custom St. Patty's Day magnet that you create together. Here's how:

1. **Find a coloring book to trace a leprechaun or woodland fairy, or sketch a shamrock onto a large piece of shrink plastic.**

2. **Let your child color it with colored pencils, cut it out, and bake it in the oven.**

   You can make several "lucky charms" this way, allowing your child to choose his or her subject.

3. **Attach a self-adhesive magnet to the back of the shrunken plastic after it's had time to cool.**

You can also attach these to many school items by punching holes in the shrink plastic before baking to make sturdy plastic fobs. Add these little mystical, miniature mementos to key chains, necklaces, and bracelets, or make mobiles out of them.

Much of your decorating — making or setting out Irish blessing cards, welcome signs, place mats, and paper shamrock garland — can all be made at one creative sitting with the whole family. With all these decorations on hand, you're bound to have plenty of things to add around the house.

Chapter 10

Rejoicing Easter

*E*aster, although rooted in religious significance, can be lighthearted and fun to decorate for as well. No meaning need be lost while decorating with cute chicks and adorable bunnies. The religious story can be told no matter what decorates your home. Welcome new, fresh life into your décor, reviving it from a long winter's nap, and celebrate the renewal that Easter brings.

Finding Your Inspiration

Easter is one of those great holidays where you can derive ideas and inspiration from the spring season as well as rely on those trusty icons, such as bunnies and baskets, associated with this holiday. So if Peter Cottontail doesn't strike your fancy, you can still add a few spring-related items into your décor. For more ideas, look over the Easter inspiration list in Table 10-1. You'll find plenty of items to get you hopping down the decorating trail in no time.

Table 10-1		Easter Inspirations	
Colors	*Fabrics*	*Botanicals*	*Accent Items*
Pastels	Easter novelty prints	Easter lilies	Candies
Blue	Cotton solids	Tulips	Bunnies
Lilac	Calicos	Roses	Chicks
Pink	White canvas	Grasses	Eggs

(continued)

Table 10-1 *(continued)*

Colors	Fabrics	Botanicals	Accent Items
Yellow	Sheers like voile or tulle	Ivy	Baskets
Spring greens		Artichokes	Chocolates
Browns		Carrots	Galvanized tin
White		Cabbage leaves	
Silver		Raffia	Cross/Bible

Write down any other items that you've always associated with spring or Easter and add any items you may already have on hand to start building your decorating scheme. Refer to my inspiration piece section in Chapter 4. You'll be designing a fantastic tablescape or a festive buffet in no time, using that Fabergé egg you treasure.

Planning and Organizing Your Holiday Decorating

Because you have so many options for Easter, the following tips can help you organize and plan better so that everything pulls together at the right time:

✔ **Decide what you plan to do for Easter.** You may want to check to see if there are any special services, plays, or other events you need to plan around. Think about whether you want to host an Easter egg hunt with family or friends or whether you want to have a picnic, brunch, or lunch at your home. Obviously, deciding on what activities you want to host or plan will have more of an impact on your decorating for this holiday.

You can have decorations placed out as much as a month in advance, but keeping activities in mind will help you place focus on what areas you really want to decorate, and which ones can include just little accents.

✔ **Know where you can get flowers.** Flowers are important items for Easter. You can use tulips, daffodils, and roses in small centerpieces or for other small accents to baskets and statuaries. So check your garden to see what should be in bloom in time for Easter.

If you don't garden or nothing is in bloom yet, call your florist or scout out home and garden centers and grocery stores for blooming bulbs. Easter lilies, tulips, and daffodils can be bought in advance and used just about anywhere you want some life or color. You can purchase them as much as two weeks in advance and keep them blooming past Easter with care and attention. Make sure that you've got plenty of extra flower pots, planters, or vases handy so that you can repot these plants and get rid of the tacky foil usually wrapped around plastic pots.

Decorating in a Flash

Running short on time? Or perhaps you just decided to add a touch of Easter around the Sunday brunch you slaved over? The following tips show you how to quickly add Easter décor for all types of settings:

- Pick up a few miniature baskets with some gourmet jelly beans for each guest. You can easily place these colorful gems at each place setting, and they make wonderful take home gifts.

  Need a more elegant touch? Many retail stores will have premade arrangements with Easter themes already done up for you.

- Buy a centerpiece for each table you'll be serving food from (for instance, a buffet and the dining table).

- Stems of fresh or faux flowers are great for tucking in baskets, vases, or around decorative accents.

- Grab a few crystal candlesticks and insert one of your decorated eggs into it. Make sure that it stays by adhering some candle wax adhesive to the bottom of the egg. Write your guests' names on the eggs with a gold marker or paint pen; add a few leaves of ivy at the base. You'll have little adorable place cards in no time using what you may already have handy.

- If you're wanting to decorate eggs fast but just don't have much time, try using rub-on transfers. Before you go "ewwwww," let me tell you — they've come a long way. Just check out some of the colorful transfers at your local craft store. You can pick up a couple of sheets of letters, Victorian art, flowers, bunnies, chicks, and so on to make your plain eggs look like they've been handpainted. All that with just a couple of rubs with a craft stick. You may read more about how to transfer art to eggs (or any surface) in Chapter 24. It only takes a few minutes to produce beautiful results!

Just remember that if you go this route, give your eggs a quick spray with a glossy clear-coat sealer — it will make any shininess of the transfer disappear into one congruent look.

✔ You can find many more Easter-themed items in catalogs, retail stores, and specialty shops. Select a few to add here and there in the house for quick touches. Wall hangings, wreaths, and special ceramic dishes can all be picked up and placed in a hurry. There's nothing better than instant décor!

If you need help making vignettes or tablescapes, refer to Chapters 2 and 3. You'll get plenty of pointers for arranging items for maximum impact.

More Splash for Less Cash

If you're looking to incorporate some holiday décor but don't have the funds to buy premade retail items or expensive bouquets of flowers, just check out the following ideas to create some holiday magic without breaking your budget:

✔ **Etch glass.** Etching glass doesn't cost a lot of money and gives fantastic results. Etch Easter egg stencils or another symbol of Easter onto inexpensive glassware items, such as bargain stemware, glass plates, egg cups, and even glass ornaments to hang on an egg tree (see how to make an egg tree in the "Involving the Family" section later in this chapter). Etching glass is easy and takes a relatively short time to do. You can find out how to etch in Chapter 27.

✔ **Decorate eggs.** Of course, you'll want to decorate some Easter eggs. At this time of year, many grocers bundle dozens of eggs at a bargain price. Buy a few dozen! The next two sections give you some ideas on how to decorate with real as well as fake eggs.

Achoo! Blowing eggs

The ancient Ukrainian form of decorating eggs, *pysanky,* starts with a blown egg. So what? Although you may never aspire to spend time decorating eggs as an art form, blown eggs are good at helping you preserve any hard work you or your family creates for Easter. Perhaps you'll want to do just a few so that you can create keepsake ornaments to mark your child's decorating skills and talent as each year progresses.

Do it for the experience! Here's how you can start blowing eggs.

Grab some eggs, a straight pin, and bowl and follow these instructions:

1. **Starting at the narrow end of the egg, gently pierce a hole through the shell and membrane with a straight pin.**

2. Turn the egg over and pierce a hole through the shell and membrane with a straight pin in the center of the bottom of the egg. Use the pin to gently start removing more bits of the shell and membrane to make a hole approximately ¹⁄₁₆ inch in diameter. Pierce the yolk.

3. Pressing your lips to the top of the egg, blow the insides of the raw egg out of the bottom of the egg into a bowl. Try not to touch the raw egg. Rinse the inside and outside of the shell with a 1:1 mixture of vinegar and water.

If you want to dye the egg, be sure to keep the raw egg intact, dye it first, and then blow out the contents. Otherwise, you'll have floating eggs on dye (nothing like bobbing for eggshells in dye!).

Oh, and don't forget to read the good ol' egg safety cautions at the end of this chapter.

Using paper or plastic — eggs, that is

Egg shapes come in various types of materials. Visit a craft store and stroll the aisles to find eggs done up not only in the plastic pull-apart type, but also in glass, papier mâché (perfect for ornaments), wood, foam (polystyrene), and who knows what else! I've even seen ceramic bisque eggs that can be painted and then fired at a ceramics studio.

Choose eggs that appeal most to you and function well for your decorating purposes. Real eggs won't last more than a couple of days, blown eggs are fragile, and faux eggs last but have their own drawbacks as well (ever try to hang a wooden egg on an egg tree?). All of them are relatively inexpensive — take your pick!

Decorating real eggs

When you start decorating eggs, decide on whether you want to boil them in a pan of water, or blow the raw egg out of the shell. You can do both! Boiled eggs are best for little hands to work with (imagine if one slips out of a toddler's hand — less mess to clean up), they take dye baths well, and make the eggs less fragile.

If you're quite the artist, have a gentle hand, don't have to worry about kids, dogs, or anyone else getting raw egg matter on them, or want to dive into a little more intricate patterned designs for your egg surface, by all means, blow away (see the sidebar, "Achoo! Blowing eggs"). Just be sure to read the egg safety information I give you at the end of this chapter. It'll come in handy.

Here are some of my favorite quick and easy ways to decorate eggs for kids of all ages!

Dyeing

Want to dye eggs without a kit that has those handy dissolving tablets? Make your own egg dye by adding 25 drops of food coloring to ½ cup of boiling water and ½ teaspoon of white vinegar. Add enough water to cover eggs. You'll be ready to dip those babies in no time.

To get a lighter color, don't skimp on the food coloring! Just take the eggs out of the dye a little earlier. Leave them in longer for a deeper shade of color.

Stamping

After your eggs are dyed, use fun stamps to decorate or customize your eggs. Emboss them if you want! Need more information? Go to the stamping section in Chapter 23.

Glittering

Who knew that a staple in kid's crafting could look so glam? Brush a light layer of craft glue on your plain or dyed eggs and roll them in pastel colors of glitter. Let them dry on a sheet of aluminum foil or wax paper.

Waxing

Before you dye those eggs, use a white crayon to write names, draw designs, or embellish any way you want. The wax resists the dye, so whatever you draw on the egg turns out to be the original egg color. Try this after you dye eggs and double-dip into another color! Lay a small stencil on the egg surface and color it in with the crayon. You'll have lots of fun playing around with this technique.

Painting

Use craft paints to add designs to plain or dyed eggs! Refer to Chapter 23 for some general tips and techniques you may want to use on your Easter eggs.

Tissue paper

Tear or cut bits of colored tissue paper and layer them onto the egg for a stained glass effect. Use watered down household glue to attach pieces to the egg surfaces and connect or layer the tissue as desired. After they're dried, seal with a few coats of clear-coat spray.

Pearlizing

Perhaps one of the most elegant ways to finish plain or dyed eggs is by dipping them in a mica substance called PearlEx Powdered Pigments by Jacquard. You can find this fine metallic powder in art supply stores, and it comes in many colors and finishes.

After dyeing your eggs, dip them into PearlEx and wipe with a soft cloth (do not brush). Rub and buff the egg, applying more PearlEx as desired until you get the desired look. Seal the finish with a satin finish clear-coat spray and allow it to dry.

Jazzing Up Smaller Spaces

If you're short on space but still want some holiday flair, see if the following ideas can give you any inspiration:

✔ A crystal candy dish filled with chocolates covered in pastel foils, a clear vase full of freshly cut tulips, or a garden statuary rabbit displayed bring touches of spring and Easter into any small area.

✔ A single potted Easter lily adds a simple and elegant touch to a bathroom sink vanity. Small pastel soaps can replace your usual hand soaps in a bathroom. Glass vials containing one stem of a single spring flower can accent a small area beautifully.

✔ If that's not enough, small baskets duded up for Easter are plenty to liven up a smaller space that needs a little holiday decorating (see "Involving the Family," later in this chapter, for ideas on decorating Easter baskets). And if you really want to be clever, decorate them for guests to take home after Easter festivities are over. It'll clear out space for decorating other holidays.

Involving the Family

Decorating eggs with the family is integral in decorating for Easter! You can always dye or paint eggs alone, but there's something about seeing what kids of all ages can create when gathered around a table full of colored eggs and art supplies. Use my suggestions for decorating eggs that I give you earlier in this chapter, but if you want more ideas for decorating with the family, here's what I suggest.

Decorating baskets

Baskets at Easter house pretty colored eggs, chocolate bunnies, or a few plush toys. Adding decorative touches to them is as simple as 1, 2, 3, and 4!

Ribbon

Add one large ribbon in a pastel color to one handle of a basket. You can purchase them premade at any craft store, or make your own using the instructions I give you in Chapter 21.

Flowers

Adding faux flowers, ivy, or other decorative blooms to baskets are pretty touches to surround the contents of a basket. For a permanent fix, hot glue blooms around the rim or all over the outside of the basket (leaving the bottom untouched). Or attach one bloom around the basket handles alongside a sheer ribbon bow.

If you want to add just a temporary touch keeping the basket in tact for future use, use florist's tape to wrap and tie a fresh or faux flower to the basket. Cover the tape with a bit of ribbon.

For faux flowers, the wire stems are usually slim enough to insert into the weave of the basket. If not, you can use scissors or wire cutters to strip any plastic off the wire and then insert them into the basket weave. With this method, you can quickly remove them after Easter has passed.

Found objects

Floral picks, Easter ornaments, religious symbols, or other objects can be tied to basket handles, or be adhered directly to the sides of the basket with a bit of glue. Use creativity when looking for things to add to your basket. A simple garland of pearl beads wrapped around a handle accents pearlized eggs beautifully.

Paint

If your basket is tired, or needs customizing for the holiday, a can of spray paint works wonders. Working in a well-ventilated area (preferably outside), spray your basket with light coats of spray paint, allowing coats to dry between applications. Because baskets are woven, turn and spray your basket all sorts of ways (including upside down), so you can be sure that the paint covers all the cracks and crevices.

If you're giving away baskets, try to decorate them according to people's tastes. If you're giving one to a child, a fun, whimsical basket is as welcomed as giving a basket with a crystal egg ornament tied on with a bow to a cherished friend. Decorated baskets don't always have to match your décor, taste, or style — especially when sending them with guests. Give them something that they'll appreciate so that your decorating efforts are worthwhile.

Making an egg tree

An egg tree, a tabletop decoration made of bare branches, is a great way to show off each family member's creativity! Purchase one to place on a table for a conversation piece, use a tree in your front yard, or make one yourself! Use a sturdy container that's weighted at the base (add a few rocks or marbles if you need some extra heft) and fill it with floral foam. Top it off with a bit of Easter grass or moss and insert small tree branches, such as willow or pussy willow, into the foam. You can hang decorated eggs, ornaments that your child brings home from school, or cookies tied with ribbon on the branches. Allow your child to decorate his or her own egg tree!

Papier mâché eggs

During the month, start making large papier mâché eggs with your child. Blow up an ordinary balloon (overinflate it a bit to give it that egg shape) and begin covering it with strips of newspaper dipped in a flour and water paste. (Start with about a cup of flour and add enough water to make a pancake consistency batter). Add layer after layer, drying each one in between, until the time comes to decorate for Easter. Stick a straight pin into the egg to burst the balloon, and you have a hollow egg to paint, decorate, add stuff to, cut open and fill, make a basket out of . . . okay, as you can see, I could go on and on. These eggs will keep your family busy for days and are great to have on hand for fun and decorative purposes.

A little time, some creative flair, and a bushel of bunnies, baskets, and bows will have you parading your home in style!

Handling eggs safely

Here an egg, there an egg, everywhere an egg, egg. Old MacDonald never had so many eggs around than at Easter time!

With all the use of eggs in Easter decorating, be sure to keep these few safety tips in mind.

✔ **Green eggs and ham are not cool to eat.** Never eat hard-boiled eggs that have been dyed and left unrefrigerated for any length of time. Although I'm sure that some people say you can eat them, I'm saying don't. Why chance it? Eggs carry bacteria that can cause food poisoning, and any egg that's been treated with a dye or paint is pretty iffy, even if the tint says that it's food safe. In the end, if the bad eggs get eaten, they won't be the only ones who are green. Be safe. Don't eat Easter eggs.

(continued)

(continued)

✔ **Blow it off.** Many intricate egg designs are made with blown eggs, which means that a raw egg is blown from the insides of the shell. Although this craft has been done for centuries, don't get careless when handling raw eggs.

If you can, blow eggs safely by investing in an egg blowing kit, or at the very least, buy an ear syringe used for irrigating and cleaning ears. You can find them at any drug or discount store. Use the ear bulb to blow air into the egg, removing the insides, instead of placing the egg to your lips. You can also use the bulb to squirt a vinegar and water cleaning solution inside the egg to clean and remove any remains. Take care to wash your hands thoroughly with an antibacterial soap after removing the insides of the egg.

Thinking about making some omelets with your discards? Well, I guess you can if you cook them immediately (and if your family doesn't mind a bit of accidental spit on the side). Otherwise, discard the eggs away from children and pets and clean the area thoroughly with a disinfectant. My favorite way of discarding eggs? Flush them down the toilet.

Chapter 11

Being True to Red, White, and Blue: Independence Day

In This Chapter

▶ Showing your patriotism

▶ Displaying the flag

▶ Paying tribute with decorations

Strike up the band! July 4 — the birthday of the United States of America — is cause to decorate. From parades and picnics to grilling and pool parties, Independence Day allows us to show our true colors and pay tribute to this great country of ours.

This chapter can help get you on your way to decorating patriotically and give you enough ideas to make you shout three cheers for the red, white, and blue!

Finding Your Inspiration

Independence Day ignites a love for country in the hearts of many. For inspiration, you need not look further than the trusty colors of our flag. However, if you need a few more items to add to your patriotic décor, check out Table 11-1. Perhaps it will spark projects or ideas to add to your crackerjack decorations.

Table 11-1		Patriotic Inspirations	
Colors	*Fabrics*	*Botanicals*	*Accent Items*
Red	Cotton solids	Roses	United States Flag
White	Sparkling lamés	Carnations	Stars
Blue	Novelty printed fabrics in patriotic themes	Gladiolas	Statue of Liberty
Silver	Red, white, and blue checked or striped fabric	Red fruit such as strawberries, cherries, or raspberries	Other symbols of freedom
Gold		Blue fruit such as blueberries, blackberries, grapes, or muscadines	Fireworks/sparklers
		Star fruit	Anything Americana

Make notes of items that you think would make good additions to this list. Add stars next to the ones you definitely intend to use or items you want to look for when shopping for decorations.

Planning and Organizing Your Holiday Decorating

Besides shooting or watching fireworks, you may be grilling, entertaining, or picnicking underneath the stars for Fourth of July festivities. So, because spending time outdoors is a big part of Independence Day, decorating your outdoors may be a major part of your planning. (You'll find other great indoor decorating ideas later in this chapter that you won't have to plan in such detail.)

When planning your outdoor festivities, keep the following in mind:

- Clean your outdoor furniture (refer to Chapter 7 for specifics).
- Make sure that you've planned on setting up enough tables for holding the ten surprise egg salads that guests bring.

✔ Purchase or rent extra chairs or get out some old quilts or blankets from your winter stash so that you have plenty of extra seating for relaxing underneath a fireworks-lit sky.

✔ Add a few citronella candles or some citronella oil to your shopping list. These items keep bugs away so that you can enjoy a lovely Fourth with as few bites as possible. Be sure to have plenty on hand so that you'll be able to burn this bug-fighting element all day and all night if need be.

Don't forget to check the candle safety guidelines in Chapter 25 and keep an eye on little ones (and big ones that act like little ones), so they don't try to light their fireworks using your decorations!

✔ Have some bunting on hand for draping. Think about all the places you might hang Christmas garland, and you discover all sorts of places to hang bunting — crown moldings, window boxes, banisters, outdoor columns, and stairways are just a few suggestions. Measure all the areas you want to cover and purchase accordingly.

✔ Check out the following flag etiquette tips so that you can display Old Glory with honor:

- The flag shouldn't be used as a drapery, tablecloth, or anything like that. Bunting of blue, white, and red stripes is available for these purposes. The blue stripe of the bunting should be on the top.

- When the flag is lowered, no part of it should touch the ground or any other object; it should be received by waiting hands and arms. When put away, the flag should be folded neatly and ceremoniously.

- The flag should be cleaned and mended when necessary.

- When the flag is displayed from a staff projecting from a window, balcony, or a building, the union should be at the peak of the staff unless the flag is at half-mast.

- Ordinarily, the flag should be displayed only between sunrise and sunset. If displayed at night, it should be illuminated.

- When displaying the flag against a wall, vertically or horizontally, the flag's union (stars) should be at the top, to the flag's own right and to the observer's left.

Call your local American Legion if you have any more questions about flag etiquette, including assistance in proper disposal of a flag.

Decorating in a Flash

Hang your flag high! You've never had a better time to install a bracket to hold a flagpole on your front porch or balcony. Choose your flag and flagpole first and then get the correct sized bracket to fit. Or buy a kit that contains everything you need. You just can't go wrong displaying the flag. This decoration is incredibly simple and easy, but left alone, it says it all.

If you want more ideas for decorating with flags, try some of these suggestions:

- **Use smaller flags to line your lawn.** Purchase 4-x-6-inch flags and spike them into the edge of the borders of your flower beds or lawn.

- **Poke small flags into window boxes or planters.** Center the flag in the middle of each window box for a minimalist statement. For planters, place flags at the borders.

- **Add small flags to wreaths.** Crisscross two flags and tie them on to the top or bottom of a grapevine or ivy wreath with strands of raffia. If you need a little extra security, use craft glue to secure them in place (hot glue may melt in higher temperatures if used outside).

Purchasing a few flags — in any shape or size — can add bursts of patriotism and beauty with the smallest amount of effort. You just can't do any better than the Stars and Stripes forever.

Here are a couple more ideas for decorating quickly and patriotically for Independence Day:

- Place GI cap napkin folds on each place setting (and yes, this goes for plastic plates, too — you can do this fold with paper napkins!). Add a few of these at the base of a loose daisy centerpiece on a kitchen table. Who says that you can't use paper hats as decorations! Go to Chapter 3 for detailed instructions on making the napkin fold.

- Make a few table toppers or table runners and add them to occasional tables. Purchase them or make them by buying a few yards of patriotic fabric from a fabric or discount store. You can find how to make any of these items in Chapter 19. If you're really in a hurry or just hate to sew, go casual and bunch the edges under or fringe (fray) the cut or torn edges.

More Splash for Less Cash

Decorating frugally for this holiday is as simple as repurposing some of your Christmas decorations (shhhhh — they'll never know!).

> ✔ Use white lights to string in treetops — they add great sparkle to your skies until the fireworks begin.

> ✔ Add red bows (no, not the velvet ones) to planters or on patriotic centerpieces.

> ✔ Use red, silver, or gold star garland to wrap in and around buffet settings. Use small bits and pieces as napkin rings — just wrap and tie around them!

Dig into your Christmas stash and see what other silver, red, or gold nonwinter Christmas items you can bring out for this holiday. I've used my grapevine Moravian star tree topper to hang over a buffet set underneath a low-branched oak tree. Gorgeous! And no one ever thought twice that it topped my Christmas tree just six months earlier. Use those patriotic ornaments for inspiration or make them into little tablescapes around the house. Instead of tucking them into a swag of evergreen, use ivy.

Even if you don't have a Christmas stash, you can use these same inexpensive ideas for decorating with sparkle. And then you'll have more items to reuse at Christmastime!

Jazzing Up Smaller Spaces

You can spice up those small spaces in your home by accessorizing with anything red, white, and blue. Here are some suggestions:

> ✔ A cobalt blue glass vase filled with some fresh red roses can be a nice touch for a centerpiece or small space.

> ✔ Many items, such as wreaths, candles, and small tokens symbolizing liberty, can be displayed in foyers, hallways, and sitting rooms.

> ✔ Adding a garland of bunting to indoor and outdoor spaces is an easy way of displaying red, white, and blue in your home without having to go overboard with many more decorations. Porches, banisters, balconies, and columns can be draped with red, white, and blue bunting. You can find bunting at stores, in catalogs, and online around Independence Day. Unless you want to wrap a column like a candy cane, I suggest that you cut or purchase smaller, more manageable pieces of bunting instead of trying to work with long, continuous pieces. You'll be able to center, drape, and add and take away pieces as needed.

The blue stripe of the bunting should always be displayed at the top!

Involving the Whole Family

Including family members is easy when you're decorating for the Fourth of July! Have children help you blow up red, white, and blue balloons. String them together to swag in doorways or gather a few together and attach them to picnic tables or fence posts with sturdy tape.

Let children hang crepe paper streamers in patriotic colors. Or have them help you wind red and blue streamers or ribbon up large white columns or banister rails. Cut stars from silver or white paper; you can string dangling stars around windows, mirrors, and doorways.

If you're decorating the outside of your home, have a spouse help light paper bag or Mason jar luminarias with a Stars and Stripes theme to surround the perimeters of your yard. (You can find out more about how to make luminarias in Chapter 25.)

If children want to make items to decorate the table, they can make paper Uncle Sam top hats from construction paper and glue some cutout stars on them. Have them make custom flags by taping or stapling school artwork to craft dowel rods. You can help children stake them in the ground or place them in centerpieces on children's picnic tables.

Including the family in decorating is as traditional as blue jeans, apple pie, and baseball. Enjoy living in the land of the free and the home of the brave and get courageous in trying new decorating ideas for your patriotic holidays.

Adapting your decorations for other patriotic holidays and occasions

One of the things I love about Memorial Day, Veteran's Day, and other patriotic holidays (besides having an occasional three-day holiday weekend) is that these holidays allow me to pull out my patriotic decorations to use more than just once a year to honor and remember those who have served our country.

These holidays are appropriate times to once again show your patriotism and appreciation. You certainly don't have to go all out; perhaps you want to display only a flag and wreath for outside décor.

To honor a family member or friend, place a photo of him or her in a small patriotic frame and glue (or wire) it to the wreath.

Set out a few of your tabletop decorations if you want. Most important, your decorating should always be a reminder of what the holiday means. Again, you don't have to do anything elaborate, but placing a few red, white, and blue candles helps you express loyalty and affection for those who served our great country so well.

Chapter 12

Creating a Graveyard Smash: Halloween

A ll you need for fabulous Halloween decorating is a great sense of humor, a good amount of energy, and a little imagination. You can make a stunning Halloween display with only a few intricately carved jack-o'-lanterns, or you can go all out making your home into a creepy castle.

If you have small children, you may want to keep the decorations on a happier, somewhat less sinister level so that you don't scare the heebie-jeebies out of them. But for the eternal kid in all of us, you can really get down and dirty with some haunted Halloween decorating.

Finding Your Inspiration

You find a list of inspiration pieces in Table 12-1 to reference when gathering your items or planning your Halloween decorating theme. Decide whether you want to go simple or sinister. Many items on this list — like ghosts — can be twisted to be either happy or ghastly.

Table 12-1	Inspiration Pieces for Halloween		
Colors	*Fabrics*	*Botanicals*	*Accent Items*
Orange	Sheers like lace, scrim, and chiffon	Pumpkins and gourds	Black cats, bats, spiders, and spider webs
Black	Satin	Raffia	Ghouls and goblins
Purple	Specialty prints with Halloween themes		Monsters
Blue			Mummies
Red			Witches
Yellow			Skeletons and graves
Silver			Werewolves and Vampires
Gold			Ghosts

Planning and Organizing Your Holiday Decorating

Halloween is one of those holidays where you can elaborately decorate your home inside and out. Obviously, you want to determine how much time, money, and effort you want to put into decorating for this holiday (as you would any other).

Make a project form (see Chapter 6), and make notes on a separate piece of paper listing key items you already have. If you're planning on hosting a Halloween party, plan your decorations around your festivities, taking every safety precaution you can when it comes to the elements that are almost always present at Halloween — darkness, fire, and weird clothing — a prescription for potential terror.

Even if you just want to spruce up the entryway with a few lighted jack-o'-lanterns, keep safety in mind with the many kids traipsing up to your door thinking more about candy than if their capes are dangling over a burning candle. Safety first, last, and always.

Keeping safety in mind

Many elements of Halloween decorating can pose hazards to unsuspecting visitors. Here are a few safety tips to keep handy when preparing for Halloween:

- **Clean up your mess.** Do your pumpkin carving on absorbent newspaper and scoop those pumpkinseeds and slimy innards into a bowl.

- **Say "No, no," to knives.** Don't let your children handle sharp carving knives and keep an eye on them while you're carving. If possible, purchase specific tools that are geared just for pumpkin carving (for your safety, too!). If the kids really want to participate in the carving, you can let them make the pattern or poke the pumpkin flesh in after you've done the carving.

- **Reconsider the candles.** If you're going to have many children around, nix the candles. It's just too much of a fire hazard. Buy a bunch of glow sticks readily available at any party supply or discount store and place them inside your jack-o'-lanterns. They cast an eerie green glow and are safe all around.

- **Pay attention.** Never leave a candle anywhere unattended, and never leave burning candles where children (or people who act like children) can reach them or accidentally knock them over.

- **Blazing fires aren't allowed.** Keep a fire extinguisher handy. You never know when a gourd will go up in smoke (no, dear, that's not a special effect).

- **Secure the perimeters.** Make sure that all props hanging, dangling, draped, staked, or set are steadily secured. Where there will be foot traffic, tape down loose wires with duct tape. You don't want people to trip. And check these places often during the course of the evening for any loose edges that need retaping.

- **Follow the package directions.** If a package of lights says that they're only for indoor use, don't string them outside. Read the fog machine directions. Take every precaution when it comes to decorating with materials you're not familiar with. Oh, the things I've seen. . . .

Getting the goods on film

If you plan to spend a fair amount of time and energy decorating for Halloween, or you love visiting old haunts in the neighborhood, you'll probably want to take a few photos. As I mention in Chapter 6, photos are also a good way of keeping a log of every year's decorating themes to keep in your decorating notebook. You can keep tally of what worked, and didn't work, as well as remember all the effort you put into one frightful event!

Most likely, your Halloween decorating will be best viewed at night when the fog machine is set, and your pumpkins are lit. But how do you capture your spooktacular decorating on film? Here are a few tips I've found that work best for photographing illuminated objects:

- ✔ Photograph your Halloween decorations right at dusk. You'll be able to see the illuminated objects, but it's not completely dark outside.

- ✔ Turn off your flash, so that your camera doesn't bounce light off the surface of your object leaving your photo bleached out and nondimensional. A lot of Halloween decorating uses lighting angles for effect — a pumpkin is lit from within, a tombstone from behind. What you want to do is capture that by artificially lighting the image from the front with lamps, candles, or other subdued lighting without using flash photography. You'll enjoy the eerie effects you get.

- ✔ Contrary to popular belief, faster film speed is not the best for this kind of photography. You want to slow your shutter speed down allowing the most light into the lens to capture your shot. Using a film speed of ISO 100 or 200 will do the trick with most point and shoot cameras. Be sure to keep a steady hand! With the shutter staying open longer, you have a better chance of blurring the images. Try mounting your camera to a tripod if you have access to one.

- ✔ If you're shooting a lit jack-o'-lantern, place a few extra candles inside so that the illumination isn't too faint when you get your pictures back.

Choosing your pumpkins

I'm assuming here that you want to at least carve a pumpkin or two to add to your holiday decorations. Before you buy your pumpkins, choose what designs you want to carve into them and take templates with you. Try to find pumpkins that are clean (so you don't accidentally pick one that's rotting where you thought was just dirt), gouge free, and have a relatively smooth surface to make carving easier.

Never carry a pumpkin by its stem; it can break and smash the squash to smithereens.

Decorating in a Flash

Halloween decorating usually takes a lot of preparation. Even a simple jack-o'-lantern can take a few hours to prepare and carve.

Never fear. Here are a few ideas you can conjure up in a pinch.

- **Lighted labyrinth:** Turn on some spooky music and turn out the lights! Make your room a labyrinth by gathering candles of every shape, size, and color that you own and place them all in one room. Light them, taking care that all your surfaces have been properly protected from any wax that may ooze its way down.

  For a different but just as eerie effect, place lighted candles on a path leading visitors or guests from one room to the next.

- **Lonesome luminarias:** Use plain paper lunch bags to make luminarias. Write haunted words like "Boo!" and "Scream!" with a black marker on them. Stamp them with Halloween stamps. Add sand in the bottom of them and place a votive candle in them for an eerie welcome into your home.

- **Haunted home:** If you have a few white sheets, you can instantly transform your home into an abandoned house. Throw sheets over all your furniture as if you've left for the season. Remove a few furniture pieces from the room to give a really "moved-out" effect. Sprinkle a light dusting of talcum powder, baking soda, or cornstarch on shelves, mantles, or other surfaces to give an accumulated dusty look (for me, I just have to leave things the way they are).

  Accent areas with wispy ghosts also made out of sheets. To make a ghost, simply blow up a balloon and center and drape a sheet over it. If you place the tied end of the balloon at the top, you can insert a safety pin through the sheet and the tied end of the balloon to suspend the ghost from the ceiling.

- **Stacked pumpkins:** Don't worry about carving a pumpkin at the last minute (some can be quite time consuming!). Grab a garden urn or flowerpot and stack two or three pumpkins, one on top of the other, to make a pumpkin topiary. Cut off stems and hot glue them together for added security so that they don't topple. Place your topiary on a buffet or sideboard for a stunning conversation piece.

More Splash for Less Cash

Novelty stores and party supply supercenters are great resources for inexpensive decorating ideas. You can buy just about anything from fake eyeballs to glowing skulls, and a lot of them for less than $10.

- ✔ **Lab specimens:** Put a few drops of green food coloring in a jar of water. Float a novelty item such as a fake eyeball or pack it with a rubber bat for a great gross-out effect. Be sure to place this eye-catcher around a light source. It's sure to cause a reaction one way or another.

- ✔ **Tombstones:** Make grave markers by purchasing large sheets of Styrofoam, found at craft and discount stores. After carving the sheet into the desired shape you want, press the edges of the Styrofoam with your fingers, making the edges look like hewn stone. Spray paint with a faux stone finish or simply use gray spray paint. Use a black broad-tipped marker to write on the front of it or use black vinyl adhesive letters found at office supply stores.

  Hang your tombstone on a door, or if you want to stake it in the ground, insert long dowel rods (available at any hardware or craft store) through the bottom of the gravestone leaving at least six to eight inches of dowel rod showing for staking into the ground. Remove the dowel rods from the tombstone, insert them into the ground, and then reinsert the tombstone onto the dowels.

- ✔ **Spooky silhouettes:** Draw or trace outlines of werewolves, bats, witches, and monsters on black poster board. Using a piece of chalk is best, so that you can easily see the lines. Cut around each shape and wipe away any chalk residue. Tape these to your windows. These spooky silhouettes transform your home into haunted just by turning on all the lights in your rooms.

Check your favorite Halloween supply stores the weekend before Halloween. Many stores deeply discount these seasonal items as much as 90 percent to make way for all the Christmas merchandise coming. Take advantage of it! Besides, you won't want to unveil your fiendish finds till right before the event.

Jazzing Up Smaller Spaces

Even the smallest room can be booootifully decorated with smaller accent items.

Use pushpins to suspend lightweight objects such as bats or spiders from your ceiling. Use monofilament to tie around the object and loop around the pin before pushing into the ceiling. It won't leave marks, the holes are small, and it's easy to tack items up and take them down.

✔ **Webs:** Fake spider webs and plastic spiders go a long way. Use these items to spook up a hall, corner, chandelier, or any other small corner you have.

✔ **Black lights or spotlights:** A black light (which, oddly enough, casts a bluish tint) makes all things white, including teeth, glow. Place one in a small room or near a window. If you're answering the door for trick-or-treaters, make sure to have one close by as your only light source. Spooky blue glowing lights coming from an opening door is enough of an effect to send shivers down some spines.

Spotlights, bought at any home improvement store in the lighting section, can be placed under plants, fake cobwebs, and other props to cast shadows on the ceiling.

Involving the Family

Scooping pumpkin guts, stringing out fake spider webbing, and making paper bats out of construction paper are activities that the whole family can enjoy doing together.

Carving pumpkins

Besides impressing your neighbors, a well-carved jack-o'-lantern easily decorates any area of your home — inside or out. Although the traditional way of carving a pumpkin is to grab a knife and carve a freehand design, I give you some variations you may want to try.

Regardless of design, here are the pumpkin carving basics to keep handy when diving into this project:

✔ **Tools:** I'd prefer that you purchase a pumpkin carving tool kit from your local discount or grocery store. These kits are usually inexpensive, are made specifically for this project, and can be thrown away if desired after the holiday. However, if you want to do a *lot* of carving, purchasing or gathering the tools I list here may be worth the investment. You can find most of these items at kitchen supply or hardware stores.

- **Punching tool:** Use an artist stylus (found at any art supply store), or an awl (found at hardware stores) for transferring designs onto the pumpkin. Sometimes, a nail or an ice pick works just as well.

- **Boning knife:** This long, thin-bladed knife is used to cut the opening and any large pieces out of the pumpkin

- **Paring knife:** Sharpen up a small paring knife to carve detail work.

- **Small serrated knife:** You'll want to use a serrated knife in a sawing motion to chunk out pieces requiring a little elbow grease. For smaller areas, try using a serrated steak knife.

- **Craft knife:** A craft knife works well for carving out intricate pattern work.

- **Bandages:** Do I need to explain why?

- **Gutting tools:** Sounds gross, eh? Really, all you need here is a large ice cream scoop or spoon to scrape out the insides of the pumpkin.

- **Large bowl:** Use a bowl to scoop seeds and pumpkin slime into. You can separate the seeds for toasting later or safely toss the goop — seeds and all — into the trash.

- **Candles, candle holders, and lighters:** Purchase white votives and tall, clear glass candleholders for placing inside your carved jack. Try to get fireplace matches or candle lighters, so that you don't burn your fingers when trying to light the candles inside the pumpkin.

- **Newspaper:** Use newspaper to protect your work surface areas and to absorb pumpkin juice or any spills you may have.

- **Fire extinguisher:** Again, do I need to explain why?

- **Tape:** You'll want to tape your patterns to the surface of the pumpkin and will need more than you think as you go along. Keep tape handy.

- **Petroleum jelly:** Sound weird? Well, to make your carved pumpkin last longer, smooth a bit of this magical jelly on the cut edges (even the inside of the pumpkin!) to seal in the moisture and prevent rapid deterioration or mold. It'll happen eventually, but petroleum jelly prolongs your hard work.

Clean your tools thoroughly and store them flat in your supply box for next year.

✔ **Patterns:** Picking a pattern for your pumpkin is one of the hardest decisions to make. Here are a few ways you can design your own or mix and match them up for a truly one-of-a-kind creation.

- **Drawing:** If you are an artist, or just want to free hand your own designs, you can draw your pattern two ways: 1) use a nonpermanent black magic marker and draw directly on the face of your pumpkin or 2) draw your design on a clean sheet of paper and tape it to the face of the pumpkin.

- **Painting:** If you've previously painted your pumpkin, simply carve out elements of your design.

- **Stenciling:** If you like a very tailored, precise look, buy lettering or design stencils at your local office supply or arts and crafts store. Design your pattern, using the drawing instructions earlier in this list.

- **Cookie cutters:** Metal cookie cutters and other vegetable garnishing tools available at a kitchen supply store can come in handy for making patterns. Place your cutter on the pumpkin and gently tap it with a mallet until the cutter scores the flesh. Then you can carve the design out using your regular carving tools.

- **Computer art:** Design and print out your pattern using your computer. If you have a graphics program, you can have a lot of fun turning photos into black and white patterns, or simply search online for pumpkin carving patterns. There are many free, downloadable designs to choose from!

After you've gathered your tools, picked your pumpkin, and selected your pattern, you're ready to dive in. Follow these easy instructions for preparing your pumpkin.

1. **Using a long, thin knife, cut out the top of the pumpkin (angling the knife inward) a few inches around the stem and remove the top.**

   Make sure that the hole is large enough to place your hand in for removing the seeds and membrane. Remove the bottom for easier removal of the pumpkin guts or if your pumpkin is missing its stem.

2. **Scrape the insides thoroughly, using an ice cream scoop or large spoon.**

   Make sure that all the membrane is removed and slather a good coat of petroleum jelly on the inside of your pumpkin to seal in moisture. (I've found that a good spritzing of vegetable oil works fine, too).

3. **Tape your pattern to the pumpkin and use a punching tool to score the lines of your design onto your pumpkin punching indentions approximately ⅛-¼ inch apart.**

   Don't poke the tool completely through the flesh. Remove pattern checking to make sure you've adequately outlined your carving lines.

4. **Using a serrated knife (or sawing tool), *saw,* don't slice, through your pattern lines with short back and forth motions. Carefully push out all the cut pieces of your pumpkin.**

   Use a paring knife to trim the edges and to cut the inside of the holes at about a 45-degree angle to allow more light to shine through. Smooth a light coating of petroleum jelly on the cut edges.

5. **Place a candle in a glass votive cup inside your pumpkin and light it.**

   Place the top back on, or leave off.

Painting pumpkins

No matter how old or young you are, painting is always a creative way to spend time decorating for Halloween. Provide plenty of colors of craft paint and disposable paintbrushes you buy at the dollar store. Have participants make their own palettes by giving them their own paper plates. Make sure that clothes and surfaces are adequately protected, and just have fun. Try having a few extra items on hand such as glitter, chenille stems (also known as pipe cleaners), googly eyes, raffia, and glue. You never know where this activity can take your works of art!

Even if older kids think that painting pumpkins is baby stuff, they can still join in on the family fun, laying out their carving pattern by painting it directly on the pumpkin in black. Because the pumpkin isn't carved yet, the design will last longer, and when they're ready to take their first stabs at carving their creations, the prep work is already done!

Cutting up at Halloween

Allow the family to help you with anything that needs to be cut or strung. Little hands can use safety scissors to help cut out black construction paper bats to string from ceilings. Set them up with orange, black, and yellow pieces of construction paper and provide paper punches in Halloween themes. They can punch out elements to insert into invitations, glue on fridge art, or add to scrapbook pages.

Bigger hands can help you cut anything else you need help with!

Manning your haunted house

Kids of all ages can plan, decorate, and man your haunted house. Never underestimate what lengths a kid will go to scare someone. Put them in charge of making sure that everything is running smoothly. They can always report back to central command if lights have shorted out, or the crypt isn't working anymore.

Have plenty of fun decorating for Halloween. Keep your audience, visitors, and safety in mind, and have a boooooootiful time! *Buwah-ah-ah!*

Chapter 13

Displaying Gratefulness at Thanksgiving

In This Chapter
▶ Reclaiming Thanksgiving as a decorating holiday
▶ Discovering your decorating focus for Thanksgiving

Some time ago, I began to notice Christmas decorating items being displayed in stores before Halloween items were even stocked on shelves. Between Halloween and Christmas, where did Thanksgiving decorating go? Thankfully (no pun intended), I'm starting to see more and more Thanksgiving merchandise, but still, these items can really get lost amid the glow-in-the dark skeletons and endless array of stockings and ornaments — so don't let yourself miss out on decorating for this holiday.

Thanksgiving is a wonderful time to cozy up your home with layers and textures for the oncoming winter months. Even if you live in a climate that doesn't really change that much, adding natural autumnal elements seems to just warm the heart and soul somehow. It's an easy look that anyone can achieve simply by borrowing elements from nature. So count your blessings, and don't let Thanksgiving get lost in the shuffle. Read through this chapter and find out how to celebrate each and every moment with grace and style.

Finding Your Inspiration

Even though Thanksgiving conjures up images of pilgrims and Indians, you can choose from a variety of colors and styles aside from this traditional theme for decorating. (However, if you're looking to incorporate that theme into your holiday decorating, check out the sidebar at the end of this chapter.)

Glance over Table 13-1 and choose from the many colors, items, and accent pieces to get ideas or inspiration for your Thanksgiving decorating. Check out the botanicals section especially for this holiday because an integral part of Thanksgiving is centered around celebrating a bountiful harvest. I'm not suggesting that you decorate with sweet potatoes or rhubarb, but you can refer to their colors when choosing accessories or accent pieces. Of course, if you want to decorate with sweet potatoes, don't let me stop you!

Table 13-1		Inspiration Pieces for Thanksgiving	
Colors	*Fabrics*	*Botanicals*	*Accent Items*
Deep tones of reds or wines	Velvets	Pumpkins and gourds	Woven baskets
Browns	Chenille	Autumn Leaves	Wreaths made of natural materials such as vines, wheat, leaves, twigs, or berries
Purples in eggplant or grape	Heavy cottons	Twigs	Metals in antiqued gold, bronze, or rust finishes (pewter is pretty for this holiday as well)
Greens: from deep sage to light pear	Fleece	Sheaves of wheat	Earthenware
Golds: from bright yellows to antiqued gold	Tweeds	Nuts	Candles in pillars, tapers, or votives
Creams: from ivory to white	Flannels	Chrysanthemums	Pilgrims
Oranges: from pumpkin to sweet potato	Wools	Roses	Native American Indians
	Tapestries	Fruit: pomegranates, cranberries, grapes, blackberries, kumquats, apples pears	Cornucopias
		Vegetables: corn, rhubarb, sweet potatoes, beets, squashes	

Feel free to make your own list of items that you associate with this holiday. Add the items here in the margins and take this book with you while you shop or plan your decorating for this holiday. When you go to the craft or home furnishings retailer, you can use your list for color and texture cues. It comes in handy when you become perplexed on decorating little areas or when choosing colors for accent pieces. You can never be at a loss for ideas if you're armed with related items that blend beautifully together.

Planning and Organizing Your Holiday Decorating

Because Thanksgiving is not only sandwiched between several other highly decorated holidays, but also follows the Jewish High Holidays, don't fret over how much or how little to do. You can produce simply stunning results, whether you do all your decorating in a day (or less) or take your time. Just remember to focus on making your surroundings comfortable and welcoming for family and guests, and keeping things simple.

Planning to decorate

Because products of nature lend themselves to great Thanksgiving decorating, you can decorate beautifully in about a day — you just have to do a little planning. Follow the suggestions in this section to make sure that all your bases are covered.

Taking a nature walk

You can get inspired by spending a day enjoying a spectrum of color and a crisp autumn breeze from a trip outdoors this season, and you can also find great items to fit your Thanksgiving decorating needs.

Use the following tips to make your nature walks successful decorating outings:

- Check your local newspaper or contact your local chamber of commerce for the best days and places to view foliage in your area.

- Take your camera, a backpack, and plastic resealable bags for storing pine cones, fresh leaves, nuts, or other items gathered from nature.

Don't touch or pick up any items unless you're absolutely sure what they are. I don't want you to pluck poison ivy or carry home anything that may be harmful to you or your family. In addition, find out the rules and regulations regarding gathering items from your nature walk areas. I know a friend who was once chased out of Central Park for gathering ginkgo leaves that had fallen to the ground — no fun eating turkey in the slammer!

Visiting a farmers market

Farmers markets are great places to places to pick up pumpkins and gourds to display, as well as delectable edibles to lay out for your Thanksgiving feast.

Try to find a market that can give you a good assortment of quality items. If you're not sure where to find the best (or any) farmers markets in your area, go to www.ams.usda.gov/farmersmarkets/map.htm and click on your state. The USDA has compiled a listing of farmers markets along with the dates and times that they're open for business.

Shopping for additional supplies

Although you can find a lot in your own backyard, candles don't grow on trees. So if you need to stock up on holiday candles, candleholders, or other supplies that you'd rather not create, shop early. As the time for Thanksgiving draws near, more and more autumnal items are replaced by their red and green relatives.

Setting aside some time to decorate

In addition to shopping for supplies, you also need to plan to make time to actually do your projects — always overestimate. On Thanksgiving morning, you don't want to stir pots on the stove while finishing the embossing on your velvet table runner (see Chapter 22), so be sure to give yourself plenty of time to enjoy as well as finish the projects you want to start.

Also schedule a day to put your items on display. The week after Halloween is a perfect time to begin setting up your Thanksgiving decorations. If you have everything you need, you should be set to prep and display lovely vignettes in a day or less. See the upcoming section, "Decorating in a Flash," for even more suggestions.

Decorating in a Flash

Short on time? No problem. Check out the following ideas that take minimal time and effort but still have a great effect.

- ✔ **Use throws.** If you have wonderful woolen throws, use these for table toppers or drape them on chair or sofa arms.

- ✔ **Use your fireplace.** If you have a fireplace, light it. Nothing's more beautiful or soothing on a crisp, cool day or evening than the orange glow of a fire. Be sure to place some cookies and tea out on a nearby table for chilled visitors to snack on. It adds to the overall visual effect.

✔ **Use candles.** Place a few autumn leaves on a surface and then start piling on a grouping of a few candles in staggering heights. (Now, make sure that you're not piling so many on that you cause a fire hazard! Be sure to refer to the candle safety tips in Chapter 25.) Toss a few nuts (in the shell), cranberries, and/or some moss at the base of the candles, and you're set.

✔ **Reuse uncut Halloween pumpkins.** If you used an assortment of pumpkins for Halloween decorations, and they remained uncut, reuse them in a fall arrangement. You can also place these in a simple grouping of three or more for an impact of color in your décor, or stack them vertically (on top of each other on a sturdy garden urn) for an instant pumpkin topiary.

Core apples and mini pumpkins for impromptu candleholders. Carve out the centers of each and place taper, votive, or tealight candles in each one. If you're worried about tipping, place each apple or pumpkin in a martini glass, or wedge them into the cups of an old muffin tin and cover the exposed tin areas with moss and small red berries.

More Splash for Less Cash

Thanksgiving really lends itself to inexpensive decorating, which is nice because we all know what a chunk the upcoming holidays can take out of the old budget. Nature provides the most wonderful decorating materials for free. A quick trip to the backyard, a farmers market, or the park can sometimes give you everything you need to decorate gracefully and sufficiently.

I give several ideas for using natural materials for Thanksgiving decorating throughout this chapter, so you can adapt these ideas to fit your needs. But if scattering leaves and nuts about makes you feel more like a squirrel than a great decorator, here are a few more ideas you can use and still decorate frugally.

Do the sweater shuffle

Do you have some old sweaters that are a little worn or outdated? Try wrapping them around an accent pillow to give them a whole new look. Stuff the pillow or pillow form inside the body of the sweater and wrap the neck and bottom of the sweater to the back of the pillow. Tie the sleeves to the back of the pillow and you have warm, snuggly pillows to place around the house. If you're good at sewing, make pillow covers out of them using the instructions I provide in Chapter 19.

If you don't want to do this with your own sweaters, grab your spouse's or visit a thrift shop or garage sale for some great finds for less than five bucks.

Create canvas art

Infuse a little color into your world — decorate with artist's canvas! That's right. You don't have to be a painter or crafter, or even be able to draw a straight line, to make gorgeous accent pieces.

Purchase a few prestretched and primed canvases at your local arts and crafts supply store. Use these as your seasonal accent pieces! You can finish them in several ways:

- ✔ **Paint them.** Paint the canvases in bold, stark hues, or try finishing them in wispy washes of color. Using leftover paint, craft paint, or artist's acrylics, you can smear a little pumpkin color with washes of burnished gold for the fall and then paint over them in the spring with fresh pastels. Reusing the same canvas over and over saves money and adds dramatic color or faux finishes to a wall easily without color commitment. (Chapter 23 is all about painting decoratively.)

- ✔ **Wallpaper them.** Have you ever seen abandoned wallpaper books at your local paint and wallcoverings store? Often, these retailers pile up discontinued wallpaper sample books available free to any takers. Here's your chance to use small samples for a big effect.

  Choose a few wallpaper samples in complementing colors. Remove the samples by cutting them from the book spine, using a craft knife. Cut them to the same size as your art canvas. Spread an even amount of household glue on the canvas and smooth that wallpaper on! After it dries, you have interesting "art" to hang or place around the house that can be changed or papered over as often as you can recover those wallpaper books!

- ✔ **Attach finds to them.** A spoon, knife, fork, pine cone, leaf, or other objet d'art can be tied or glued to the center of a blank canvas for a three-dimensional piece of art. Change the objects to reflect each season.

You can paint, paper, or attach and reattach findings to them for each season. Because canvases are inexpensive, you can replace them when needed or add to your collection as desired. Use these little pieces of art to color block a wall or use where you'd normally place a picture.

Jazzing Up Smaller Spaces

If you have a small room to decorate, or you live in cramped quarters, you're at an advantage.

Thanksgiving is an understated holiday, so less is more. Try the following ideas for adding a cozy touch to your small space.

- **Add a table runner to a dining or sofa table.** Purchase or make one in velvet or soft, scrumptious chenille in autumnal colors such as mustard or aubergine. (Check out Chapter 19 to find out how to make your own table runners, including the no-sew option.) Whether you add beading (see Chapter 26) or nothing at all, this tiny splash of color adds a big punch to your décor.

- **Arrange a few bare branches in a pot or urn.** Place them in a corner or on top of a dining table for a dramatic statement. If you have a chandelier, weave the branches in between the arms to reach toward the ceiling. The light will cast shadows and highlight the branches beautifully on a cool Thanksgiving evening.

- **Gather birch logs, twigs, and pine cones in large baskets.** Set them by the fireplace. Not only are they great for stoking the fire, but they also add a casual touch of nature in a beautiful way. Scent them by adding a few drops of cinnamon or vanilla oil for an added bonus!

- **Add small touches in neutral colors.** Filling a tall clear glass vase with acorns, pecans, and other assorted nuts in shells adds an autumnal touch that really makes a big statement in smaller spaces.

Involving the Family

You can do more with the family than turn a child's handprint into a picture of a turkey (although that's always fun). Check out these fresh ideas that involve the whole family.

- **Gather autumn leaves.** Rake and create! Shove a rake in the hand of every willing and able body to gather autumn leaves for decorating. Freshly fallen leaves are perfect — flaws and all — for spreading out on a table around candles and centerpieces or stringing one on top of the other for a stacked leaf garland. (See Chapter 21 for instructions on making garland.) To help get everyone psyched up — after all, when the rakes come out, it signals chore time not fun time — be sure to rake up a separate pile of leaves that the kids, and the kid in you, can take a tumble in. The plus? You get your yard raked.

✔ **Create centerpieces.** You may think that putting kids in charge of making centerpieces is an outlandish idea, but this project is quick and easy to do — perfect for placing on small tables and keeping little hands busy.

Gather an assortment of mini pumpkins, gourds, nuts, candles, and baskets or plates for each child. Place a large pillar candle in the middle of the basket or plate and then let each child start placing the items around the base of the candles until her she gets the desired look. Chapter 21 talks about using botanicals in centerpieces.

Just make sure that nothing can pose a fire hazard when the candles are lit.

Taking on the traditional

Let's face it: You've successfully decorated your home for a beautiful Thanksgiving season, but Suzy comes home each week after Halloween with Thanksgiving art displays, such as her hand traced into a turkey (an old stand-by that you can count on *every* year). Your heart melts over her handiwork, and you know that she'd be crushed if you didn't prominently display it for all the world to see somewhere within the house. But, alas, you feel torn. Where in the world can you display this artwork so that her feelings aren't hurt but so that you don't throw off the beautiful vibe you have going and have worked so hard to achieve? Aside from displaying it on the ol' fridge, let me count the ways:

✔ Frame your children's art. Find some simple frames that complement your décor and give the frames a special place in your home, which can be a corner in the family room.

✔ Make a special "brag box" for the crafts to be placed into. You can bring out this brag box to show off your children's handiwork to visitors.

✔ Decorate the infamous "children's table" at Thanksgiving with children's art or promise to display it on the dessert table.

✔ Display your children's handiwork in the room that's designated just for kids — such as a playroom. Those rooms can always benefit from a decorator's touch, and if it caters to children most of the time, why not use your children's pilgrims and turkeys to get them into the holiday spirit?

Chapter 14

Decking the Halls at Christmas

*O*ften, when people think of holiday decorating, they automatically think Christmas. Whether or not you decorate for Easter, Halloween, or Valentine's Day, chances are you deck the halls for the Christmas season.

Christmas is special. It has meaning, traditions, and tons of decorating options and opportunities, and you can find decorations in abundant supply for any budget.

But just where do you start, and when? And how much, or little, do you do? Read this chapter and start making notes on some of the ideas you want to implement in decorating your home for Christmas. You can have a holly jolly start on a wonderful tradition.

Finding Your Inspiration

Christmas is a wonderful holiday for building decorating schemes from many interests, hobbies, items, and themes. You may find a ribbon in an amazing color that sparks a whole decorating scheme, or you may find that your antique toy collection is all you need to make an old-fashioned Christmas.

Table 14-1 gives you a general list of items traditionally associated with Christmas as well as a things you want to keep in mind when choosing your decorating theme.

Christmas is one of the few holidays where you can easily decorate each room in a different theme and it all goes together because you still have consistent items from room to room. The consistent pattern of green garland and trees throughout the home pulls it all together. So, you can go all out decorating with themes throughout your home.

For example, you may choose to decorate your child's room with a Sesame Street theme, using character ornaments, primary colored bows, and themed merchandise on a small tree or tucked into a green garland, but that doesn't mean you can't have resplendent traditional red and green décor surrounding your home.

Table 14-1		Christmas Inspirations	
Colors	*Fabrics*	*Botanicals*	*Accent Items*
Reds	Plaids	Poinsettias	Ribbon
Greens	Novelty Prints	Holly	Ornaments
Golds	Satin	Mistletoe	Nativity
Silvers	Taffeta	Evergreen trees, boughs, garlands, and wreaths	Collections
Blues	Organza	Amaryllis	Snowflakes
Purples	Tulle or netting	Paperwhite narcissus	Snowmen
	Felt	Cranberries	Toys
	Fleece	Pomegranates	Santa
	Fur	Pine Cones	Sleighs
	Tapestries		Reindeer
	Moire		Elves
			Crystal, silver, and gold items
			Candy canes
			Gingerbread houses
			Lights, tinsel, candles

My best advice is to take a piece of paper and start making your own inspiration piece list. You may have a favorite theme already in mind, a favorite ornament handed down to you, a hobby that you want to do a themed tree around, or any other great idea. Divide your piece of paper into four columns and label them Colors, Fabrics, Botanicals, and Accent items.

Because Christmas is so popular for decorating one's home, many themes and decorations are at your disposal to explore. If you don't already have a particular style that determines your Christmas décor, if you're looking to try something new, or if you're simply looking to expand your holiday decorating into another room but want to do something different, check out the themes in Table 14-2 and see if you can find some additional inspiration.

Table 14-2	Choosing a Theme
Theme	*Description*
Music	Lots of scrolls of sheet music, musical instruments, brass horns
Patriotic	Plenty of red, white, and blue ribbon or lights on the tree, Americana ornaments, flags
Victorian	Beaded ornaments, lace, ribbon, roses, pearls, baroque pieces, cameos
Kitchen	Wooden spoons, gingerbread ornaments, copper cookie cutters, punched tin ornaments, miniature molds, tin measuring spoons
Nature	Gilded or glittered pine cones, berry and fruit garlands, preserved fruit slices, raffia bows, grapevine garland
Nautical	Shell ornaments, shell garland, miniature ship-themed items, blue and white bows

Planning and Organizing Your Holiday Decorating

Some people start planning for Christmas a year in advance. Unless you coordinate major events, you don't have to start planning for Christmas until around October. Don't worry, you won't have to tie a ribbon around your finger to remember, either — in case you haven't noticed, this is about the same time that retail stores start stocking Christmas items. As soon as you see signs of Christmas, it's time to make a project form (see Chapter 6 for more information on project forms) and get started.

In order to figure out the best time to start your planning, ask yourself these questions:

- ✔ Do you plan to host any open houses at your home?
- ✔ Do you plan to help decorate your child's classroom?
- ✔ Do you plan to decorate for any parties other than at your home, such as office parties?
- ✔ Do you plan to decorate in a formal or whimsical style?
- ✔ Do you plan to decorate someone else's home for the holidays, such as an aging parent's?

These questions can get you thinking about all your commitments, plans, and ideas for the Christmas holidays — make notes for all your plans on your project form, and if you have specific dates for completing any of these items, you need to note them as well. You can use this initial list for planning your decorating schedule. Say, for example, that you're hosting an afternoon open house the day after Thanksgiving so that neighbors can stop by for cider, coffee, or a snack after braving a day of shopping. You'll probably need to plan on decorating your house before Thanksgiving, depending on how much you do.

Keep specific dates for scheduled events at the top of your list. If you need to enlist any help to carry out your decorating plans, ask those people as soon as you know that you'll need their help. Purchase supplies and set them aside in labeled boxes, such as "front door decorations," and "lights for the second floor," or whatever else you have planned. Make sure to list tools you'll need for each individual project. Although you won't want to pull them together inside each box just yet, a simple index card with the list of tools needed will help you hit the toolbox right before you dangle about 50 feet of extension cords to the second floor. You don't want to be out in inclement weather without the right tools to do the job. And if people are helping you, they'll think that you're an organizational guru when they see that you have everything you need on hand and ready to go!

Keep in mind that you also need to plan your outdoor holiday decorating ideas. Use the information I give you in Chapter 17 to help you lay out and plan what you want to do with your exteriors and lawn. You may find this information particularly helpful if you want to change up what you normally do or add outdoor decorations to your home for the first time.

Planning ahead allows you to feel more at ease (and hopefully a little less stressed) when the time comes to decorate for the holiday. So you can spend more time hitting the sales and hosting fabulous parties and less time untangling the tinsel and searching for ornaments.

Choosing and caring for a live Christmas tree

If you like to buy live Christmas trees instead of using faux ones, follow these simple guides from the National Christmas Tree Association for buying the best Christmas tree:

✔ When you find a tree that you like, do a freshness test to make sure that it's worthy to come home with you. Gently grasp a branch between your thumb and forefinger and pull it toward you. Very few needles should come off in your hand if the tree is fresh. Shake or bounce the tree on its stump. You shouldn't see an excessive amount of green needles fall to the ground. Some loss of interior brown needles is normal and will occur over the lifetime of the tree.

✔ After you've chosen your tree, keep it in a sheltered, unheated area, such as a porch or garage, to protect it from the wind and sun until you are ready to decorate it.

✔ Just before you set up your tree, make a fresh, straight cut across the base of the trunk (about ¼ inch up from the original cut) and place the tree in a tree stand that holds a gallon of water or more. If you don't cut off some of the trunk, the tree won't be able to absorb water, and it will dry out and become a fire hazard.

✔ Keep the tree stand filled with water. A seal of dried sap will form over the cut stump in four to six hours if the water drops below the base of the tree. If a seal does form, you'll have to make another fresh cut, which is much harder to do when the tree's decorated.

A tree will absorb as much as a gallon of water or more in the first 24 hours and one or more quarts a day thereafter. Water is important because it prevents the needles from drying and dropping off and the boughs from drooping. Water also keeps the tree fragrant.

✔ Keep your tree away from heat and draft sources, such as fireplaces, radiators, and television sets.

If you purchase a live Christmas tree, locate a recycling program in your area for when you need to get rid of it. Log on to www.real christmastrees.org or www.earth911 .org or call 800-CLEANUP and enter your zip code, and you can get a list of local drop-off points or pickup programs.

Decorating in a Flash

More often than not, decorating quickly for Christmas will never be a challenge. Adding small touches here and there are enough to pull even the largest room together quickly and easily — just check out some of my suggestions below:

✔ **Hang some stockings.** Even if you only hang one or two, these babies say Christmas without a doubt.

✔ **Hang a wreath.** A purchased wreath — bow or not — hung on the door says, "Welcome to our holiday home!"

✓ **Dim the lights and light some candles.** Lit candles give the same twinkle effect as strung lights, and they take a fraction of the time to set up.

✓ **Throw a holiday tablecloth or table runner on the dining room table.** This simple touch adds instant holiday cheer.

✓ **Put on some Christmas music.** Although music isn't decorating per se, a little "Jingle Bells" is all you need to create a festive mood.

✓ **Pick up a few poinsettias.** Placing a few of these beauties around your home may become one of your favorite fast decorating tricks.

Poinsettias work well around doorways and staircases, under windowsills, and in corners of rooms where you need a little color. They also dress up your holiday buffets. If you do decide to put them on tables with food, just make sure that you remove any wilted leaves or petals so that they don't fall into food items. Poinsettias can be poisonous.

✓ **Pick up a few pine bough branches and some garland.** These items dress up your home in no time. Couple them with a few premade bows and you're ready to start slinging pine needles everywhere. Here are a few ideas for using these evergreen decorations.

- **Use garland to swag or wrap around staircase banisters.** Add bows where the greenery meets the handrails, and you have no-fuss decorating in a flash.

- **Remove everything from your fireplace mantel and place a long piece of garland on it, letting it drape down both sides of the fireplace.** Don't have a fireplace? This trick works for tops of bookcases or shelves, too! Wire in a few ornaments, attach cascading oversized bows to the draped edges, and reassemble your fireplace mantel decorations, moving the garland in and out of your décor. Place a few tall candlesticks on one side, and you have a lovely focal point to your room.

- **Attach a long piece of garland about a foot over the top of a large mirror or painting hanging over your fireplace.** Drape and attach the sides of the garland to surround the painting or mirror. Add a beautiful wreath at the top or an oversized bow to complete the picture.

- **Weave garland in an out of casual chandelier arms.** Swag the garland if you like. Add a beaded garland to give it sparkle. I like to purchase crystal chandelier pendants and hang them from the garland. The light sparkles through them and adds a hint of Shabby Chic to the room.

- **Weave and wind lush strands of garland in and around the tiers of your buffet table (see Chapter 3) before you set out the food.** Tuck sprigs of berries, ornaments, fruits or vegetables, or other decorative items into the greenery, or just leave it alone. It's beautiful plain and simple.

- **Place a few pine bough branches around a tall pillar candle on a table runner.** You now have an instant centerpiece.

- **Add pine bough branches as a decorative swag over doorways or on the edges of bookshelves.** It's funny how slapping out a bunch of evergreens in a hurry starts putting the spirit in the season.

More Splash for Less Cash

You can easily decorate for Christmas without breaking the bank. Folding napkins in decorative ways, snipping a few pieces of boxwood from your hedges to insert into arrangements, and taking a little more time to creatively wrap presents to display underneath the tree are just a few ways that you can make the most of little things that have to be done, but done in extraordinary ways. Here are some other ways to get the most bang for your buck:

✔ **Shop smart.** You can find Christmas décor gems at many places that you may never have even thought of before. Just check out the following possibilities:

- You can find some quality Christmas decorations at mass market retailers such as Target, Wal-Mart, and K-Mart, that stock plenty of trendy to traditional merchandise. Because these retailers have incredible buying power, they pass those savings on to us.

- Don't forget that craft stores keep beefing up their holiday merchandise selections in home décor. No longer do you have to make everything from scratch if you purchase from a craft store. Many premade items are constantly being put on clearance even during the height of the holiday shopping season. Check for discount coupons on major craft store Web sites, direct mail pieces, and in newspapers. Often, these retailers have 40 to 50 percent-off coupons that can save you a bundle if you're investing in larger purchases.

- Silver is notoriously associated with Christmas. A few silver or galvanized containers purchased at a home improvement center can help you decorate. Buy silver mud trays, normally used to hold drywall joint compound, and transform them into easy silverware trays on buffets. Seal the joints with a silicone sealant and use them as low-lying centerpiece containers. Fill them with aquarium gravel or beach glass, and let paperwhite narcissus bulbs bloom in them. Place them on mantels, shelves, or any place you need a filler.

  Silver paint buckets, found — you guessed it — in the paint section can double as ice buckets for wine, decorative pots for planting beautiful blooms, or decorative containers for party mix, bread sticks, and other nibbles. Wrap a red ribbon around the middle of the container, and you automatically dress it up for the season.

✔ **Makeover ornaments.** If you have a stash of old ornaments that need some livening up, or you want to change up the whole look of your tree without reinvesting in all new ornaments, you can spruce up old ornaments by trying some of these cost-saving tricks:

• Spray paint them with pearlescent paint to give them a unified look. Hang ornaments outside on a suspended line to spray paint from all sides. Use light layers and several coats to eliminate dripping.

• Bead them by using small amounts of craft glue in a design or pattern and then dipping the ornaments in tiny beads. Set them on wax paper to dry.

• Stencil them. Use the stencil instructions I give you in Chapter 23 to stencil new designs onto your ornaments.

• Dip them in glitter. Spread an even coat of school glue on the ornament with a sponge brush and dip and roll into glitter. Set them on wax paper to dry.

• Add swirls or stars in dimensional paint. Using a squeezable tube of dimensional paint, free hand swirls on your ornament. Create whimsical stars and fill them in with the paint. Work on one side and set the ornament in an empty egg carton to dry; come back later and finish the other side.

• Take the shine off the surface by spraying with a glass frost spray paint, or dip them in an etching bath. For more information on etching, you can go to Chapter 27.

Jazzing Up Smaller Spaces

Because of the variety of supplies and décor you can find just about anywhere during the Christmas season, you should have no problems decorating your smaller spaces. Just check out some of my suggestions:

✔ **Use smaller trees in smaller spaces.** Miniature trees that fit on tabletops, bay windows, or are halved to hang on walls are great options for those living in smaller spaces or who are resolute to have a tree in tight spaces. Decorate these trees with smaller ornaments, or forego ornaments altogether and simply string with lights and beaded garland.

✔ **Change out any temporary wall hangings to include an Advent calendar.** An Advent calendar is a countdown calendar that you can tuck 25 little presents in — one for each day in December till Christmas morning. Usually, you can find these calendars premade in holiday departments in retail stores.

✔ **Display lovely fruit topiaries in urns.** Flip to Chapter 21 for instructions.

✔ **Use a small space to display your Christmas cards received.** Line them up on a mantel, tape them with removable tape to a wall, or frame them in small frames. Christmas cards add instant art to a room and are a warm remembrance of friends and family who cared enough to send you a holiday greeting.

✔ **Try gathering a collection of some sort into a small space.** A Christmas village tucked into a cozy corner brings detail to a small room. A compote full of glass ornaments in holiday colors, a favorite collection of toy trains, or one simple stocking from your childhood hung with care bring small spaces to life.

✔ **Hang a mistletoe kissing ball in the doorway and drape fresh garland around a doorway with a bright, ruby-red bow at the top.** Adding touches of little things brings style, grace, and meaning to otherwise overlooked areas of our homes.

Involving the Whole Family

Christmas is very kid friendly. From trimming the tree to making ice lights or luminarias for the walkways, you can get the whole family involved in tons of different ways.

Making paper chains out of construction paper, stringing popcorn and cranberries, cutting out paper snowflakes — all these activities can be done on a lazy afternoon of listening to Christmas carols or on a family night sitting in front of the TV watching *It's A Wonderful Life.*

Making gingerbread houses is a great way to decorate while spending time with kids. If you're a purist, you'll probably want to go through the painstaking details of mixing everything from scratch, but if you're hurried — take heart. Now, you can find all kinds of gingerbread cookie mixes, patterns available online (so you don't have to be an engineer), and prebaked kits that you just assemble (now we're talkin'). Splurge a little and try your hand at whatever suits you best. Your kids will love it!

Spouses can help you test and string lights in hard-to-reach areas. Other ways they can help is by generally occupying the rest of the family while you decorate!

If you're lucky enough to have a blanket of snow on the ground around Christmastime, enlist the whole family to decorate your lawn with snowmen! A snowman set against a backdrop of beautiful Christmas decorations brings the season to life. And it's a fun way to spend time with the whole family.

Christmas safety tips

Follow these tips to keep your Christmas safe and merry:

- When decorating Christmas trees, always use safe tree lights. (Some lights are designed only for indoor or outdoor use, but not both.) Larger tree lights should also have some type of reflector rather than a bare bulb, and all lights should be listed by a testing laboratory.

- Never use electric lights on a metal tree.

- Follow the manufacturer's instructions on how to use tree lights. Any string of lights with worn, frayed, or broken cords or loose bulb connections should not be used.

- Always unplug Christmas tree lights before leaving home or going to sleep.

- Place candles well away from Christmas tree branches, and *never* use lit candles to decorate a tree.

- Try to keep live trees as moist as possible by giving them plenty of water daily. *Do not* purchase a tree that's dry or dropping green needles.

- Choose a sturdy tree stand designed not to tip over.

- When purchasing an artificial tree, be sure that it's labeled as fire retardant.

- Children are fascinated with Christmas trees. Keep a watchful eye on them when around the tree, and don't let them play with the wiring or lights. (The same goes for pets!)

- Store matches and lighters up high, out of the reach of children, preferably in a locked cabinet.

- Make sure that the tree is at least 3 feet (1 meter) away from any heat source, and try to position it near an outlet so that cords aren't running long distances. Do not place the tree where it may block exits.

- Safely dispose of a live tree when it begins dropping needles. Dried-out trees are highly flammable and shouldn't be left in a house or garage or placed against the house.

Source: National Fire Protection Agency

Chapter 15

Decorating for Kwanzaa

Kwanzaa, meaning "first fruits" in Swahili, reaffirms African-American heritage, pride, community, family, and culture. Celebrated seven wonderful days — from the day after Christmas to the new year — this culturally rich holiday, has many special decorating attributes to add to your holiday home, blending a multitude of activities, principles, and elements that are both modern and ancient.

So when preparing for your *Karamu* (Kwanzaa feast), don't forget some of these kuumba (creative) ideas to decorate your home. And don't worry — you'll get used to reading the parenthetical translations.

Finding Your Inspiration

You're lucky. Not only does this holiday have specifics for decorating, you can draw inspiration and decorating ideas straight from Africa to include in your holiday celebration. Keeping these things in mind, you'll never be at a loss for how to decorate. Check out Table 15-1 for help.

Table 15-1		Kwanzaa Inspirations	
Colors	**Fabrics**	**Botanicals**	**Accent Items**
Black	African print fabrics	Corn	Kinara (candle holder)
Red	Kente cloth	Vegetables, any kind	Mkeka (mat)

(continued)

Table 15-1 *(continued)*			
Colors	*Fabrics*	*Botanicals*	*Accent Items*
Green	Natural cottons or linens	Fruits, any kind	Candles
Gold or yellow	Kuba raffia cloth	Dried grasses	Kikombe cha umoja (communal unity cup)
Brown		Raffia	Baskets
Orange		Bamboo	African art and artifacts
Purple			Bendera (African flag), beads, masks, carvings

For the most part, I've given you some general items and themes in the previous table. From there, you can research any particular item that sounds interesting to you. The beauty of this holiday is connecting with your African roots. The more research you do to find out the story behind a piece of *kente* cloth, or *Asafo* (war tribe) flag, the more it enhances the true meaning and principles of Kwanzaa.

But don't think that you have to make a trip to the library for basic decorating ideas. This chapter provides you with plenty of suggestions that allow you to decorate for Kwanzaa easily and with style.

Planning and Organizing Your Holiday Decorating

Planning for Kwanzaa should begin about the same time you start planning for Thanksgiving and Christmas decorating, if you celebrate them, because many items from these two holidays can be repurposed for use in your Kwanzaa decorating as well. Plus, I find that it's always nice to include bits of Kwanzaa or African heritage decorating into other major holidays that take place around the same time. By thinking and planning ahead, you can blend elements from these holidays together while still keeping them separate and distinct holidays.

Keep in mind, though, that you do need some basic supplies that are specific to Kwanzaa. Check out the following tips to organize and plan for your Kwanzaa decorating:

✔ **Repurpose red and green items from Christmas.** Red and green are the colors of the African flag, so you may want to invest in solid-color items such as napkins, tablecloths, planters, and so on, so that you can use them for both Christmas and Kwanzaa.

✔ **Repurpose harvest items from Thanksgiving.** Harvest items you may readily find at Thanksgiving, such as corn, wheat sheaves, gourds, and squashes can be pulled into Kwanzaa as well. Just make sure you only repurpose vegetables and fruits. Put the cornucopia away! It's only associated with our Western holiday and is not part of African culture.

✔ **Gather basic supplies for Kwanzaa.** The following are basic supplies you need to celebrate Kwanzaa:

- *Mkeka* (place mat usually woven of straw or raffia)
- *Kinara* (candleholder)
- *Mishumaa saba* (seven candles — one black, three green, three red)
- *Mazao* (fruits and vegetables representing crops)
- *Vibunzi* (one ear of corn for each child in the household)
- *Kikombe cha umoja* (communal unity cup)

These items are the staples you should never be without when decorating for Kwanzaa. You'll be adding *zawadi* (gifts that are enriching) later and will want to plan on shopping or making these to add to your Kwanzaa table. For now, concentrate on finding these items for decorating. Look for Afro-centric stores in your area or search online. You can also make items like the kinara (see the instructions later in this chapter). Finding candles and fruits and vegetables to place on your table is as simple as visiting your local grocer.

✔ **Spend some time discovering and practicing the rituals for your karamu that takes place New Year's Eve with all your family and friends.** Research the meanings for things you want to know a bit more about, so that you can make your celebration as enriching as possible.

Decorating in a Flash

As long as you have all the supplies you need (see the list in the previous section), decorating for Kwanzaa takes almost no time. You just need to know how to lay out the items properly on your table.

The kinara should always be a focal point for the room it's in. I suggest putting it in a room other than where you put your Christmas tree, preferably the dining room.

Here are some other tips for setting up your Kwanzaa table:

- ✔ To protect your wood surfaces, place a red or green tablecloth on your table and then center the mkeka on top of that as either a table runner down the center, or as a large square table topper.

- ✔ Place a kinara as the centerpiece of your mat. The black candle, which represents the people, goes in the middle. The three red candles, which represent continuing struggle, belong on the left. And the green candles, which represent the future, go on the right. You may also alternate the green and red candles — one green, then one red — if you like.

  Together, all seven candles are called the *Mishumaa Saba*.

- ✔ Place baskets and wooden bowls of fruit and vegetables around the kinara.

- ✔ Arrange ears of corn — one for each child in the household — around the bowls in an attractive manner. Even if you don't have any kids, you should use at least one ear of corn to represent the African concept of social parenthood.

Besides the basic table setup for Kwanzaa, you can get creative and inspired by creating an African-themed room where your table resides. Purchase some African art posters to hang. If you find African-inspired masks at import stores, or interesting carvings or beadwork, you can place these items around the room as well. Tropical plants can add a little life to your room and be used on buffet or dessert tables. After all, the feast is a major part of the holiday celebration; you'll want to have plenty of items to accessorize your delicious spread.

More Splash for Less Cash

Interestingly enough, one of the principles of Kwanzaa is exercising your Kuumba — meaning that if you *can* make it, you *should* make it. This admonition opens the door to making several of the items necessary for a happy Kwanzaa, as well as other accents that you may want to add to your festive occasion.

Sprucing up inexpensive finds

You can use craft stamps and stencils with African motifs to decorate many items you buy premade at a discount or import store. Look for woven baskets, mats, wooden trays, pottery, chargers, and cups. You can find these items pretty inexpensively at several bargain stores and then spiff them up to match your theme with a little paint. You can find help with stenciling and stamping in Chapter 23.

You might also transform pieces of pottery, vases, trunks, or metal trays with transfers of African art. Find postcard sizes of African art or artifacts and flip to Chapter 24 to find out how to make transfers.

Making your own kinara

You can make a kinara out of any wooden item. Try using a birch log, a piece of drift wood, or even a 2-x-4-inch board cut to size and perhaps sanded and painted black. You can find screw-in-type candleholders at hardware stores, and, if all else fails, drill holes where the candles will need to be placed. If you're working on a flat board, candleholders can be glued to the board with wood glue. Use your imagination. In a pinch, I've even used painted 2-liter soda pop caps screwed into wood to make candleholders for a child's personal kinara.

Taking a little help from Thanksgiving and Christmas

As I mention earlier in this chapter, if you decorate for Thanksgiving and Christmas, you may want to repurpose some of the decorative elements into your Kwanzaa celebration. For instance, a red or green tablecloth used at Christmas can do double duty if you place it under the mkeka.

Thanksgiving incorporates many harvest- and autumnal-themed elements such as corn, other vegetables, fruits, baskets, hearty bowls, and such. Kwanzaa, by definition, means "first fruits." You can decorate frugally by reusing and restyling faux fruit or vegetables for Kwanzaa by just taking out any cornucopia designs or references. Natural items, such as straw place mats or raffia items, also work well as long as they don't have a Thanksgiving theme plastered on them.

Jazzing Up Smaller Spaces

Kwanzaa is the perfect holiday for small-space holiday decorating. All you really need is a place to set up your Kwanzaa items.

If you live in an apartment, dorm room, or other small space where dining room tables are out of the question, purchase a large straw mat to place on the floor as your mkeka. Place all your Kwanzaa items on it just as you would a table and throw plenty of cushions made of woven straw or leather onto the floor for your guests to plop down on and enjoy some sweet potato pie and other food that's good for the soul. Just because you're in a small space doesn't mean that you can't host a feast and celebrate African culture! You'll have a great gathering place to share good food, conversation, and the principles of Kwanzaa.

If you want to take your decorating a step further, here are some other tips that may come in handy to help you celebrate:

✔ Hang the Bendera (African flag) on a porch or patio to welcome guests or to signify the seven days of your celebration. Flags of all sizes can be used in small spaces that need just a small touch of African heritage.

✔ For a modern touch, grab three art canvas boards at a local craft store and paint them red, black, and green — one color for each board. Prop them up on a mantel, or hang side by side (representing unity) to display the colors of Kwanzaa. This color-blocking technique is a simple yet bold effect that demands attention in a smaller space.

✔ Make a wall hanging or a table runner out of kente fabric, a traditional African printed fabric in silk or cotton, or other African-inspired prints to jazz up otherwise lifeless spaces. Make a few throw pillows to place on sofas or window seats to coordinate with your other kente fabric accessories. (Chapter 19 is all about making things such as table runners and pillow covers, providing sewing how-to as well as no-sew options.)

Involving the Whole Family

The basis for Kwanzaa is built on family and community. Here, getting the whole family involved in decorating is both fun and almost a prerequisite! Kids can make heritage symbols as well as small decorative items that can be used throughout the house. Clean coffee cans and oatmeal canisters can be painted and decorated or wrapped with scraps of kente cloth to make tribal drums. (You'd better have some aspirin handy.)

You and the kids can stamp woven place mats for everyone at the table. You can also stamp plain craft paper with African symbols or elements of the Nguzo Saba (the seven principles of Kwanzaa) for wrapping zawadi.

Try to help them carry out Kwanzaa's principles by incorporating it into other holidays. Making Afro-centric ornaments to go on a traditional Christmas tree can be another way to show heritage and culture in other decorations. Just make sure that you aren't trying to display the tree in the same room as your Kwanzaa feast. You don't want anything to distract from the meaning of Kwanzaa or its ceremony.

A gorgeous Valentine's Day tablescape.

Lots of candles, fiery red roses, and a drawn bubble bath turn up the heat for this romantic holiday.

An inviting Easter table setting with fan-folded napkins, creative centerpiece, and elegant table runner.

A lovely, simple Easter tablescape.

Traditional Easter basket with charming painted eggs.

Halloween is the perfect time for an over-the-top vignette, but if you prefer simplicity, a jack-o'-lantern or two on the porch or in the window works perfectly.

Using standard fall fruits, vegetables, and other botanicals, you can create a Thanksgiving centerpiece that's either traditional or contemporary.

An intimate table setting provides an alternative to the huge Thanksgiving table, and the elements of red and green let guests know that Christmas is on its way.

If you celebrate the Jewish holidays, you have plenty of opportunities to incorporate symbolism with elegance.

Outdoor decorations, such as luminarias and wreaths, greet holiday revelers and let them know that the festivities are about to begin!

A traditional Christmas theme conveys warmth and holiday cheer, but if you're tired of the traditional, these contemporary arrangements in white, gold, and silver should provide some inspiration.

Decorate for your Kwanzaa feast, using the traditional elements (candles, kinara, and so on). The arrangements here provide guidance, but are by no means the only way to go.

Another great aspect of Kwanzaa is that its colors are also red and green, so you can reuse many of your Christmas items.

Chapter 16

Celebrating Jewish Holidays

• •

In This Chapter

▶ Renewing at Rosh Hashanah

▶ Donning white for Yom Kippur

▶ Building and decorating a sukkah

▶ Having a happy Hanukkah

▶ Celebrating Purim

▶ Honoring Passover

• •

I'll be honest. As someone who was completely unfamiliar with Jewish holidays, when I began to tackle decorating for them, I was incredibly humbled and intimidated all at the same time. Jewish holidays have remained unchanged for centuries, unlike every other holiday in this book. Easter gained bunnies, Christmas acquired Santa, and so on (thank goodness there's nothing like a Hanukkah Harry for me to contend with).

Decorating for Jewish holidays is a form of celebrating heritage and tradition. It should never compete, as no holiday decorating should, with the reverence or meaning of the holiday itself.

I don't tell you how to celebrate in this chapter. Chances are you already know how to do this, or you know where to get that information. But, I *do* give you some ideas how to creatively decorate, using things that you're familiar with, or items you want make yourself or acquire. So whether you've just blended into a Jewish faith family, have been Jewish all your life, or are new to the traditions, you can decorate for each important holiday throughout the Jewish year with style and creativity.

Finding Your Inspiration

A wonderful undercurrent supports all Jewish holidays. Symbols, rituals, flags . . . most of your inspiration pieces have been chosen for you. Plus, special items are involved in each holiday. In Table 16-1, I list those inspiration pieces or specific color schemes that I like to use to decorate each holiday in each section.

Still, if you want to get a bit more creative, look for additional items to add to your standard decorating fare. Also, take out a pencil or pen and add items that I may have overlooked. You can refer to this list often when looking for additional touches to add to your home.

Table 16-1		Jewish Holiday Inspirations	
Colors	*Fabrics*	*Botanicals*	*Accent Items*
Blue	Cottons	Palms	Star of David
Silver	Silks	Miniature trees	Hebrew words
Gold	Organza	Herbs	Silver accessories
White	Velvets	Pomegranates	Judaica accents
Black	Linens	Grapes	
Purple	Fabrics with Judaic motifs or accents olives/olive branches	Greens	Spices
Accent colors in reds, yellows, and greens		Tulips	
		Tuberose Freesia Iris Crocus	

Observing the High Holidays

This period from Rosh Hashanah to Yom Kippur is one of the most challenging to decorate. Known to be incredibly introspective and mindful, spending any time concentrating on decorating seems almost frivolous. But I found that a good way to decorate for these holidays, which are full of fasting, feasting, and preparing for a blessed year ahead, is to decorate once and add as you go along.

My favorite underlying color scheme for the month of Tishri is white because it signifies purity of the new year and a fresh slate on which all other things can be added. It's also an uncomplicated color that allows your mind to think and contemplate when you're surrounded by it, which is important at this time of year.

Rosh Hashanah

Rosh Hashanah, the beginning of the Jewish new year, shows much promise for decorating. Because this holiday occurs most often in the month of September (sometimes going into October), you have nature's bounty to add to your all-white décor.

Planning and organizing your holiday decorating

Read the holiday decorating ideas covered in this section while you are planning your traditional Rosh Hashanah observation. You'll find ideas you can easily implement.

Because not everyone lives close to running tributaries, I suggest incorporating a running garden fountain somewhere in the house or garden for this particular holiday to make the practice of *Tashlikh* (casting off) a bit easier for guests.

To make a beautiful fountain, follow my instructions in the "Jazzing up smaller spaces" subsection later in this chapter. If you decide that you want to construct one, you may want to plan weeks or even months ahead, so that you can have time to enjoy it, maintain it, and prepare it for the High Holidays.

Plan to pop your new year's greetings in the mail before Rosh Hashanah, but remember that you can still send them through Sukkot. If you can't find any cards you like, try making your own. Chapter 20 gives you creative ideas for making your own greeting cards.

Keep the cards that are sent to you by placing them in a scrapbook. You can also decorate your home with them during the holidays. Cards are artful (and smart) ways of decorating, especially throughout this season.

Decorating in a flash

Rosh Hashanah is a perfect time for decorating quickly and easily, so you may concentrate your focus on personal preparation for the new year. Here are some quick tips:

- ✔ **Don everything in white.** If you're planning to have a feast at your home, coordinate plates, linens, flowers, and accents in shades of white.

- ✔ **Purchase or gather some lovely birch logs to stack in the fireplace in anticipation of the first frost.** They add just the right touch of woodsy white to a room.

- ✔ **Spotlight pomegranates (fresh or preserved) in baskets or bowls around the house.** Encourage guests to take them!

- ✔ **Use baskets as much as possible when decorating.** Serve out of them, place buffet utensils in them, or put potted plants in them. Try to decorate with as much organic materials as possible, which should be widely available at this time of year.

More splash for less cash

One great way to save money when decorating is to use food as a decorating tool. Make the honey used for dipping bread and apples into decorative additions to your table. Gather a few decorative vials or bottles (you can find them at an import store). Divide and pour honey into them. Flavor each bottle by drizzling a few drops of flavored oil into it. Cork them and then tie a piece of raffia next to the vial opening and dip just the top in melted beeswax. Tie the remainder of the raffia to the stem of a small apple for a sweet treat. You can also write the names of guests on these bottles with a paint pen. Set the apples and honey in the middle of your place settings for a unique touch.

Jazzing up smaller spaces

Small spaces decorated for Rosh Hashanah should be simple and uncluttered. Check out the following ideas for ways to make the most of your small space:

- ✔ One of the common greetings at this time of year, "L'shanah tovah" (meaning "for a good year"), is one of the best ways of decorating a small space. Display this greeting proudly by printing it on specialty paper and inserting it into an elegant frame. Alternatively, you may want to paint it on a wooden plaque, attach it to a dried pomegranate wreath, and hang it on your front door.

- ✔ Small tablescapes with items reminding you of the new year are very appropriate. An important symbol of Rosh Hashana is the shofar (the Ram's horn), which is blown on that day several times to announce the new year. It is a very decorative symbol, and papier mâché replicas can even be made and placed around the house.

Days of Awe

Days of Awe can be one of the most wonderful times to dedicate your decorating to being purposeful and meaningful — bringing beauty and comfort to those who enter your home. If sincerely approached in the right way, it's a wonderful and respectful thing to commit yourself to in the upcoming year.

While you're mending relationships, donating to charities, increasing the level of acts of kindness, and preparing yourself for a wonderful new year by returning to your best self, don't forget to include a mere mention of mindful decorating. It's not sacrilege. It's a wonderful and beautiful thing to do for yourself and others.

Having a fountain present in a small space is another creative way to practice the ritual of Tashlikh, or casting off. Depending on your space, you may choose a tabletop fountain, wall fountain, or a larger version that will fit in either your home or garden. I give you instructions on how to make your own, but you can find a wide selection of ready-made fountains or kits at garden supply or retail stores. If you want to make the fountain for which I've provided instructions, choose an area for your fountain by selecting level, firm ground. If you select an entryway or other indoor area, be sure to protect your floors from occasional splashing that can occur with any fountain.

Most large water garden fountains cost a bundle, but you can make yours for less than a few hundred bucks. Here's how!

First, gather the following materials:

- Large galvanized metal tub
- 1 cinder block
- 1 bag river stones
- 12–18-inch-tall lightweight foam garden urn
- Water garden plant
- 1 foot of ¾-inch PVC pipe
- 2½ feet of black tubing that's ½ inch in diameter
- Silicone sealant
- Heavy-duty scissors
- Water pump

When you have what you need, follow these instructions:

1. **Seal the metal tub cracks and crevices with silicone sealant.**

   Allow the sealant to dry and cure for 24 hours, or according to the manufacturer's suggestions.

2. **Insert the PVC pipe into the center of the urn through the drainage hole, leaving a few inches exposed for connecting the pipe to the water pump.**

3. **Center the cinder block in the tub.**

4. **Place the water pump next to the cinder block and attach the black hose to the pump and then to the PVC pipe at the bottom of the urn.**

5. **Fill the tub with water and test the pump to make sure it works.**

6. **Pull the pipe up to the rim of the urn; divide and pot the water plant around the pipe and top with a few inches of river stones or aquarium gravel.**

7. **Spread the rest of the river stones at the bottom of the tub.**

8. **Place the urn on top of the cinder block, turn it on, and enjoy the soothing tranquility of your own water fountain.**

If you want to make your fountain permanent, add garden stones to the sides of the galvanized tub. Stones mask the galvanized metal and add stability to the sides of the tub.

Involving the family

Most of the decorating ideas I've given for Rosh Hashana are perfect and safe to do with the whole family.

- ✔ Allow children to fill baskets or bowls with pomegranates while you explain how these first fruits are simple reminders to be as abundant in good deeds for the year ahead as the number of seeds in them.

- ✔ Design your greeting cards for the new year with your children, mother, or grandparent.

- ✔ Let children help you make the decorative honey jars and bottles, allowing them to sop up the leftovers in mixing bowls with a nice piece of challah bread.

- ✔ Involve a spouse in gathering materials and assembling a beautiful fountain for your home or garden (see the previous "Jazzing up smaller spaces" for detailed instructions).

Whatever you choose to decorate with this Rosh Hashana, let it be yet another occasion for sharing with those you love.

Yom Kippur

This most important holiday observance at the new year deserves the very best. Read on to get some practical tips and inspiration.

Planning and organizing your holiday decorating

Because Yom Kippur follows so closely behind Rosh Hashanah, you can follow the same decorating schemes used for Rosh Hashanah for your Yom Kippur decorating.

You can retain the all-white color scheme that I discuss earlier in "Decorating in a flash" for Rosh Hashanah — just upscale the accents, taking out or paring down the colors and amounts of decorative items used. Everything should remain light, just as the types of foods your meals for this holiday are. Also take a few spare moments during the days between Rosh Hashana and Yom Kippur to weed out the unnecessary material items. Polish your silver candlesticks and set your table well in advance in preparation of your feast breaking the fast.

Taking a few minutes to pare down and freshen your décor will get you off to a great start for the new year.

Decorating in a flash

White represents purity and newness — and is perfect for decorating for the new year. Check out the following ideas for adding some quick touches of white décor around your home:

- One large bunch of white gladiolas, fanned and placed in a vase, is a beautiful sight to behold. These flowers last a long time as well. If you purchase barely opened blooms at the end of Rosh Hashanah, you'll be able to enjoy them through Yom Kippur.

  Alternatively, a small bunch of white tulips, mums, daisies, or roses are easy to pick up while shopping and need little or no arranging. White flowers, no matter how casually arranged, upscale the look of a room.

- Slipcover your dining chairs in white. Drape chair runners over them in sheer fabrics and cinch with long lengths of wide tulle ribbon tied in bows on the back.

- Outfit your dining table in crisp white cotton linens. Use special napkin folds to add texture (see Chapter 3).

More splash for less cash

No matter what your budget, the following ideas can give your home a nice touch without breaking the bank:

✔ **Use lots of candles.** Place all-white candles in your best candlesticks. Gather and group pillar candles or votives on a tray and add a touch of greenery to the bases of them. Adding other accents of simple white items brings the all-white look together. Because it's traditional to light a memorial candle for deceased loved ones, make these special by making them a different size from the rest.

✔ **Etch special dishes or glassware for Yom Kippur.** The frosty white designs echo an all-white feel and add elegance to a buffet or table setting. You can find out how to etch glass in Chapter 27.

Jazzing up smaller spaces

You don't have to forego decorating for Yom Kippur just because you have some space constraints. A great way to celebrate Yom Kippur is to chart the growth of plants, representing your own personal growth, in the upcoming year. Something as small as a new ivy plant or miniature rose bush set out around Yom Kippur brings a touch of life to a small space. Invest in a very special planter you'd love to look at daily over the next year. Charting your plant's growth can be a meaningful, decorative gift that reminds you how fragile life is, yet how abundant when you nurture it.

Involving the family

Etching special glassware, potting a new plant, paring down decorations, setting the table, arranging flowers — all these things can be enjoyed with the family.

When you involve the family in any of the decorating suggestions I provide, you have yet another opportunity to focus on the many wonderful things in life, which is so much a part of this holiday.

Sukkot

Congratulations! You get to build something!

Build a sukkah tent to honor the 40-year period during which the Children of Israel wandered in the desert. In this section, I give you some creative ideas for making the walls and ceilings of your sukkah, plus ideas for decorating it beautifully.

Planning and organizing your holiday decorating

For Sukkot, your planning and organizing revolves around building and decorating your sukkah. You can pop up a sukkah in about an hour, using one of the new-fangled pop-up, transportable kits, or you can take your time over a week building a larger, more elaborate sukkah. Estimate how much time you'll need and pencil this "building and decorating" time in on your calendar. You don't want to wait until the last minute.

The lulav (a woven or bound sheath containing branches of the myrtle, willow, and palm) is a staple for blessing the sukkah along with the etrog, a citrus fruit. Be sure to order them in advance, either from a Judaica store or your synagogue. You may also order your lulav and etrog online and have them shipped to your door. Home delivery is a great convenience because you'll be making several other preparations for Sukkot.

The myrtle and willow are great for decorating your sukkah when gathered and made into garland. Although all etrogs and lulavs are grown and imported from Israel, you may want to source additional myrtle and willow branches locally for decorative purposes only. They're significant and beautiful when shaped into natural decorative items to include in your sukkah.

Save a place in your refrigerator to store your lulav and etrog set and keep them in the sealed plastic bag until ready to use. Willow wilts quickly (thus the significance), so if you use willow branches to decorate, it's best to have them preserved or dried in advance. Follow the instructions in Chapter 21 to do it yourself.

Checking out restrictions for the sukkah

Building your sukkah to eat meals and even sleep overnight in for the seven days of Sukkot will be the beginnings of your decorating plans. But you need to remember some special restrictions on building a sukkah. For example:

- **The sukkah must be three walls.** You may use an existing building wall for one of the three.

- **The walls may be built out of any material.** Lattice, plywood, galvanized metal, clear corrugated polycarbonate board, canvas, and other cloth are just a few examples of materials you can use. A visit to a home improvement store can give you plenty of ideas.

- **The roof must be made of organic materials, such as items grown or cut from the ground.** I give you examples later in this section.

- **You cannot use staples, nails, or wire to assemble or secure your roof.** Instead, use cotton string or jute twine, if needed.

- **Keep your sukkah away from trees.** Remember that you must be able to see the stars through the roof of your new dwelling.

Your materials don't have to be waterproof. The roof's made of loosely gathered organic materials that allow sun, wind, and rain to come through. Going to great lengths to make sure that your walls are waterproof is also unnecessary. Making them out of material strong enough to last throughout the week is the most important criterion at this point.

If you need materials cut to a particular length to build your sukkah, ask a clerk if he or she can cut the materials for you. Often, you can get some or even all the cuts done for free. Take advantage of such services because they save time and money and often yield more accurate results.

Finding a place to build your sukkah

According to the restrictions listed earlier, your sukkah shouldn't be underneath a tree, but beyond that, any of the following provide a great place to build your sukkah:

- ✔ If you live in an apartment with a balcony (fire escapes don't count), you can easily build one, using the exterior wall as one of the walls of your sukkah.

- ✔ If you live in an apartment complex with roof access, you can use that if your landlord gives approval.

- ✔ If you have a backyard, build your sukkah there. Camping in your backyard is fun!

- ✔ If you want to get away, look into campgrounds, public parks and beaches, and other such facilities. Cabins can provide shelter during the day, and you can spend your evenings in your sukkah dwelling built nearby.

Wherever you intend to build your booth, just make sure that you've checked all rules or regulations before setting up. Letting your non-Jewish neighbors in on what you're doing is also a good idea, in case they aren't familiar with Sukkot. Many people may scratch their heads in confusion — enlighten them!

Decorating in a flash

If you find yourself running low on time and still need to decorate your sukkah, just try some of the following ideas:

- ✔ **Purchase premade wall hangings or decorations found at Jewish markets and Judaica specialty shops for instant décor.**

- ✔ **Decorate the ceiling and walls of the sukkah with fruit, as is the custom.** Follow the instructions in Chapter 21 to find out how to make garlands to hang. For a quicker option, you can individually tie fruit to your sukkah ceiling, using ribbon. Just wrap a long piece of raffia or ribbon around the fruit and tie it in a knot at the top. Secure the ribbon to the fruit with floral picks. Tie to the ceiling as desired, being careful not to weight it too much.

- ✔ **Make a fruit topiary.** You can place this topiary in the center of your table to emit a citrus fragrance while you feast in your temporary dwelling. You can find instructions in Chapter 21.

✔ **Pay particular attention to your table settings, even if you do nothing else.** You'll be sharing many meals for seven days in your sukkah, so make sure that you decorate your table with style. It's a quick thing to do that adds so much.

More splash for less cash

Of course it's not necessary to spend lots of money decorating your sukkah. Here are some easy ways to save some money while still decorating beautifully.

✔ **Choose creative materials for the roof of your sukkah.** The only requirements are that the materials chosen must be grown and cut from the ground.

Bamboo, twigs, palm leaves, floral garland, vines . . . all these items can be used for the ceiling. Add a shabby chic chandelier (holding candles at a safe distance away from the ceiling), and you have an elegant dwelling that's a pleasure to spend your seven days in.

✔ **Make your own etrog box.** Although I've seen very elaborate etrog boxes — beautiful casings made of pewter or engraved silver to hold the fruit that symbolizes the human heart — you can easily make your own. Purchase a heart-shaped papier mâché box and silver foil the outside. You can refer to my gilding instructions in Chapter 23 for directions. Line the inside with a little polyester fiberfill covered with soft velvet to cradle the fruit. You can enjoy this item for years to come.

✔ **Make your own lulav bag.** Decorative lulav bags, made of canvas and lined with plastic to prevent leaves from turning brown too quickly, are great additions to your décor.

Gather the following materials to make your own lulav bag:

- 1 yard of cotton canvas fabric

- 1 yard of vinyl

- 18 inches of matching ribbon for hanger (optional)

- The following tools: Sewing machine, iron/ironing board, scissors, yardstick, needle, thread to match, straight pins

Use the following instructions to make your own lulav bag:

1. **Place vinyl on wrong side of cotton canvas; pin in place. Trim edges to match.**

2. **On one short edge, trim vinyl 1 inch from the edge of the canvas. Fold the canvas edge in ½ inch and press, then fold in again ⅜ inch; press.**

3. **Sew short edge, using straight stitch on sewing machine.**

   Turn fabric and vinyl over.

4. Fold fabric in half with right sides of canvas and hemmed edges matching. Pin through all layers of vinyl and canvas on all raw edges (one long edge, and one short edge). Using a ½-inch seam allowance, sew raw edges, leaving hemmed top open for turning.

5. Remove all pins, trim the fabric to ¼ inch from seams, and clip bottom corners.

6. Turn the canvas bag right side out. Whipstitch a ribbon hanger to the back, if desired (see Chapter 19 for instructions and an illustration).

Embellish your lulav bag with sew-on patches or beading, which you can find out how to do in Chapter 26.

Jazzing up smaller spaces

Your sukkah is naturally a small space, so everything I've suggested so far applies to small-space decorating. But here are some more ideas:

- ✔ Fill your sukkah with comforts such as floor pillows and throws for brisk autumn nights.

- ✔ And add twinkle lights to the perimeter of your booth, lighting the way for visitors to stop in.

- ✔ Keep the vertical rule in mind: When you can't go out, go up.

    Decorate your walls and ceiling with lovely things. Bring the focus to the ceiling with beautiful hanging items. Hang beautiful crystal prisms or translucent beads to reflect the light showing through. Items that bring the focus up give you many wonderful things to gaze at through the night.

Involving the family

Building and decorating a sukkah as a family is a natural way of sharing this holiday. Have kids help with as many things possible. Gathering and carrying items to build your temporary dwelling is important. Having them work with natural materials, like making garlands or topiaries with you, is another great idea.

If you happen to enjoy the custom of setting aside a chair in the Sukkah for the guest of the day, have the kids decorate the chair with things you make together.

Children can also help you package wonderful baked goods in bags they decorate themselves. You'll be able to send guests on their way with a sweet treat for a blessed new year.

Having a Khalohm (Dream) of a Happy Hanukkah

Hanukkah is another Jewish holiday that can take on several looks. Whether your taste is kitschy and fun, or unbelievably elegant, you can really have a great time decorating for the festival of lights.

Planning and organizing your holiday decorating

The same planning and organizing holds true for this holiday as any. Make lists of those people you want to invite to your home for a party, prepare to have plenty of candles on hand for your menorah (you'll need at least 44 — that's a lot) and polish, make, or buy your own menorah for celebrating this wonderful season of miracles.

Make a trip to the bank to get some gelt, and decide which items you want to make yourself this holiday, if any. Perhaps you'll have some time to make a simple floral arrangement or to craft your own gelt bags. Bone up on your dreidel game (as if you need to), purchase goodies for the kids, and get ready to have some fun. Hanukkah is a joyous time to share the light that resides within you as well.

Decorating in a flash

Sparkly silver and blue anything can light up a home in a flash. My favorite items to place together for a nice Hanukkah setting are cobalt blue ones on silver plated trays. The following tips incorporate Hanukkah colors as well as other ways to decorate your home in a flash:

- **Purchase cobalt blue items.** Cobalt blue stemware is great for whipping out when company comes. A simple cobalt blue vase filled with a casual arrangement of white roses is an elegant statement. Set it between a pair of candlesticks or in front of a sunny window, so the light can stream through it. Stunning!

- **Make the colors of Hanukkah the main theme of your décor, along with a perfectly positioned menorah.** This makes any room elegantly stated.

✔ **Make an impromptu menorah.** If you receive a one-night surprise visit from mamaleh, go to a grocery or discount store and purchase eight votives and one pillar candle. Line them up on a tray, four votives on each side of the pillar candle (*shamash* or *shammus*), and fill in the area around the candles, so that it doesn't look so stark. You can use organic material, such as green lentils (also picked up at the supermarket) or fresh flowers plucked right from the stem. Or go really stark, filling in the space with something like rock salt to match a more upscale or minimalist look.

✔ **Go the really easy route and purchase a Happy Hanukkah paper banner.** String it up on the wall, and you have an instant holiday! Visit the paper goods store or a great Judaica store, and you'll come up with all sorts of paper goods to decorate your home. Have fun!

More splash for less cash

Check out the following ideas to give your home the Hanukkah touch without spending too much gelt:

✔ **If you do happen to be giving gifts in an adult crowd, make a beautiful display on an occasional table.** Puddle silver organza or satin on top of a table and place beautifully wrapped gifts on it. You can upscale the gift wrap in silvers, shiny blues, or simple whites adorned with beautiful ribbon with handmade gift tags. Get great gift-wrapping ideas and gift tag instructions in Chapter 20.

✔ **If nothing else, purchase one decorative platter and arrange blue velvet embossed gelt bags on them.** You can make your own bags for a song by embossing the velvet first (see Chapter 22) with a six-pointed star, Hanukkah menorah, or dreidel stamp. One yard of velvet can make about eight or more small bags. Simply cut out rectangles, fold them in half, stitch on two sides, and then hem the top — piece of cake!

Jazzing up smaller spaces

Really, all you need to decorate a small space, a tiny window, or a personal space is one small menorah, but if you're looking for other ways to decorate in rooms that your Hanukkah menorah won't be in, remember that this holiday is the festival of lights. Use the following ideas to create a beautiful atmosphere when you're short on space:

- ✔ **String paper lanterns or twinkle lights along a small rooftop or patio.**
- ✔ **Fill your room with candles, and line walks with lanterns or themed luminarias.**

Try this idea for making special Hanukkah luminarias: Trace the outline of a menorah, with lit candles, on one side of the bag. Cut out the flame portions from the bag at the top, so when lit from within, the flames appear brighter than the rest of the design. For more about making luminarias, see Chapter 25.

Involving the family

Allow the kids to decorate one room together, their way, for Hanukkah. Ask them to make color choices, banners for the Maccabee tribe, dreidels, clay menorahs, candles . . . anything that celebrates the holiday.

While they're waiting in anticipation of delicious potato latkes and doughnuts, they can enjoy a wonderful bout of creative play decorating refrigerators, bedrooms, and windows with their art.

Celebrating Purim

I've always known Purim as the Jewish Mardi Gras. Celebrating how Queen Esther and Mordechai saved the Jews from extermination, and from the wicked Haman (boo, hiss, grogger shake here), is one of the most fantastic decorating holidays that completely blows my mind every time.

If you want to hold a Purim celebration in your own home, opposite one held at your temple, you can go wild festooning in elaborate color schemes and festive decorations. Use wonderfully rich colors such as garnet, topaz, emerald, sapphire, silver, and gold to mimic the regality of the life the unexpected Queen Esther must have had as the queen of Persia.

Using the idea of a Persian palace as a theme or inspiration, you can make your home of any size a castle of festive celebration.

Planning and organizing your holiday decorating

In addition to your minor fast before Purim, you'll probably be looking for, finding, or making outlandish costumes. Besides other tasks you undoubtedly have planned, keep track of these few little things that do affect your décor for this holiday.

Make sure that you have a decorative bowl to hold lots of change for tips when your deliveries begin arriving! Add a little sweet treat for the delivery person by giving him or her a chocolate coin or two, and you'll do double duty! Multicolored fruit candy is also a winner and is pretty when placed in a clear glass dish next to a light source.

Although you're only required to give one gift of food and drink (*shalach manot*), you may want to make many for friends and family. Decide on whether you want your family to pay a visit to a nursing center or other charity during Purim to give gifts and make an extra gift for the staff. They'll enjoy it. In addition, decide whether you want to make additional packages to give at your Purim festival. You can incorporate the packaging into your décor.

Will you want to decorate your door? Will you want to make a special wall hanging or wreath in festive colors? If so, either purchase them or go to the craft chapters in Part IV to find out how to make them.

Decorating in a flash

There are many ways you can quickly decorate for Purim. Following are a few of my favorites:

- ✔ Normally, you might send out your parcels of food and drink in gift baskets. Why not creatively use them as your décor around the house? Look through the creative gift-wrapping section in Chapter 20 for some great ideas to make ordinary gift packages look out of sight. You can set stacks of these on ends of buffets, or if you think that it's safe, you can make a large centerpiece in the center of the table, tucking in festive flowers, groggers (noisemakers), or other party favors in between packages.

- ✔ Twist and tape up crepe paper streamers in festive colors to canopy your ceiling. This task takes only a few minutes and adds instant (and inexpensive) color. Blow up a few balloons and gather and tie them in large bunches. Place them in any corner where you need some color, and don't expect them to last but a few hours.

- ✔ Decorate a tiered assortment of *hamantaschen* with paper ribbons. Make paper ribbons in festive colors, following the directions in Chapter 20, to tape to the sides of your tiered stands.

More splash for less cash

Perhaps you're short on cash but still want to add a little Purim décor to your home. The best, least expensive, and most functional way to decorate is to use tzedakah boxes. Check out some of my ideas on how to use them:

- Decorated and stacked high on an entry table, or gathered in an over-sized basket placed on a buffet, these gifts to guests become great filler decorations.

- Besides the cardboard and metal ones that are so common, try getting a few papier mâché boxes at a craft store that can serve the same purpose. They're so easy to decorate and can match each person's personality or tastes if you want. Simply slit the top of the box with a craft knife to make a coin slot and then decorate them as you like.

- Make tzedakah boxes part of table settings for Purim. Small ones open to hold tiny chocolate treasures or yummy after-dinner mints. You can personalize each one with a paint pen, and they double as fun place cards (as well as a passive-aggressive way to hint giving to charity).

- Give away handmade tzedakah boxes at the end of a festive evening. Line them with wax paper and stack hamantaschen in them. They'll love the goodies to eat on the way home.

Jazzing up smaller spaces

Although Persian palaces may be your inspiration, you don't have to have a castle to decorate for Purim. You can re-create Persian delight no matter how small your space. Simply lay out beautiful rugs; throw tons of multihued floor pillows down; drape a faux canopy of tulle, voile, or other sheer fabric from the ceiling; and set the table with loads of fruit, pastries, and other finery fit for a king — or, in this case, a queen. Add palm trees, several candles, a mini-bar setup, and *voilà* — a Persian delight.

Involving the family

No Purim would be complete without a good grogger to blot out the name of Haman. Here's where you and the whole family can use your creativity to design and embellish your own.

I especially like that you can make them out of just about any recycled container: plastic film canisters, empty oatmeal boxes, plastic soda bottles, paper towel cardboard tubes, coffee cans, and so on. Challenge the kids to get creative with the materials they use.

My favorite super-easy grogger to make is to purchase a wooden candlestick (found at craft stores) with a wide base. Turned upside down, this can serve as a sturdy handle to which you can attach any of the previously mentioned items by gluing, screwing, or taping the noisemaker portion on. Fill the container with beans, rice, beads, change, or unpopped popcorn and seal the container shut. Decorate the outside by painting, adding stickers or, streamers, and just about anything else you can think of. Although this is a tried and true craft you've probably done since you were a kid, it's still worth doing year after year with the family — for the sheer fun of it, if nothing else!

If you have a few umbrella stands, long and slender vases, or deep baskets, have your kids make extra groggers and bouquet them in these containers. Your guests will love the party favors and the extra noise they can make. You'll love keeping your kids busy for hours.

You may want to design and craft tzedakah boxes for your party, but your kids can make their own, or the one you choose to use for your household. I know that it's traditional to have some sort of bank-type container to slip coins into, making that awesome clink when it hits the pile of change below, but anything that can hold change for charities will do.

A charity collection can start in something as meager as a beautifully colored drinking glass or a painted pickle jar. See just what your kids can come up with.

Honoring Passover

Decorating for a beautiful Seder at your home is enriching and rewarding. My favorite design for an elegant Passover Seder includes gathering inspiration from the very items that bear so much significance at this time at the Seder table: wine, matzah, a green vegetable, bitter herbs, apples and nuts (haroset), salt water, a roasted bone, a cooked egg — all placed on the Seder plate — and a beautiful wine cup. The food items symbolize the story of Passover.

I choose a combination of colors from these items to include burgundy, greens, browns, yellows, white, and ivory. Normally, most of these colors reflect a more autumnal palette, which is awkward because Passover happens in the spring when everyone is ready to lighten home accents. So I simply switch up my fabric and flower selections to make it more light, ethereal, and springy. You get many ideas in this section on how to do just that. Read on!

Part of the honor of decorating a beautiful table for a Seder is that I can really go all out, sparing no luxury — not as a garish spending spree but treating it as the incredible occasion it is. You'll be sitting at the table for a while, so why not make it luxurious and comfortable?

Planning and organizing your holiday decorating

In addition to your normal tradition of giving your home the white glove treatment — cleaning to remove all traces of leavened bread *(chametz)* — and preparing for your special Seder before Shabbat, you may want to decide what other items you want to design for your Seder.

If you plan to use candles on your table, I highly recommend using long-burning, dripless candles. Freeze them at least 24 hours before burning to make them last even longer.

Plan for low-lying floral arrangements on your table because you want even small children to see the over them. My all-time favorite Seder table arrangement is in the "Decorating in a flash" section, but you can also read the floral arranging ideas in Chapter 21.

And make sure that you read Chapter 7 on caring and cleaning your silver, china, and other special Passover dishes that you'll be pulling out for this special event. You can also find linen care there, too.

Decorating in a flash

I mention earlier that you'll want to make a low-lying centerpiece to place at your Seder table. This Shield of David centerpiece can be made in any size and lies flat on the table, so even the smallest child can peer across.

For each large centerpiece, you'll need the following:

- 3 bricks of floral oasis foam
- 1 oversized platter or large mirror
- Flowers — red or white roses are my favorites (miniature ones work well, too)
- Green filler material — use parsley, dill
- 2 packages green moss
- Floral pins
- Knife

When you have what you need, follow these instructions:

1. **Soak floral oasis foam in a sink of water until completely soaked.**

2. **Cut each foam block into quarters.**

3. **On platter or large mirror, arrange floral foam into a six-pointed star.**

   Wrap moss over each piece and secure with floral pins as needed.

4. **Begin tucking in flowers, starting at each point, and then progress around the centerpiece.**

   Fill in with parsley or sprigs of dill as desired.

For a soft flicker of candlelight, you may insert a round pillar candle or a gathered bunch of candles in the center of the star. If you do, be sure that you use dripless, long-burning candles. Seders can take a while, and you don't want to risk hot-wax drips on natural materials.

More splash for less cash

Although no luxury should be spared for this holiday, you don't have to pay luxury money to have a beautiful Seder table. Here are some suggestions to get you started:

✔ **Potted bulbs and plants are the simplest and quickest way to add accents to your Seder table area.** A tropical palm plant, which fills a bare corner more than adequately, can be up lighted for a dramatic effect. Wrap ordinary containers of potted bulbs or houseplants in a yard of fabric or metal mesh screen from a hardware store. Wrap it all together by tying a ribbon around it and fluff as necessary.

✔ **A matzah cover, a beautiful linen tablecloth, napkins, linen coasters — all these can be purchased to match, then embellished by hand as desired.**

✔ **If you purchase plain white cotton hem-stitched table linens, you have about an inch border to work with on any of these items.** You can attach a vibrant-colored ribbon to the edge; bead, embroider, or paint this edging to reflect your theme.

Just be sure that you take into consideration that these items will be packed away year after year for this one special occasion. Make whatever time you invest in handiwork be of heirloom quality to last for generations. Just look to Part IV for instructions on how to make or embellish these items.

Jazzing up smaller spaces

Although you may be spending a lot of time around the table, you aren't confined to decorating the Seder table only. Adding simple and elegant touches throughout the home is easy. Just keep your color theme in mind and carry it from one room to the next, including all the small quiet spaces of your home. Following are some suggestions to decorate these smaller spaces:

- **Accent a bench, a cozy nook, or a small living area in your home with simple silver accents to match your Seder décor.** Use lush yet simple accent pillows in reds, greens, browns or whites done in cool silk fabrics.

- **Canopy off a small area for reading by temporarily draping a sheer voile fabric from the ceiling or doorway.**

- **Add a silver or clear glass vase, resembling Elijah's cup, on an entry table. Fill it with a fresh bouquet of wine-colored roses.**

Involving the family

Preparing the table or centerpieces, folding the napkins, or placing a welcoming wreath on the door are all wonderful ways of getting the family involved in preparing for a Seder.

As I mention in the preparations section, many children may make invitations or place cards in preparation for this occasion. Spend some playtime with paper and paper crafting supplies.

Here are a few other ways smaller children can have fun:

- They can make their own version of a Kiddush cup. Have your child color a paper cup and tape or glue it on top of a spool of thread.

- Another activity is to decorate the Haggadahs (the story of Passover books read on the Seder night) and personalize them.

- They can make frogs or crickets out of clay to represent one of the plagues that hit Egypt. It's a way to bring home a message while having some fun *and* making something decorative (attach them to napkin rings at the kids table).

Sing songs that will be sung the night of your own very special Seder while you create. It's a wonderful time to have open conversations about a wonderful event in your home that you're preparing and decorating for.

Chapter 17

Taking the Holidays Outdoors

In This Chapter

▶ Coordinating your themes

▶ Planning your outdoor decorating

*Y*ou can't forget to decorate the great outdoors! You have many great opportunities to dress up your home for any holiday with simple touches or extravagant ideas. Finding out where to start, how to plan, and simple preventatives to keep that siding in shape are included in this chapter.

Show your holiday spirit inside and out. Decorate your porches, lawns, and patios with style.

Coordinating Your Interior and Exterior Themes and Décor

Contrary to what you may hear (designer gods forgive me), you don't have to match decorating themes and ideas from the inside out, if you don't want to. I know, I know: I do believe it's always nice to have one consistent style from the curb to the cellar, but I can face reality. It's just not always practical! Nor is it always desired. You may want an entirely traditionally decorated home, but you also want to have animatronic reindeer and Santa in the front lawn at Christmas.

Choosing your outdoor style

Unless you have a custom-built home, the exterior style and architecture of your home was determined long before you came along. You have to work with that exterior to coordinate your outdoor décor's styles and themes; otherwise, your outdoor décor won't blend and will stick out — in a bad way.

As opposed to interior holiday decorating, where it's sometimes easy to change up themes and styles from room to room, your entire exterior should maintain a congruent theme. That means that if you have a traditional home, and add traditional garland, wreaths, white lights, and topiary reindeer at Christmas, you probably won't want the 12-foot-tall inflatable snowman in your front yard no matter how cool you think it is. You'll also want to stay away from the flattened Santa attached to the tree, although you laugh every time you see it.

Whatever you do on the outside, keep that theme or style consistent. You can add to whatever you have, but make sure that your additions look like they belong and weren't afterthoughts or impulse buys. If you have a lawn full of plastic snowmen, reindeer, Santas, elves, and sleighs, adding multicolor candy canes to line your walkway won't hurt. If it fits with your theme and doesn't detract from what you've already got going, buy it, build it, display it.

Whether you're decorating the inside of your home or the exterior, this simple guideline holds true: Keep it consistent.

Planning your outdoor décor

Deciding that you want to dress up your outdoors with some holiday décor is easy, but after you make that decision, you may then sit at the kitchen table and wonder what in the world to do because you don't know where to start planning. I've also seen some good ideas go all wrong because the style and planning didn't match. After all, accumulating decorations over time is more the norm than buying everything all at once. Besides putting less of a dent in your budget, new things that you'll want to consider come out constantly. But that can make planning your outdoor decorating seem insurmountable. In this section, I give you some great ideas to make your planning easier.

Giving your exterior the once-over

You may find it hard to visualize what will look good on the outside of your home because you probably don't spend a lot of time standing back and surveying it (who does?). The most you probably ever looked at the outside of your home — really stood back and took a good look — was before you bought it. So stand back from your home and look at it from all angles. Better yet, take a picture — it lasts longer.

Seriously. Take photos of your house, especially straight on. Mount them to a regular sheet of paper (you don't have to be all archival-safe here) and slip it into a plastic sheet protector. You may already have this in your decorating notebook (see Chapter 6). These handy-dandy photos will help you plan all your outdoor decorating schemes beautifully.

A-sketching we will go

Now that you have all your photos in front of you, you can get down to sketching out your décor to help you envision what the outcome of your ideas will be.

You should get your ideas down on paper (or plastic in this case!); your sketches don't have to be picture perfect. You just don't want to get up to the second floor, stringing lights, and realize that you don't have enough — or end up coming face to face with a cold, wet spouse and having to admit that you don't have a plan. Sketches make you better organized and better equipped by having an outdoor decorating plan in advance.

To make the most of your sketching:

1. **Measure the lengths of areas of your home you want to cover, and record the measurements on a separate piece of paper.**

    You can easily add this information to your decorating notebook, so that you can have it on hand to refer to when barking out the decorating orders!

2. **Take a write on/wipe off felt-tip pen and draw the outlines of what you want to have added to your house right on your plastic sheet protector.**

    Don't stress. You don't have to have any artistic ability. Draw circles for wreaths, straight lines for icicle lights, and curved lines for swags. Xs work for designating where you want bows. If you want to add lawn ornaments, you can indicate them by drawing rectangles where you think that you want your items to be — you can probably manage drawing sleighs if you have to, but a rectangle box can work just as well for blocking the area.

3. **Erase lines by wiping them off with a dampened tissue if you don't like what you've done, or it ends up being just too much.**

    This way you can know exactly how much is enough or start making a list of items you need to purchase.

4. **Switch your mounted photos in and out of plastic sheet protectors to sketch out different looks or different decorating ideas for other holidays.**

Adding simple touches

When planning your outdoor decorating scheme, bear in mind that you don't have to take out a second mortgage to pay for a litany of animated or lit Christmas décor. Simple touches often provide enough outdoor sparkle and won't get you in trouble with your neighbors.

A wreath on the front door for Christmas, a menorah in the window for Hanukkah, a flag hung out for Independence Day, and an eerily lit jack-o'-lantern at Halloween all are simple touches that you can add to bring holiday decorating to your exteriors. Whether you live in an apartment or a mansion, small things can be enough to add a sense of style and décor to the outside of your home.

Small and simple can be your preferred style always, as it is mine. I like to have just enough items decorating the exterior of my home to say happy holidays, but not enough to distract from the natural beauty of the home. Also, I don't like to get too stressed out trying to do the exteriors along with the interiors more than twice a year. A few things grouped together makes a nice vignette that works for me. You can read more about how to make vignettes in Chapter 2.

Deciding how much is too much

You know that your house has too many decorations if:

- Your neighbors have to wear sunglasses to look at your house at night because so many lights are on your house.
- You have to hire off-duty police officers to direct a single line of traffic past your house.
- The city commissioner just fined you for the construction additions to your house without a city permit.
- Astronauts can see the glow of your house from outer space.
- You have to use a leaf blower to blow a path to your door from the fog machines you placed "for effect" at Halloween.
- The Easter bunny lives in your backyard he's so at home.
- People start knocking on your door to ask, "How much for the hayride?" at Thanksgiving.
- You can't get in your own front door without changing path directions.

Okay. So you know where I stand on decorating issues. The designer in me says, "Keep it simple," yet I know that, for some holidays, over-the-top decorating is completely acceptable — even desired. Halloween and Christmas fall under this category. Still, you want to ask yourself these three questions when decorating:

- When you step back and look at the overall décor, does it have a unified look and theme or style?
- Do you find yourself trying to look at too many things at once, unable to find one focal point?
- Do you have so many things gathered or grouped together that you can't tell what it's supposed to be?

Use the sketching idea I give you earlier in this chapter as much as possible, but even if you just dive into decorating the exteriors, you can still use these three questions as your checkpoints for how much is too much.

Decorating, whether or not it's for special occasions, is a system of adding and subtracting elements to reflect tastes, style changes, or even complete overhauls. Think of your outdoor décor the same way. Even if you throw it all out there, step back, look at it, and try taking pieces away and see if it still works. You don't have to throw pieces away that don't work or never use them again. In fact, if you have a lot of decorations and you're ready to pare back some, you can divide your decorations into groupings and change up the style every year.

Considering Your Options

You have many options for purchasing outdoor holiday decorations and for how you want to install them. Here, you find considerations for using both real and faux and can make a better decision on whether you want to put a hole in your siding.

Real or fake

Choosing between real or faux decorations is simply a style and budget decision. In the past, faux greenery looked fake, and you could spot a fake rose from a mile away. Plus, the cost of a fake tree ran into several hundreds of dollars, while a fresh tree offered at the local Christmas tree lot ran a little under $50.

With the popularity and quality of faux botanicals increasing, the costs are decreasing. You can find great-looking faux trees, garland, and wreaths for surprisingly low costs. Now, some faux — *really* good faux flowers — may cost more than twice the amount of the real things, but for outside decorations, the inexpensive kind will do just fine, and you may actually save money (and time) by going the faux route. The upside to having faux is

- ✔ You can pull them out year after year with minimal cleaning and caring.
- ✔ You never have to worry about accidental poisoning from ingestion or allergic reactions from handling them.
- ✔ They never die; they just fade away.

You may want to consider faux if you have an aversion to harvesting trees for holiday decorating. No need to skimp anymore! Faux is a great alternative. It's a natural selection for decorating for certain holidays year after year.

Using faux instead of real botanicals does, of course, have a few drawbacks. For instance, you may not get any shedding from faux trees or garland, but you also miss out on that fresh evergreen scent that just smells like Christmas. The same goes for flowers.

If that's a problem for you but you still prefer faux, faux botanical manufacturers have formulated scents for fake flowers and greenery that you can just spray on to get a lovely fragrance — not that you'll need that scent for outside décor.

For outside, you can use either real or faux or a combination of both. For instance, you can put real evergreen wreaths on all your windows and have faux holly bushes and poinsettias in your window boxes to put a little holiday color outside without having to worry about ice and snow damage.

Deciding between the real thing and the faux thing comes down to budget (invest once, use again and again), style (does it look real enough for you?), and personal taste (will you have time to water those potted tulips again and again for Easter?). You can benefit from using both.

Temporary or permanent

Many decorations I mention in this book offer temporary or permanent installations.

For instance, I suggest, at times, hanging art canvases on walls and switching them out season by season or holiday by holiday. Wreaths, banners, and flags can be switched out seasonally as well, making those nails you put in the wall worth it.

If you think that you'll be decorating your outside areas with hanging planters or other decorating items, such as windsocks or wind chimes, go ahead and permanently install a hook for ease in installing new décor each holiday or season.

Follow the "three or more" rule before deciding to permanently install fixtures, brackets, hooks, or nails to your exteriors. If you can envision three completely different occasions for which you can decorate a specific area with three completely different looks, or you'll be keeping a specific decoration up for at least three months or more out of the year, go ahead and install permanent fixtures that allow you to do that. A hardware store has many options that you can choose from. Otherwise, install your decorations temporarily, minimizing damage, wear, and tear to your home.

Securing Decorations Without Harming Your Exteriors

Many products on the market today are designed especially for protecting surfaces from the damage that hanging a few decorations can possibly do. Here are a few of my favorites that you may want to consider to protect your house from minor holes, scrapes, or wear and tear.

Fishing line — ahem, I mean monofilament

Use sturdy monofilament or fishing line for tying wreaths to exterior windows and doors, hanging lighted ornaments in trees, or for anywhere you'd want to normally use rope. Fishing line — especially 40-pound test line and above — is fine for securing almost any kind of holiday decorations. It protects the exterior finishes of your home, tree bark, and other finishes from scratches. Plus, monofilament stretches, making it flexible in case of high winds or storms. It doesn't deteriorate as natural fibers do, either. Try to use it as much as possible for securing or hanging decorations. Refer to Chapter 2 for tools for hanging decorations while protecting your interiors — the same rules apply here, too!

Sandbags

Instead of putting holes all over your lawn to secure a few large yard ornaments, (besides that, they may still fall over with the strongest of stakes), buy a few sandbags from your local hardware store. Place these at the backs of the bases of large wooden cutouts to secure them in place. Spray paint them with a few coats of paint to match the bases of the yard ornaments or spray them the color of your lawn so that they'll blend in if you hate the looks of regular old sandbags around your ornaments. These little gems are sure to keep your yard décor in place.

Thumbtacks

Thumbtacks are a staple in my toolkit. If you're working with a wooden surface and something needs hanging, reach for a thumbtack to make an instant hanger, so that you don't have to go looking for a hammer and nail. Thumbtacks, surprisingly strong, come in all sorts of colors, so you can find a color that matches the exterior of your house. Thumbtacks leave smaller holes than nails do, so you run a lesser risk of damaging property. Plus, you can just dab a bit of silicone sealant or wood putty on them if you want to repair holes quickly.

Duct tape

Call me tacky, but using duct tape helps eliminate the need to staple or nail, and it holds up well under inclement weather conditions. Duct tape now comes in several colors and widths, so you can pick some up that blends in better for taping down extension cords or taping up paper or plastic decorations.

To easily remove any sticky residue, dab a bit of vegetable oil onto a clean rag or paper towel and wipe the residue, scrubbing as necessary. You can just go back over the surface with a vinegar and water solution (or use a glass cleaner) to remove any oils that may make surfaces slippery.

Electrical tape

Besides using electrical tape for wrapping around joined extension cord sockets, it's great for taping around any wires that may be sticking out from floral arrangements or wreaths. It also comes in handy for securing items around banister railings because it leaves a less sticky residue than other kinds of tape.

Other great items

Here are just a few additional items that really come in handy for temporary decorating both indoors or out:

- Plastic clips that slide onto gutters or shingles to hold strands of lights
- Plastic or metal wreath hangers that slide over doors
- Suction cup-type devices that can hang items from windows and glass doors

Today, you can find all sorts of innovative products to help you protect your exteriors from temporary installations. A quick trip to a holiday section — paying close attention to the ends of the aisles and hanging merchandise next to items on shelves — gives you the latest innovations for hanging, securing, and protecting your home from exterior decorating damage.

Try your own solutions, too. A ribbon can substitute for an over-the-door hanger as long as you counterweight it with another like item. For example, take a long length of ribbon, tie or staple one end to the top of a wreath, and the other end to the top of another wreath and slip the center of the ribbon over the door. The equal weights of the wreaths keep everything in place.

Embellishing Exteriors

You can decorate the exteriors of your home in many ways. If you look around the interiors of your home, you'll find many nooks and crannies just waiting for something special to happen. The same holds true for your exteriors. However, you need to think on a grander scale for your exteriors, keeping in mind that the larger your home is, the larger your decorations should be and vice versa. Scale and proportion for outdoor decorating are two very important points.

Whether you live in temporary housing or on your own estate, here are a few other things to keep in mind.

Balconies, patios, lanais, and porticos

Outdoor sitting areas are great spaces to bring the indoors out. If you live in an area that has year-round mild temperatures, you can consider these areas as extensions to your indoor living areas and decorate them just as you would the rest of your home. Well, you'll want to make sure that you keep outdoor inclement weather in mind, so no fake snow or aluminum Christmas trees, okay?

To decorate a balcony, drape garland, lights, wreaths, or bunting. A balcony is a gathering place for barbecues and after-dinner drinks, so you'll want to use the small-space decorating ideas I sprinkle throughout the holiday chapters for decorating these spaces. Make sure to adapt any ideas for weather-proof decorating.

Small arrangements on patio tables do just fine, too. Hang flags for appropriate holiday occasions, if you're allowed to attach a bracket to your exteriors. Be sure to check with your housing management staff or community association before attaching anything permanent to your exterior siding or brick.

Windows

I touch on many things to hang in your windows from the inside in all the holiday chapters, yet you can add several things to the outside of your windows around the holidays.

For Independence Day, there's nothing like seeing a swag of bunting underneath each window. At Christmas, a wreath hanging on each window of your house makes it look like a Currier and Ives Christmas card. When you glance through the list of other exterior decorating ideas, check each one to see if you can add any of them to the your exterior windows.

Window boxes, if appropriate for your home, are great additions to add curb appeal to your house — unless you display dried-up plants as I do occasionally. They require a lot of upkeep, watering, and replanting to reflect seasonal and holiday changes, but they really do add a lot to windows.

Try layering interior and exterior holiday decorating for a great look. For instance, I have a combination at Christmas of hanging wreaths on each window, doing arrangements of holly and evergreen in the window boxes, and displaying a candle light inside each window. It's a layered effect that works for me.

Lawns

If you have a large lawn, you'll probably want to take advantage of decorating it as well as embellishing your home. Here's where you can get really creative, go large scale, and let loose with your imagination.

Remember to plan and take all kinds of proper precautions when using lighting or anything electrical outdoors. You may want to consider installing some exterior spotlights, so that you can highlight decorated areas or items for best viewing at night.

If you have a few lovely trees in your yard, you can light up the night by stringing them with lights. The best way of doing this is by starting at the base of the trunk of the tree and following these instructions:

1. **Test the lights to make sure that they're working, and then leave them plugged in while you work to get an accurate idea of how the lighting will look.**

2. **Secure an extension cord supplying electricity to the tree at the base by staking a dowel rod into the ground.**

3. **Tape the female end of the extension cord to the dowel rod with electrical tape.**

   After plugging in and stringing lights, you may cover this part of your extension cord with a plastic bag; tape the bag to the dowel rod to prevent moisture from seeping into the connection making it a fire hazard.

4. **Start winding lights up the tree.**

   Enlist others when necessary — and keep adding strands as needed, making sure to wrap each connection thoroughly with electrical tape.

Make sure that you string a maximum of only three strands of lights or less to one extension cord to reduce fire hazards. I don't want your holidays to go up in smoke, or all your hard work to just short out only moments after lighting it up.

Look for other types of lights that are netted together to cover bushes. They're perfect for giving a unified look, and you won't have to worry about stringing the right coverage of lights on a particular bush. Netted lights do the design work for you.

Safety information for outdoor lighting

Here are some tips to keep your outdoor illumination glowing safely:

- Inspect electrical cords for wear and tear and replace any cords that are beginning to fray; if any of your lights have been exposed to snow or other winter conditions, be extra careful when inspecting them for damage.

- Avoid cluttering outlets. String no more than three strands of lights together, and make sure that all lights have been tested by an independent organization, such as Underwriters Laboratories (UL) or Canadian Standards Association (CSA).

- Before leaving home or going to bed, unplug all your outdoor lights.

Large wooden cutouts

You can purchase large, life-size wooden cutouts that are decoratively painted at many department stores, garden centers, or specialty stores. Lighted from the front at night and on display during the day, these items can add a personalized touch to your lawn décor. Depending on what you can find, I've seen large lawn ornaments for announcing new babies, birthdays, and other special events besides the Christmas holidays.

Wire forms

Wire-formed dimensional shapes come prelighted for easy holiday decorating. Reindeer, Santas, sleighs, trees, stars, pumpkins, flags, and more usually come in plastic-coated one- or three-dimensional shapes. The one-dimensional shapes can be hung; the 3-D shapes are usually staked into the ground. Be sure to refer to the section earlier in this chapter that gives you alternative ideas for securing your lawn ornaments.

Topiaries

A new breed of wired-formed, lighted objects to decorate the lawn has emerged. *Topiaries,* real or fake foliage covering three-dimensional forms, are becoming more and more common for holiday decorating. I've found hearts, reindeer, and trees so far, but I'm sure that as the popularity of these increases, so will the selections. Look to topiaries as an alternative to the skeletal wire forms. You get a slightly more upscale look, and you can easily see them daytime or night. They're a graceful addition to a holiday landscape.

Pinwheels and flags and reindeer, oh my!

I am always simply amazed each time I make my trek to the garden center to see what new and innovative décor just came out! The selections just keep getting bigger and bigger each year as materials and product design keep getting better and better.

Around your favorite holiday — yes, even in cold winter months — visit garden centers to browse their selection of holiday merchandise. Even discount stores reserve garden center sections as one place to change out merchandise to fit the holiday or season. By visiting these centers often, you'll be able to find themed gazing balls, pinwheels, stepping stones, statuaries, banners or flags, flowerpots, and other outdoor decorations.

Craft and fabric stores are getting in on merchandising for the holidays as well, so don't forget to check there for some great lawn decorating items.

Part IV
Crafting for the Holidays

The 5th Wave   By Rich Tennant

You're not impressing anyone, Chiklit!!

In this part . . .

This part is packed with basic how-to instructions and ideas for crafting holiday decorations and seasonal home furnishings. Each craft idea can be adjusted to fit any holiday decorating chapter and is a quick reference for those wanting to find out more, do more, craft more, save more, or play more.

Chapter 18

Getting Started Crafting

In This Chapter

▶ Getting rid of common crafting misconceptions

▶ Finding the tools and materials you need

▶ Following necessary safety precautions

▶ Clearing up space for your craft projects

Creating your own holiday decorations is rewarding. You can produce outstanding results with just a little effort. You can breathe new life into old items by sprucing them up with some paint, create new holiday items from scratch, or customize premade items with your own little touch.

Although crafting can, at times, be downright frugal, it's not just for those with a tight budget. Knowing a few craft basics (like the no-sew techniques I give you in Chapter 19) can empower a holiday decorator. You can hem a tablecloth, create seasonal pillow covers in a flash, and make a table runner without picking up a needle and thread! Crafting is no longer for people with nothing better to do.

Crafting is therapeutic by nature (unless you're a superperfectionist wired for stereo). It allows you to slow down, it gives you control over something in a sometimes frenetic world, and it helps boost your self-esteem. Hearing someone say, "You *made* this?" is always great. You feel real accomplishment when you conquer yet another project you never thought you could do.

If you're feeling uneasy about crafting, check out the first section in this chapter, where I put to rest common misconceptions about the hobby. However, if you're psyched and ready to get started crafting, skip that section and read the rest of this chapter. I let you know what materials you should generally have on hand, alert you to important safety precautions, and provide suggestions for getting and staying organized. Roll up your sleeves and prepare to have fun. Crafting isn't your grandmother's hobby anymore!

Busting Common Crafting Misconceptions

I've talked to many people who don't try to craft anything because of their preconceived notions. In this section, I discuss (and disprove) the top three misconceptions I've heard over the years.

You need to be talented

Are you kidding? I'm never going to ask you to sculpt a masterpiece to complete your holiday decorations. If you can wash and iron your clothes, use a ruler and perhaps a hammer, sew on a button, make a copy on a copier, cut with scissors, or trace outlines, you have the skills necessary for making many crafts for the holidays. You don't have to possess artistic ability or even appreciate fine art to craft simple things.

Folks of all ages can craft the projects I include in this book.

You need a lot of space

If you have a little kitchen table, an ironing board, or a bed tray, you can craft most of the projects I feature in this book. I take care not to list anything that is going to take a lot of space to complete. Flowers can be arranged next to a sink; fabric can be laid out, cut, and assembled on a bed; paper crafts can be created on a desk.

I like to work on craft projects in my spare time. I may have a few minutes here and there to work a little on my project, so I don't want to have to drag out a lot of supplies every time I'm ready to dive in, or have to eat off a TV tray because my project is taking up the whole dining room table. Most everything I include in the crafting chapters that follow can be crafted on a small work surface, a floor, or a desk. The supplies you need to complete most projects are minimal, and they can be tucked away in a basket, drawer, or box.

Crafting through the generations

Remember to include your family when planning your craft projects. You can really enjoy wonderful moments when sitting around a table as a group, making something by hand. Many of the craft projects I list in this section of the book are perfect for family projects.

A grandparent and child can create paper garlands. A mom and her kids can create gingerbread houses or string ornaments on the tree. An older teenager can help his younger brother carve the most wicked pumpkin ever.

Provide creative time for many generations of family and friends. Remember that you don't have to include only your family.

Your synagogue or church group can prepare a day of crafting with seniors at a nursing home to deck out rooms at the holidays. (You may be surprised at all the crafting shortcuts they can show you.) You can volunteer to help a teacher decorate her classroom for a holiday. You can ask one of your social groups to decorate a town green or public space together. You can also host a neighborhood ornament-decorating party.

Crafting helps bring generations together. When glancing through the projects mentioned in each holiday chapter, or while perusing through this section, see if you can think of anything that will help you share the holidays together with others. When you craft with others, you're able to accomplish several things: making time for others, sharing or swapping stories, catching up with friends and family, and crafting really neat stuff that can used to decorate with and to cherish for years to come.

You need a lot of time

I won't kid you, crafting can take up some time depending on what project you're working on. But you can complete many of the crafts in this section of the book in just a few hours, or over the course of a weekend. To tell you the truth, some projects may take more time to shop for than they will to put together. Most of the crafts in these chapters can be made while you're watching TV. I believe in multi-tasking, and crafting is the one thing I can do while watching my favorite TV shows.

You only need to set aside an hour to begin crafting. Start with a project or technique that's quick and easy and then go from there.

Getting the Right Tools and Materials

Each craft technique requires different tools and materials. You don't have to worry about acquiring a massive list of supplies to begin crafting fabulous items. In each chapter, I tell you the tools and materials you need to complete each project. In general, I provide you with a list of supplies along with any additional materials that may be helpful for prepping your project. Some other easy-to-stock things you may want to have on hand are:

- **Rubber, plastic, or latex gloves for protecting your hands.** Some people are allergic to latex, so use what is best for you. Use heavy-duty cotton or leather gloves when working with metal, wire, or metal mesh.

- **Newspaper or newsprint to protect your work surfaces.** You can use the stack of newspapers meant for the recycling bin as inexpensive surface protectors.

- **Cardboard cutting board.** You can find corrugated cardboard cutting boards at your local fabric store. These boards are great for the holiday decorator. They're printed with grid measurements for laying out fabric and other flat materials. Use one of these inexpensive cutting boards to make small surfaces large (place it on a small table or bed), pin fabric in place, and protect your surfaces. (I don't want you to cut up your best down comforter to make throw pillows, you know.) Folded up, these cutting boards easily store under a bed or stand upright in a closet.

- **Self-healing cutting mat.** These mats are great to have on hand when cutting items with a rotary blade or craft knife. Made from a rubber/plastic surface that essentially "heals" (or repairs the cut) itself after you cut on it, these mats come in all shapes and sizes, and store flat. You can find them at craft and fabric stores.

Taking Precautions

Although most of the craft projects you're going to be making for the holidays are safe and easy for most everyone, you still want to pay attention to safety precautions.

Make sure that you read the directions for each of the craft projects from beginning to end and note any precautions I give you for protecting your skin, your surface, or your household.

Take these additional safety measures:

- **Keep sharp objects and cutting devices away from children at all times.** I like to use safety scissors (don't laugh — they cut really well!) when crafting around my little boy. I know that if he picks them up while my head is turned, they'll be much safer than my sharp fabric or embroidery scissors. Plus, they're compact enough to throw in my crafting basket, and they won't poke holes in plastic resealable bags if I need to take them with me.

✔ **If you craft holiday decorations with children, make sure that you use age-appropriate materials.** Precut as many items as you can.

✔ **Keep hot items, such as irons or glue guns, out of reach of animals or children, and never leave them unattended.** Make sure that you unplug them after use and let them completely cool before storing them away.

Making Room for Making Stuff

Just like everything else, craft supplies can quickly get out of hand if you don't manage and organize them. Tiny beads, loose glue sticks, and sewing needles that seem to vanish into thin air only to later reappear stuck to someone's behind are no fun. You need to keep your creative stash in order, just like you do all your other decorating supplies. You also need to decide on a special place to complete your project, so that you can keep everything together and have the room that you need.

Organizing for playtime

Try to keep your tools and supplies together, organizing as you go. Here are some of my favorite items for storing stuff — projects and all.

✔ **Plastic resealable bags:** I use plastic resealable bags for keeping small supplies or projects together. They're especially helpful for keeping everything nice and dry (not to mention clean). You can use them to sort out individual projects or keep supplies separated when placed in larger plastic bins.

✔ **Baskets or boxes:** Use baskets or boxes to house works in progress. Keeping your projects in baskets or boxes is key when you have to stop and start projects often or you have to shove a project into a closet when company comes over. I keep a large basket for hand-sewing projects beside the sofa. All my messy projects go into boxes that I can throw away or recycle after I'm finished using them.

✔ **File folders or plastic filing bins:** If you do a lot paper crafting, such as making holiday cards, invitations, place cards, and many of the projects I mention in Chapter 20, you may want to store your handmade and specialty papers in file folders. Add them to a home office filing system, or purchase a plastic filing bin specifically for your paper crafting needs. Many special organizers are geared specifically for paper crafters or scrapbook enthusiasts. Look for these organizers at your local craft store.

✔ **Specialty organizers:** Crafting is so hot now that you can usually find an organizer for any space restrictions you may have. You can find many different types of flexible storage systems on the market today. Creative Gear, which is made by Plaid, is one craft organization line that's made up of a heavy-duty, canvas-covered hard case bag that houses interchangeable storage compartments. These organizers are specifically manufactured to hold craft paint bottles, brushes, craft punches, specialty scissors, yarn, or whatever! You simply buy the inner storage compartments a la carte.

The beauty of these specialty storage systems is that they are made especially for the crafter who wants to keep things put. The roll about systems make it easy for arthritic or hurried crafters to move supplies easily from room to room. If you're interested in using these systems to store your craft supplies and tools, you can find them at your local craft store.

✔ **Stackable plastic bins or boxes for storage:** I like to buy inexpensive clear shoe boxes so that I can easily stack and store my supplies. Most of the supplies you need for holiday crafting can easily fit inside these compact organizers.

✔ **Labels:** It doesn't matter if you use a high-tech labeling machine or you write directly on a box, bin, or folder. The point is, you need to label your creative supplies for quick and easy identification.

You may find it helpful to keep a list of the craft supplies you have on hand. Take a sheet of notebook paper and list each craft item with a short description. Keep this list in your decorating notebook with everything else. When you run out of something, cross it off the list or purchase more. That way, when you approach a craft project, you'll know what you have on hand and what you need to purchase.

Claiming space for crafting

You want to clear a space big enough to complete your projects. Here are some suggestions for some of the best places to craft that don't take up a lot of room:

✔ **Take it outside.** Being outdoors automatically gives you more open space with which to work. And sunshine and fresh air (especially when spray painting) always do a body good.

✔ **Use the kitchen table.** Clearing off the kitchen table for a night can give you enough surface to complete just about any project in this book. You can also set up the kids for crafting for the holidays here while you prepare holiday feasts, treats, or meals — a great way to keep an eye on them (oh, and spend more time with them, too).

✔ **Go to your room.** Use a desk, a bed, or the floor. Just make sure that you protect all your surfaces from accidental spills, cuts, or burns. (That glue gun'll get ya!)

✔ **Keep it in the garage.** Many tools and projects, especially painting projects, are best completed in a garage or tool shed where spills and splatters may not be as big of a problem. In areas such as this, you can concentrate on crafting and having fun and not have to worry so much about being messy.

Some projects, such as beadwork, hand sewing, and embroidery, are completely portable. I recommend storing the materials for these types of projects in a covered basket or in a plastic resealable bag to keep them clean and organized.

If you're really tight on space, you can always purchase a piece of foam core (a sturdy, lightweight, poster sized piece of laminated foam) at your local art and craft supply store. Store it in a closet, under a bed, or behind an armoire and pull it out for an instant crafting surface that you can carry just about anywhere, inside or out.

Going with the Flow

Above all, remember to allow yourself some flexibility when creating your projects. Most of the projects I mention in each chapter are simple starting points for you to expand upon.

Go with your creative flow. Try new things, and tweak instructions the way that works best for you. Creating something from nothing is a very cool process to experience. Have a blast.

Chapter 19

Crafting with Fabric (Sewing Optional!)

Fabric furnishings are a large part of home and holiday décor. Dressing up a table with a tablecloth, switching out pillow covers to match the season, and adding chair covers are just a few ways you can add holiday touches in a flash.

But fabric furnishings aren't only decorative — they're protective, too. A table runner easily slides under a metal candleholder or a scratchy greenery centerpiece, a chair runner protects expensive upholstery, and a place mat keeps water rings from circling your dining room table.

You can find many of the items in this chapter premade; I firmly believe in using premade items when you can during the holidays — it saves time. However, you may find a bargain on some cool fabric, want to repurpose a stained heirloom tablecloth into a table runner or napkins, or need a different way to display that thrift store drapery you couldn't pass up.

Well, here you have it. In this chapter, you can find quick-sew, low-sew, and no-sew techniques for making wonderful fabric furnishings for the holidays.

Choosing Fabrics for Your Holiday Projects

Most home decorating fabric stores have a good selection of cotton and cotton-blend fabrics to choose from in many prints, solids, or patterns. My advice is to find a fabric that you can machine wash and dry for the easy care, cleaning, and storage of your holiday fabric décor. You can find the manufacturer recommendations for cleaning fabrics on the end of a bolt of fabric. The manufacturer recommendations should also indicate fabric content.

Many synthetic fabrics resist wrinkling and have a good *hand,* meaning that they feel good when resting in your hand. (The synthetics of long ago felt scratchy and coarse.) You may want to consider using synthetic fabrics for projects that you want to be a bit more stain resistant, such as a chair or table runner, or a table topper overlay.

Don't forget to look at dressweight materials, too. You may be able to find microsuedes, special occasion fabrics, and other unique blends that are perfect for some of the projects in this chapter. Dressweight materials are lighter than home decorating fabric; they won't stand up to as much wear and tear, but holiday decorating items are only used for a short amount of time anyway. Dressweight materials often hold up better in the wash and resist wrinkling well. Don't overlook these little gems when shopping for fabric.

When choosing fabrics for projects, pick blends for your holiday finery that can be easily washed, dried, and ironed — that way you'll get many uses out of them, and you won't have to stress over the minor (or major) spills that are predestined to visit your home at the holidays. (By the way, you may want to refer to Chapter 7 for stain removal, ironing, and storage tips.)

Prewashing fabrics before crafting

Prewashing your fabrics before crafting is always a good idea if you're going to wash your item often or attach a trim to it. If your fabric has a sheen, or the manufacturer indicates that it should be dry-cleaned only, take it to a dry cleaner and have it preshrunk before you begin your project. This preshrinking will keep the finish intact and prevent puckering.

Sewing a Chair Runner

Protecting a chair's upholstery or wood finish is as easy as pie. All you need is a chair runner, which is incredibly easy to make.

You can use the following measurement guide to determine the amount of fabric you need for each chair runner:

1. **Measure the width of your chair: _____ inches.**

   Your fabric will need to be cut to this width.

2. **Measure the *drop* (the length from the seat of the chair to the floor): _____ inches.**

3. **Measure the depth of the seat cushion: _____ inches.**

4. **Measure the height of the seat back (measure from the cushion to the top of the seat back): _____ inches.**

5. **Add the height of the seat back (Step 4) to the drop measurement (Step 2): _____ inches.**

6. **Add up the measurements for Steps 2, 3, 4, and 5, and then add 2 inches: _____ inches.**

7. **Divide your answer for Step 6 by 36 inches to determine the total yardage of the fabric you're going to need for each chair.**

   Your fabric will need to be cut to this length.

To make a chair runner, you need

- Fabric cut to size (use the measurement guide in this section)
- Matching thread (For a no-sew option, use fabric glue.)
- Scissors
- Straight pins
- Sewing machine (not necessary when using the no-sew option)
- Tape measure
- Iron/ironing board

After you collect all the materials you need, follow these instructions to make your chair runner:

1. **Press all edges ⅜ of an inch to the wrong side.**

2. **Press again ½ of an inch to the wrong side.**

3. **Use a straight stitch to sew all edges approximately ⅜ of an inch from the edge of the fabric.**

For a no-sew option, you can use fabric glue to fuse the hem into place.

When your chair runner's complete, place it on the chair and cinch it up with a wide ribbon bow or a tasseled cord.

For a designer variation, sew cording, welted beading, or other decorative trim to the edges of your chair runner.

Creating Place Mats

Making place mats is like making a pillow without stuffing. Instead of filling the two pieces of fabric full of stuffing, you just fuse them together. The instructions in this section show you how to make place mats out of the same type of fabric, but you can use different types of fabric to add more variety to your place mats. For example, you can make color blocks or create reversible place mats that you can flip.

To make four place mats, you need

- 1½ yards of 45-inch-wide fabric
- 1½ yards of 22-inch-wide nonwoven, double-sided, fusible interfacing (with paper backing)
- Matching thread (For a no-sew option, use fabric glue.)
- Scissors
- Straight pins
- Sewing machine (not necessary when using the no-sew option)
- Tape measure
- Iron/ironing board

Making good time by creating your own patterns

In several of the instructions in this section, I tell you to cut a number of fabric shapes (squares, rectangles, and so on) that have to be a certain size. Save some time. Make a pattern out of newspaper and pin it to your fabric before you make your cuts. With this method, you only have to measure once. You can then cut accurately sized shapes as many times as you want.

Save a trip to the recycling pile: Before you store it away, write the measurements of the pattern and what the pattern is for on the newspaper.

After you gather all the materials you need, you can follow these instructions:

1. **Cut eight 13-x-19-inch rectangles from the fabric.**

2. **Cut four 12½ x 18½-inch rectangles from the fusible interfacing.**

3. **Center and place each piece of fusible interfacing on the wrong side of four of the fabric rectangles. Adhere the interface to the fabric by ironing according to manufacturer's suggestions.**

4. **With right sides facing, align the edges of a fused fabric piece to a plain fabric piece and pin them together.**

5. **Using a ⅜-inch seam allowance, sew or use fabric glue to bind the edges, leaving approximately 6 inches open for turning.**

6. **Clip corners near the seam and remove the paper backing from the fusible interfacing.**

7. **Turn the place mat right side out and carefully push the corners out, using your finger or an unsharpened pencil.**

8. **Making sure that the top piece of the place mat is centered over the bottom piece, begin pressing and fusing the two pieces together. Fold the edges under at the opening and press.**

9. **To close the opening, either *whipstitch* (shown in Figure 19-5) or glue it closed, using fabric glue.**

Fashioning Tablecloths

Tablecloths are an easy item to switch in and out at the holidays. They protect tables, mask ugly scars, or hide unsightly plastic card tables that are used for additional serving stations or seating.

Round tablecloths

Making your own tablecloths is really quite simple — you just have to handle and sew (or glue) a large amount of fabric. Measure the diameter and height of your table (see Figure 19-1) and then use the measurement guide in Table 19-1 to determine how much fabric you need.

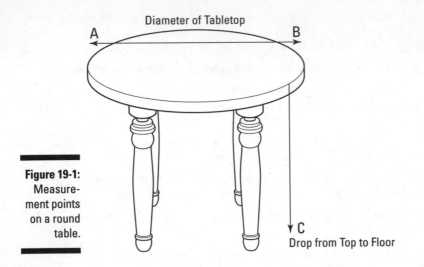

Figure 19-1:
Measure-
ment points
on a round
table.

Diameter of Tabletop

A   B

C
Drop from Top to Floor

TIP

If the diameter of your tabletop differs from the sizes listed in the chart, just take your table measurements (refer to Figure 19-1) with you to the fabric store, and the salesperson there can help you calculate how much fabric you need.

Table 19-1	Measurement Guide for Round Tablecloths				
Table Diameter	Yardage Amount for a 10-inch Drop (45-inch-wide fabric)	Yardage Amount for a 10-inch Drop (54-inch-wide fabric)	Trim Amount for a 10-inch Drop	Yardage Amount for a 30-inch Drop (45- or 54-inch-wide fabric)	Trim Amount for a 30-inch Drop
30 in.	2⅞ yards	1½ yards	4½ yards	5 yards	8 yards
36 in.	3¼ yards	3¼ yards	5 yards	5½ yards	8½ yards
48 in.	4 yards	4 yards	6 yards	6 yards	9½ yards
54 in.	4¼ yards	4¼ yards	6½ yards	9½ yards	10 yards
60 in.	4½ yards	4½ yards	7 yards	10 yards	10½ yards
66 in.	5 yards	5 yards	7½ yards	10½ yards	11 yards
72 in.	7¾ yards	5¼ yards	8 yards	11 yards	11½ yards

If you need two lengths of fabric to achieve the width, cut the fabric in half crosswise, and then cut one piece in half lengthwise as shown in Figure 19-2.

Diagram A

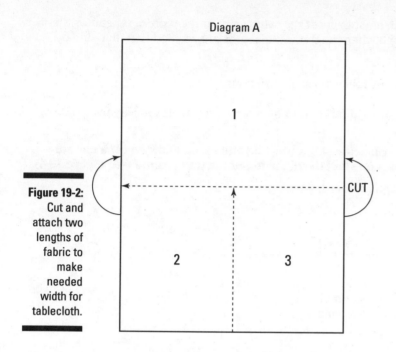

Sew 2 and 3 on either side of 1, as shown in Figure 19-3, thus avoiding a seam
running down the center of the table.

Diagram B

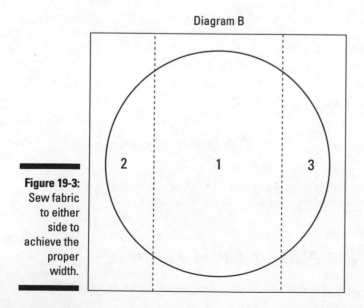

Each cut length must begin at the same point in the pattern repeat for the pattern to match when the three cut lengths are seamed together side by side.

To cut your circle, follow these instructions:

1. **Fold the seamed fabric into quarters and pin all four layers of fabric together.**

2. **Place a yardstick at the centerfold and pivot, marking off a measurement that is one-half the diameter all the way around (see Figure 19-4).**

3. **Cut through all four layers.**

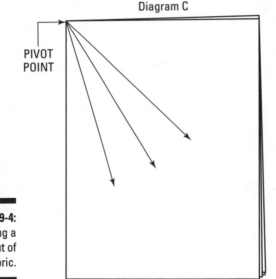

Diagram C

PIVOT
POINT

Figure 19-4:
Cutting a
circle out of
fabric.

After you've cut your circle, hem with a ¼-inch double hem and add any desired trims.

The cording or trim yardage listed in Table 19-1 allows for *ease* as you sew to ensure that the trim will lay flat. Do not pull the trim tight.

Square tablecloths or table runners

Before making square tablecloths or table runners, you need to determine how much fabric you're going to need:

1. Measure the length of the table: _____ inches.

2. Measure the *drop* (height from top of table to floor) and then add 2 inches for seam allowances: _____ inches.

3. Add the measurements from Steps 1 and 2 to determine the total length of fabric you need: _____ inches.

4. Measure the width you want your tablecloth or runner to be (add 2 inches for seam allowances): _____ inches.

5. Add the drop to the total inches in Step 4 (add 2 inches for seam allowances): _____ inches.

6. Add Steps 3 and 4 to determine the total length of fabric you need: _____ inches.

7. Divide your answer from Step 6 by 36 to get the total yardage amount of fabric.

   Your fabric will need to be cut to this length.

If the fabric isn't wide enough, refer to Figures 19-2 and 19-3 to find out how to cut and sew fabric together.

To make a tablecloth or table runner, you need the following materials:

- Fabric cut to size (refer to the measurement guide in this section)
- Thread (For a no-sew option, use fabric glue.)
- Scissors
- Straight pins
- Sewing machine
- Tape measure
- Iron/ironing board

When you have all the materials you need, follow these instructions:

1. Press all edges ⅜ of an inch to the wrong side.

2. Press again ½ of an inch to the wrong side.

3. Use a straight stitch to sew all edges approximately ⅜ of an inch from the edge of the fabric.

   For a no-sew option, use fabric glue to fuse the hem in place.

For a designer variation, sew cording, welted beading, or other decorative trim to the edges of your tablecloth or table runner.

Making Napkins

If you happen to find a good cotton fabric that's really cheap, you may want to make your own napkins. If you have leftover fabrics from other decorating projects, you can make napkins — even a single one made from the same fabric — that can be used in dinner roll baskets, wrapped around wine bottles, or covered over a stack of books to heighten a floral arrangement for a *tablescape* (see Chapter 2). Using the instructions I provide in this section, you can turn remnants into a nice decorating prop.

To make four napkins, you need the following:

- ✔ 1 yard of fabric (any width)
- ✔ Matching thread (For a no-sew option, use fabric glue.)
- ✔ Scissors
- ✔ Straight pins
- ✔ Sewing machine (not necessary if using the no-sew option)
- ✔ Tape measure
- ✔ Iron/ironing board

After you collect the materials you need, follow these instructions:

1. **Cut four 18-inch squares from the fabric.**

2. **To finish the edges with a narrow hem, fold all edges of fabric approximately ³⁄₈ inch to the wrong side and press.**

3. **Fold the edges in again ³⁄₈ inch and press again.**

4. **Use a small straight stitch on the sewing machine to hem the edges using a ¹⁄₄-inch seam allowance.**

   For a no-sew option, use fabric glue to bond the edges.

Managing mitered corners

In this chapter, I tell you how to press and hem the edges for all kinds of fabric items, but if you want another, less bulky alternative at the corners of your fabric creations, try *mitering*. A mitered corner is just a 45-degree angle formation at the corners of your fabric. Sound technical? Don't worry — it's easy.

After folding in the edges of your fabric item the first time (as I pretty much instruct in all my projects), press each corner in to make a triangle, just like I show you in the first accompanying figure. Fold the edges in again (see the second accompanying figure) to make the miter. Now hem away.

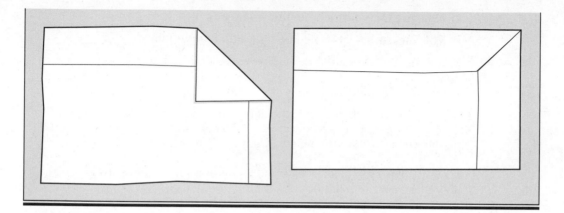

Crafting Pillow Covers

Pillow covers provide you with an easy way to change the look of outdated throw pillows. They're made to be slipped on and off for easy care and washing. You can make several pillow covers to match any holiday or season without having to purchase and store a million different kinds of throw pillows.

Make a pattern for each pillow that you think you'll want to update during the holidays. You can save time by knowing exactly how much material you're going to need when that luscious fabric you're eyeing goes on sale!

To make a removable pillow cover, you need the following materials:

- Fabric for the pillow top and backing
- Hook and loop tape
- Thread (For a no-sew option, use fabric glue.)
- Scissors
- Straight pins
- Sewing machine (not necessary when using the no-sew option)
- Tape measure
- Iron/ironing board

To determine how much fabric you're going to need to cut for your pillow cover, use the following measuring guide:

1. **Measure the width of the pillow and add 1 inch.**

   This measurement should be the width of your fabric.

2. **Measure the height of the pillow and add 2 inches.**

   This measurement should be the height of your fabric.

After you calculate the width and height, cut two pieces of fabric to serve as the front and back of the pillow cover. Then cut one piece of hook and loop tape the same width as the pillow (don't add 1 inch).

After you collect all the materials and figure out how much fabric you need, follow these instructions:

1. **Fold the bottom edge of the pillow top ½ inch to the wrong side of the fabric and then press with the iron. Fold the edge in ½ inch again and press.**

   Repeat this step for the pillow backing.

2. **Using a straight stitch on the sewing machine, hem the folded edge of the pillow top in place, using a ½-inch seam allowance.**

   For a no-sew alternative, use fabric glue to bind the hem in place.

   Repeat this step for pillow backing.

3. **Separate the hook and loop tape, and then center and pin one piece on the hemmed edge of the pillow top.**

4. **Sew around the edges of the hook and loop tape or glue the tape in place. Remove the pins.**

   Repeat this step for pillow backing, using the remainder of the hook and loop tape.

5. **Place the right sides of the pillow top and backing together, making sure to align the bottom hemmed edges together. Pin the pillow top and backing together around all edges.**

6. **Sew or glue around three sides (using a ½-inch seam allowance), leaving the hook and loop tape edges open. Remove pins.**

7. **Clip the sewn corners and turn the pillow cover right side out.**

8. **Insert the pillow and press the hook and loop taped edges closed.**

To sew a pillow, nix the hook and loop tape and all the hemming on the bottom edges. Start at Step 4 in the previous set of instructions and adjust the pillow bottom as needed. After inserting the pillow, just *whipstitch* the opening closed (see following instructions as well as Figure 19-5) or use fabric glue to adhere everything in place. *Voilà!* Instant permanent pillow!

Here's how to make a whipstitch:

1. **Thread a sewing needle with coordinating thread and knot the end.**

2. **Insert your needle at the beginning of an opening that needs to be sewn together close to the edge of the fabric on one side.**

3. **Pass your needle through the other side of fabric straight across and pull thread till taut.**

   Repeat until opening is sewn closed by inserting needle on the same side of the fabric each time and placing stitches close together.

4. **Finish by running the needle and thread in and under a few stitches and knotting the thread before snipping the thread away from the fabric.**

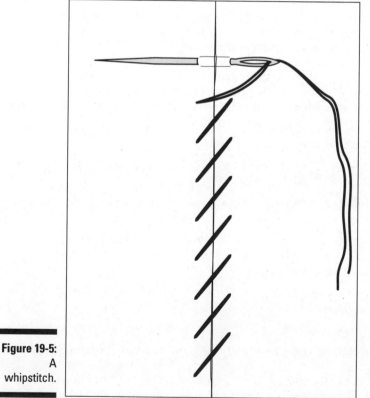

Figure 19-5:
A
whipstitch.

Designing Throws

A throw is a great decorative accessory that you can drape on the back of a chair or fold and place over the arm of a sofa. You can make several throws for snuggling under during the cold winter months.

How do you make a throw? Psst. Check out the instructions for making square tablecloths (see "Square tablecloths or table runners," earlier in this chapter).

If you decide that you want to make quick reversible throws that don't require any sewing, follow these simple instructions:

1. **Cut two pieces of fabric the same size and place them wrong sides together.**

2. **Cut 6-inch fringe strips on all sides through both layers and knot the layers of fringe together two at a time, using one piece of fringe from the bottom layer and one from the top.**

If you need to tack the top and bottom layers together to keep them from sliding, you can use a coordinating color of thread and stitch randomly through the layers. I've found that polar fleece works really well for this project and seldom requires you to tack the layers together.

Chapter 20

Providing a Finishing Touch with Paper Crafts

In This Chapter

▶ Souping up store-bought decorations

▶ Getting creative when crafting paper

▶ Taking gift-wrapping tips from the pros

Do you remember cutting out hearts, snowflakes, or paper dolls when you were a kid? Perhaps you uniquely folded a note in high school to pass to your sweetheart. Did you love to make paper airplanes or hats?

Paper is probably one of the most versatile craft mediums you'll use during the holidays — especially for decorating. In this chapter, I tell you how to embellish and utilize premade paper decorations, and I also give you instructions on how to make your own. What tools are you going to need? Well, other than a good pair of scissors, you won't need much. I also give you tips on other supplies that may make a great addition to your paper crafting stash.

And, you're in luck. Paper crafting is continuously gaining popularity, so you'll be able to find the most unique embellishments, tools, patterns, templates, and crafting accessories. No longer do your paper crafts have to look like they were made by grade school kids (even though this is one of my favorite family crafts to do) — your holiday designs can be stylish; not cheesy.

Using Store-Bought Decorations

You don't have to always make everything from scratch. Take the easy route and buy premade paper decorations in holiday themes or motifs. You can decorate instantly!

But, you can also begin with some plain paper items and make them a little better (or more your style). This section shows you how to embellish paper goods of all kinds to your heart's desire.

Finding products in a pinch

Sometimes, during all the holiday rush, you just don't feel like doing a bunch of crafts to decorate your home. Thank goodness for store-bought paper goods! A quick visit to a stationery, party supply, card shop, or craft store can yield a bounty of paper decorations or supplies.

Holiday shapes or figures with springy pleated tissue bodies, arms, or legs are quick and easy to pop out and set on a table for a quick holiday touch. Banners provide a quick and easy way to wish someone a happy holiday and paper streamers strung on tables, chairs, around doorways and on tables are a great way to add holiday colors in a pinch.

Embellishing the plain

Even though simple is good, you may want to add a little of your own holiday style to a few of the items you'll be using at your holiday gathering. Scan the supermarket or discount store paper-goods section. Standard paper goods like napkins, paper plates, and cups are readily available to embellish. Around the holidays, stores usually carry a good selection of paper decorations in holiday-related themes or colors. After you find what you're looking for, try using a few of the following ideas to help you make plain paper items your own.

Paper napkins

Napkins can be stamped or stenciled with a motif to help change the ordinary into something really cool. If you want to try something like this but need a little more direction, refer to the stamping and stenciling instructions in Chapter 23.

Here's one creative idea that can save you time from stamping a lot of napkins: Purchase a large quantity of napkins — dinner or beverage — with your monogram or a motif of a specific celebrated holiday that you invite guests over for year after year. You can get the napkins at a wedding or party supply store that does personalized napkins. If you don't include dates, you can use the napkins for years to come.

Printed napkins usually come boxed or shrink-wrapped, so you can store them with your regular paper goods. You can save money by buying in bulk. You can have the napkins professionally custom printed so that you can use them for special occasions.

Paper tablecloths

Paper tablecloths are a lifesaver for protecting tabletops and making cleanup a cinch. You can perk up boring or lifeless creased paper tablecloths by adding other one-dimensional art to it.

Believe it or not, you *can* iron paper. Just be sure that the paper you're ironing isn't plastic backed (it will melt), and that you use your iron on the lowest setting possible with no steam. You can gradually increase the temperature of your iron if the creases are not ironing out. Never leave an iron unattended, and make sure you keep that bad boy moving across your paper! You don't want any scorching.

Decorate your paper tablecloth just as you would any other type of paper. Instead of place cards (which would be odd anyway, because you're using paper), write directly on the tablecloth for a touch of whimsy.

You may also want to provide crayons at your table (just like restaurants do for kids) and then encourage your guests to draw before, during, or after dinner. Who says adults can't have fun?

Paper cups

If you're going to be serving your guests with paper cups, you can add a few touches here and there. Ribbons, markers, paint, stamps, or attached paper adornments are creative ways that you can customize your paper cups. You can write initials or names on them or attach stickers that you print from your computer or buy specifically to suit the guest's personality. You can also use them as place cards at a casual table setting. Just make sure that you don't spend too much time or effort on them, because they're also disposable.

Don't stack the paper cups inside one another after you embellish them: You may mess up the design or leave smears of craft paint or other residue inside the cups — which isn't good when you're trying not to poison your guests. Instead, try making a unique holiday decoration by stacking them in small pyramids at your beverage service.

Making vellum table runners

Vellum, a translucent paper, can be bought in large rolls at office supply or architectural drafting supply stores. To make a quick custom table runner that you can later pitch in the trash, simply roll out a length of paper down the center of your table and trim the edges as desired. Stamp motifs or designs on the edges of your runner, or grab a paint pen in complementary colors and write along the edges to wish your guests a happy holiday, give them a blessing, or remind them of a favorite quote. Vellum is a bit more expensive than plain paper, but the results are beautiful and well worth it.

Anything you do to embellish your paper cups can usually be added to real glass. You may need to make minor adjustments with adhesives, paint, and so on; check labels to make sure that they're appropriate to use with glass. You can practice on paper cups, first. If you really get going, you can always decorate glasses and then give them out as nifty take-home gifts.

Paper place mats

Paper place mats, just like all paper craft projects, are easy to make and are wonderful for quick cleanup. If you don't like laundering fabric place mats again and again, try making place mats out of paper.

Place mats usually measure 10 x 14 inches. Cut 11-x-17-inch paper down to size, or get creative and use other paper products, such as unique shopping bags, handmade paper, mat board, or poster board. If you like a particular type of paper, but it's not big enough to make a 10-x-14-inch place mat, you can piece odd-shaped strips of paper together to make the proper size place mat, and then tape them together on the back sides.

Keep embellishments on your paper place mats to a minimum; your place mats will mainly be used for protecting your surfaces. Decorate the edges with paint, stamps, or stencils, but keep the accents flat so that you won't have to arrange flatware around any three-dimensional attached pieces.

Paperboard food containers

Chinese food containers come in different colors and sizes and are great to have on hand for guests to take home leftovers.

You can use these containers for party favors, too. Stack gourmet cookies, pile in party mixes, or include nice little personal items like bath salts or small lotions and potions. You can put whatever you want into the containers.

You can leave them plain, but you have four sides — four blank canvases — to work with if you want to doll them up. Embellish them with paper cutouts, markers, paints, ribbons, stamps, iron-on monograms (yes, you can iron paper), or anything else you can come up with.

Decorated containers are pretty when stacked together on a tray for guests to pick up as they leave.

Paper portion cups

Paper nut cups can be a party favorite when they hold tiny tummy yummies, such as almonds, peanuts, mints, or chocolate truffles. Plus, they're sort of retro and cool.

You can use these cups as the base for your place-card attachments. Simply attach your place card to the outside of the nut cup and then fill it with whatever you like. These little darlings provide a quick and inexpensive way to decorate your holiday table.

Paper doilies

I don't recommend embellishing doilies if you're going to use them in a traditional sense (such as for placing under food). However, you can spice them up with paint, glitter, ribbon, or beads if you're going to use them to embellish other things. Use paper doilies to wrap up items like compact discs, tickets, or other small items. Roll a doily around the item, or wrap the item up burrito style — with side flaps folded in first, the bottom folded in next, and the top folded in last. Tie a ribbon around the doily to secure it, or stamp a big wax seal on it for a more delicate and distinguished look.

Streamers

I used to think that crepe-paper streamers were only used in the high school gymnasium for prom night. Lately, I've been using crepe-paper streamers as oversized ribbon accents. At summer gatherings, I use them to act as faux canopies for shading my outdoor buffets and seating areas. I string them from trees to secured poles — whatever suits my mood. And they're inexpensive and easy to make.

You can get creative during Halloween by roping off doorways as crime scenes, and, of course, you can always use white crepe paper to "mummy-up" a teddy bear for a sweet little accent next to the Halloween candy dish.

Other creative ideas for using streamers range from garland around a doorway to impromptu colorful napkin rings. Because of their size and stretchability, crepe-paper streamers are really good for wrapping around the stems of hand-tied bouquets of flowers or cinching up paper tablecloths at the edges. And, because they're made out of paper, you can draw, write, stamp, label, or accent them any way you want. Try writing favorite sayings on them before you hang them up. You can write out a verse, poem, or quote on a crepe-paper streamer to help accent the holidays.

Paper lanterns

White Chinese paper lanterns are beautiful for stringing up at holiday gatherings, indoors or out. Try embellishing them with holiday colors or motifs. You can easily add stripes of color by gluing strips of crepe paper around them. You can also randomly glue paper metallic stars on them for a twinkling effect.

Spruce up plain paper lanterns to reflect the holiday you're celebrating. Attach items, paint designs on them, and string 'em up!

Creative Paper Crafting

Not only can you make decorations from paper, but you can make invitations, containers for holding goodies, and gift wrap to boot. No wonder paper crafting is booming right now — just look at what you can do!

If you like the idea of crafting holiday items with paper, or you just like to embellish the goods you've got, invest in a good paper-crafting stash of items. With all the good stuff on the market today, your list of items can stretch for miles. Here's a list of good items to help you get started:

- Ribbon
- Paint
- Paint pens
- Markers
- Stickers
- Grommets
- Adornments
- Precut shapes
- Stamps/Pigment pads
- Stencils
- Wooden stylus
- Small light box
- Paper punches
- Specialty-edged scissors
- Adhesives (archival-quality and acid-free adhesives, glues, fusible web, and specialty dimensional foam squares or dots)
- Desktop paper cutters
- Hole punch
- Laminator
- Binding tools
- Die-cuts

Paper garlands

Using die-cut holiday motifs, cutouts, or combinations of individual letters, you can create your own holiday garland in just a few minutes time.

Line up the cutouts side by side on a flat surface. Tape or connect them together with string and then hang them around doorways, on the front of buffet stations, across front porches, and so on.

Cut out beautiful paper snowflakes at wintertime and string them together for a one-of-a-kind garland. Use your own imagination, as well as current offerings at your local craft store, to piece your garland together.

Paper ribbons

Tape paper ribbons to the edges of open shelves, around cake plates, or to gift wrap.

The easiest way to make paper ribbons is to cut 1-to-2-inch-wide strips of paper with a paper cutter and then follow these instructions:

1. **Trim one edge of the paper strips with decorative-edged scissors.**
2. **Use a hole punch or craft punch to cut out designs every few inches.**
3. **Adhere double-sided tape to the back top edge of your paper ribbon, and join the edges of the lengths of ribbon together as needed.**

Place Cards

Place cards on your holiday table can be anything but boring. You can make your own place cards out of index cards or specialty paper. Make them so that they tent fold, or insert flat place cards into place card holders.

Inserting hand-lettered or printed place cards into small silver or brass picture frames (or any other color of frame) is one of my favorite ways to display place cards. These frames, which are normally used to show small wallet-sized photos, add a great effect to the dinner table, and they can be repurposed for any occasion or holiday.

Notecards, greeting cards, and invitations

The myriad of styles you can use for greeting cards, notecards, and invitations are just too numerous to mention in this chapter! Overlays, attached grommets, findings, wire, stickers, and die-cuts are just a few things that you can easily add to these stationery items.

If you want to make your own stationery items, decide how detailed you want to get. Do you want to cut and score your cards yourself, or do you want to just embellish premade blanks?

Pay a visit to your local office supply and craft store to check out the selection of premade items you can feed through your inkjet or laser printer, and then go from there. You can often find enough open-stock merchandise to experiment with layering or compiling your stationery design right there in the store.

If you decide that you really want to get into creating stationery items, find a class that educates you on the many choices you have.

Gift tags

You can make gift tags from scraps of your best paper, hang tags from an office supply store, or use metal foil cutouts!

To create holiday motifs, trace the outline of a cookie cutter onto paper and then cut out the design and embellish it as desired. Punch a hole at the top of your design and string yarn or ribbon through it.

You may also want to try using adhesive labels — the ones that are normally used for shipping or addressing envelopes — as gift tags. These stick-on buddies allow you to creatively embellish the labels just as you would any other paper; plus, they never come off after you attach them to the package. Check discount and office supply stores for the right size label to suit your needs.

Pinpricking paper

Pinpricking paper is a technique that Victorians used to punch decorative designs into paper. By using a simple pattern and a pushpin, you can create pretty, impromptu paper chandelier shades that fit over your regular ones for the holidays.

Pinpricking paper is quick and easy, and it looks best when wrapped around a light source. Try applying this technique to luminarias, glass votive wrappers, and window shades. Tiny holes of light shining through a design is subtle and sweet.

If you want to try this fun and easy craft, follow these instructions:

1. **Place the paper on a soft but sturdy piece of corrugated cardboard.**

   The cardboard keeps your paper flat and provides a soft surface for the pin to pierce through.

2. **Position your pattern (such as a line drawing or stencil) on top of the paper as desired.**

3. **Using a thumbtack, prick through all layers as you follow the outline of the design.**

4. **Remove the pattern and then finish cutting and designing the paper craft as desired.**

Decoupaging

Decoupage, or the Victorian art of cutting out images and pasting them to surfaces, is one of the easiest ways to decorate with paper. You can decoupage many things for the holidays, such as Easter eggs (after dying), gift boxes, tins, furniture, lampshades, and even art canvas.

To use this technique, you need nothing more than pretty pictures or artwork (greeting cards or calendars work well), or beautiful tissue paper or napkins, a surface on which to glue your treasures, and a good *decoupage medium* (a special glue, used for this particular craft, that dries clear). It's as simple as that.

Brush a layer of decoupage medium onto your surface and then position your artwork on it — singly or layered — as desired. Brush another layer of decoupage medium over the art and allow it to dry. Continue to add layers of decoupage medium until you're satisfied with the sheen or sealed surface. You may gently sand the surface of the glue in between coats for a super-smooth finished surface.

Making paper shades

For a nice holiday decoration, you can temporarily wrap your existing chandelier shades and lampshades with paper shades in holiday colors.

Make a pattern for your shade by placing the seam at the edge of a large piece of newsprint. Place a marker at the bottom edge of the shade and mark the pattern as you slowly roll the lampshade on the newsprint, stopping when the seam meets the newsprint again. Repeat this process by using the marker at the top of the shade. Use a ruler to connect the top line of the

pattern to bottom line of the pattern. Cut out the pattern. Double-check the accuracy of your paper lampshade pattern by rolling it around your shade again; note how much you need to extend your pattern for an overlap.

Place the pattern on the back side (the side that won't show) of the paper you're going to use as a shade; trace the lines of the pattern. Cut out the shade. Roll the paper into a shade and overlap the short edges; glue with a glue stick. When you're finished, slide your new shade over the existing shade.

Creating collages

Collage artists create a picture or design by adhering a number of flat items (such as newspaper, wallpaper, printed text, illustrations, photos, cloth, string, cutouts, and so on) to paper, canvas, or frame using everything from glue to waterslide transfers to paints. Because of the layered effect, collages are viewed as being one-dimensional to three-dimensional works of art. The goal is to craft a message or feeling through the patterns or textures used in the content or overall design.

Holiday collages can turn into large, extemporaneous pieces of artwork that the whole family can enjoy. Lay out a large canvas with random holiday items gathered from your home (make sure that the items are one dimensional) and have your family paste on the items any way they want. You may find that making a collage is like putting together a puzzle — you just can't leave it alone. This collage can become a work of art that you bring out and hang on the wall year after year.

If you're interested in just the basics of putting together collages, I encourage you to take a few classes in scrapbooking to get your feet wet. Knowledgeable instructors can help you with design, layout, cropping, and the selection of paper and embellishment items. The information from the class can help you with all your collage work. Find a scrapbooking or craft store in your area and ask if they offer a class.

Wrapping Gifts Like a Pro

The gifts you give at the holidays and other special occasions can also be used as quick decorating items. In that case, they need to look pretty, right?

In order to make your gifts look like they've been wrapped by department store gift wrappers, you need to have a little patience and skill.

How do the department store gift wrappers get their packages to look so good? They wrap gifts on big worktables, work with perfectly sized boxes, and have the right supplies and tools for the job at their fingertips. Oh, and they also take the time to get it right. No wonder I'm not able to make my packages look so pretty! I doubt that my dog-hair dusted floor counts as a proper work surface. And I guess I can't say that I'm the most attentive gift wrapper, because I usually try to watch TV and cook dinner, too.

So, after observing what the professionals do right, here are some key points to keep in mind when wrapping your next gift:

- ✔ Select a large, clean, hard surface (that means the back seat of the SUV is out). Try using your kitchen table.

- ✔ Have a clean, empty box nearby to hold rolls of paper when they're not in use. (Too bad we can't have those giant stationery rollers attached, right?)

- ✔ Keep a small basket or plastic bin nearby with sharp scissors, gift tags, pens or markers, ribbon, bows, and anything else you like to use for adornments.

- ✔ Get an office tape dispenser and load it up with double-sided transparent tape.

- ✔ Because scissors never seem to cut a straight line (yes, I'm blaming it on the scissors), do what the pros do and fold a small amount of paper under to make a straight edge. Your wrapping will look tidier, and you'll be able to match up the pattern.

- ✔ Make sure that you use plenty of bows and ribbons, and consider attaching sprigs of greenery, bells, silk or real flowers, cookie cutters, or any other embellishments that seem appropriate.

Making your own wrapping paper

Brown craft paper or white butcher paper (which are both available at restaurant supply stores or paper warehouses) provide you with a cost-effective alternatives to sometimes high-priced wrapping paper.

You can purchase a single bulk roll, which varies from 800 to 950 feet long. That's a lot of wrapping, my friend. You'll rarely pay more than twenty bucks for the whole roll, and you can design your wrapping paper as you go along.

Can't find the right box? Make your own!

If you've ever searched for small boxes for the little treats you give out at the holidays, you know that finding them is not that easy. What's up with all the shirt boxes? You'd think that retailers and manufacturers would figure out that, sometimes, we like to give gifts that are thicker than two inches deep.

Thankfully, you can purchase kits that contain patterns, box blanks, and everything you need to craft your own boxes. You can find them in craft stores or you can order them online.

Painting, stenciling, and stamping are popular ways of customizing your wrapping paper, but you can also try using stickers, press-on tattoos, beads, or other creative finds. Because these papers are neutral colors, you can design them to match any theme or color scheme. You're only limited to your imagination.

What's black, white, and read all over?

Newspapers are often used in a pinch to wrap presents inexpensively. Instead of looking cheesy and cheap by wrapping up a gift in the comic section, try using newspapers in an artful way.

Simple black-and-white newsprint provides a great backdrop for a striking red fabric bow to *pop* off of. Add a handmade tag, and your chintzy wrapping will look tailor-made.

Use cool or unusual newspapers, like the stock market section of *The Wall Street Journal,* to wrap up a gift for a money-conscious friend or relative, or use a Chinese newspaper to wrap up gifts for a Chinese New Year celebration. A little thought — and a buck or two at your local newsstand — can provide a wrapping bonanza.

Chapter 21

Taking Advantage of Flower (and Botanical) Power

There's nothing like adding fresh or faux botanicals to a room to make it complete. What is it about adding leaves, blooms, and even weeds like Queen Anne's Lace (which can be found on the side of the road) that makes a room perk up?

Botanicals — whether real or fake — capture the essence and beauty of nature while adding an element of life to your surroundings. Enjoy creating with these elements and try infusing as many as you can into your holiday decorating.

In this chapter, you find ways to create your own floral arrangements, wreaths, and garland. You also discover how to tie a florist bow and preserve botanicals. So dive in. You'll find more ways to create, decorate, and have fun at the holidays, naturally.

Creating Arrangements

Arrangements can be made from many things, but floral designs seem to be the most popular. A beautifully arranged floral design can make a holiday even more extraordinary. I provide my favorite simple arrangements in the following sections. Try making these arrangements for your holiday table.

Single stem arrangements

Single stem arrangements aren't necessarily made up of only one flower — instead, they consist of only one *type* of flower. A simple single stem arrangement of fresh tulips in spring colors, cut at the same height and placed in a water glass, can be just as stunning as an over-the-top, five-foot-tall centerpiece on a buffet.

Single stem arrangements come in many forms; read on for some examples.

Urn arrangements

You may want to start arranging flowers by trying your hand at a simple yet elegant faux flower *urn arrangement.* Urn arrangements can be big and bold, but I like to arrange blooms close together following a geometric shape of some sort for a tailored look. These arrangements are particularly nice to have at your next upscale party for accent pieces in smaller spaces.

Simply place a small Styrofoam ball into an urn and insert roses with 2-inch cut stems side by side until the urn is completely full. The shape of the Styrofoam provides the design for the arrangement, so you don't have to worry about heights or placements.

Flower topiary

You can make a *flower topiary,* an arrangement of flowers in a geometric shape, with fresh or faux flowers.

Try arranging a fresh flower topiary. Cut a piece of foam to fit snugly in a watertight container. Soak floral foam in water until it is thoroughly absorbed. Gather a large bunch of flowers and cut the stems so that they are all the same height. Insert the stems into the foam very close together and tie a piece of raffia or ribbon close to the blooms (this will help keep them together). Cover the foam with layers of moss and you have a beautiful centerpiece that takes little time and effort.

Everlasting arrangements

Everlasting arrangements are made up of flowers that will last a week or so. Long-lasting fresh flowers, such as gladiolas, work well for an impromptu floral arrangement. Cut the stems all the same length at an angle, and then fan them out in a large vase. The stems will last for at least a week or so. This tall arrangement will stand out in an area that needs a little height.

Try arranging other everlasting flowers, such as daisies or carnations, in loose bouquets. Everlasting arrangements can be made a few days in advance of any holiday event and still look gorgeous the day of.

Multi-flower arrangements

I love arranging bouquets that contain a variety of flowers. In this section, I discuss some of my favorite floral arrangements that use multiple kinds of flowers and fillers.

If you're short on time, visit your local supermarket or florist and grab a bunch of prearranged flowers so that you can simply cut off the stems and place the flowers in a vase of fresh water with flower preservative.

Something as small as a teacup can be used to start a terrific little arrangement. All you have to do is cut the stems of a multiple variety of flowers and filler materials (such as leather leaf fern, caspia or wax flower) at about the same length, place a few glass marbles or river stones in the bottom of a teacup, and then fill the cup about half full of water. Place several mixed flowers into the teacup, wedging the stems in between the marbles or stones. When you're finished, you'll have a perfect little arrangement to set on top of, or at the head of, a place setting for Valentine's Day, Thanksgiving, Christmas, Yom Kippur, or Mother's Day (not in this book, but still important).

Flower arranging should be fun. Don't be intimidated by trying to figure out which height you should cut each flower, or where you should place your flowers based on their height. Flowers are beautiful by themselves. Just cluster them together and place them throughout the house. You can't go wrong!

Picking fruits and vegetables for arrangements

Adding an artichoke, asparagus stem, a bunch of grapes, or any other vegetable or fruit to a flower arrangement provides a certain punch and a touch of the unexpected.

Think about arranging fruits attractively on layered trays or stringing them as garland. A topiary form can easily be covered with lemons or limes and then filled in with fresh basil or salal leaves (use floral picks to attach fruits, veggies, and herbs to the forms). A glass vase shines when filled to the brim with fresh cranberries and water. Try displaying and arranging fruit that seems out of the ordinary. You may never look at your produce stand in the same light again.

Allergic to flowers?

I include many ideas for making other types of arrangements in each holiday section. Here are some more ideas:

✔ Cluster glass ball ornaments in a decorative dish.

✔ Arrange seashells in a layer of sand on a long decorative tray.

✔ Group a collection of wooden dreidels in a silver bowl.

✔ Make your party favors into an arrangement. If you're passing out party horns or noisemakers, arrange them in a tall, slender basket with the bottoms facing out. This arrangement will resemble a bouquet.

✔ Put some pine cones into a basket for a rustic wintry arrangement.

These are just a few idea starters. Look at ordinary objects in a whole new light. Making arrangements to showcase them can be fun and easy.

Making Wreaths

As you probably already know, wreaths are perfect for any holiday or season, not just Christmas. They can be used indoors or out, and you can make them out of just about anything.

The easiest way to make a wreath from greenery, moss, flowers, faux berries, or dried leaves is to start with a foam base. You can choose from a variety of shapes, including squares, hearts, rings, or stars. Visit your local craft store. They supply just about everything you need to make beautiful wreaths for indoors or out.

To make a wreath, you need the following materials:

✔ Foam base wreath form

✔ Primary wreath materials, such as

- Moss
- Silk flower blooms
- Berry or floral picks
- Greenery
- Dried leaves
- Ribbon

✔ Floral paddle wire

✔ Floral pins

✔ Wire wreath hanger

✔ Metal floral picks or small wooden picks

✔ Wire cutters

✔ Scissors

✔ Hot glue/hot glue gun

To make your wreath:

1. **Lay the foam shape on a flat work surface and insert the wreath hanger at the top back of the shape.**

2. **Separate the primary wreath materials into manageable chunks and cut the stems with scissors or wire cutters.**

   If you're using moss, simply separate it by pulling it apart with your hands.

3. **Attach floral picks to the stems of the gathered bunches that need extra support to insert into the foam wreath.**

4. **Insert picks, stems, or leaf clusters close together on the wreath form until it is completely full.**

5. **Fill in holes with smaller "picked" clusters (floral picks attached to the stems), or use metal "U" shaped floral pins to attach individual small botanical fillers to the wreath.**

Check out these additional wreath-making tips:

✔ If you make a wreath out of one material that's nonseasonal, such as bay or magnolia leaves, moss, or ivy, you'll be able to change the look of it regularly by switching out different colored bows or ribbons that reflect the holiday seasons. You can add and take away picks of seasonal berries, flowers, and themed items to give it a fresh, new look regularly.

✔ Making fresh or faux evergreen wreaths is easy. For a large and full evergreen wreath, use long lengths of evergreen garland (see the instructions for creating garland in the following section). Starting at the back of the wreath, secure one end of the garland with a floral pin. Begin wrapping the garland in and around the wreath base, shoving the garland as close together as possible. Use floral picks as necessary on the back of the wreath to prevent the garland from slipping. Wind the garland all the way around and then cut and pin the end to the wreath base.

✔ For a different, simple look, wrap a spool of satin ribbon around the wreath base, starting at the back. Use a floral pin with a dab of hot glue to secure the ribbon to the back of the wreath base. Add a small arrangement of flowers and a bow to the bottom of the wreath.

Assembling Grand Old Garland

Garland isn't only used at Christmastime, nor is it always made of evergreen or tinsel. You can string anything end to end, making beautiful garlands to use anywhere for any season and any holiday occasion. You can use paper shamrocks for St. Patrick's Day, paper hearts for Valentine's Day, or dreidels for Hanukkah — any icon or object that can be threaded is game.

To make your own garland, you need the following items:

- Any materials you want to make into garland, such as
  - Leaves
  - Flowers
  - Berries
  - Popcorn
  - Paper shapes
  - Beads
  - Flags
  - Ornaments
- Needle
- Florist paddle wire, thread, and/or monofilament (or fishing line)
- Floral tape
- Scissors
- Small nail or thumbtack

To make your garland:

1. **Punch holes in the materials you're going to use for the garland with a nail or thumbtack.**

   Punch the holes at the top of the items for layered garland, or punch holes at the opposite ends of the items to string them end to end.

   For items that are soft (such as popcorn) or items that already have holes in them (such as macaroni and beads), no hole punching is necessary.

2. **String your items together.**

   If you want to string your items together end to end, thread a needle with monofilament or thread and then string the items, weaving in and out of the punched holes.

For beads, popcorn, berries, or any items that you don't want to string end to end, simply string the items together and knot the ends close to last item. Cut the thread or monofilament approximately 12 inches from the tied knot.

To make garland out of evergreen, herbs, or flowers, make a small grouping of flowers and wrap paddle wire tightly around the stems. Add staggered groupings of flowers, wrapping them with wire as you go. Finish by wrapping the last stems with wire and then taping them together with floral tape.

Here are some more garland tips:

- ✔ To thread hard objects, such as seashells or nuts, use a power drill with a small bit to drill holes for threading.

- ✔ Drape garland on banisters, around chandeliers, on mantels, or on ceilings. You can also try finding other interesting places, such as windows or mirrors, to drape a swag of garland or two.

Topping off your arrangement with the perfect bow

Including bows in your wreaths, garlands, and other decorating projects can add a certain touch of elegance and texture to the overall look of your project. Adding bows to floral arrangements and centerpieces also adds a finishing touch. Tying a bow isn't nearly as difficult as it looks. If you can make loops, you can make beautiful bows.

Finagling a flat bow

You can make flat bows with ribbon that's hard to knot or gather. Use them on packages and napkins. To make a flat bow:

1. **Make a small loop of ribbon, and then fold layers of ribbon back and forth, lengthening each layer until you have the desired thickness. (See Figure 21-1.)**

2. **Staple the layers together in the center and then wrap the center with a coordinating ribbon or trim, securing the backing with tape or a small amount of hot glue. (See Figure 21-2.)**

For an upscale designer look, insert a stemmed flower (live or silk) in between the bow and center ribbon, or slip an ornament, bell, or other find onto the center ribbon before wrapping it with the flat bow.

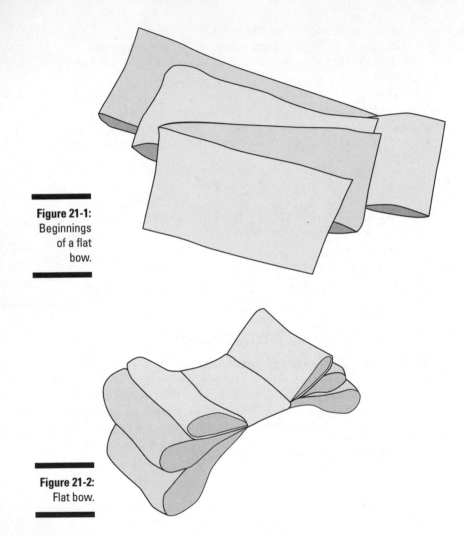

Figure 21-1:
Beginnings
of a flat
bow.

Figure 21-2:
Flat bow.

Fluffing up your arrangement with a florist bow

Fluffy looped bows are best made with a good fabric ribbon. Give extra volume to your bow by choosing a wire-edged fabric ribbon. To make a florist bow, follow these steps:

1. **Make a small loop of ribbon and hold it with your thumb and forefinger.**

   This loop will be the center of your bow. (See Figure 21-3.)

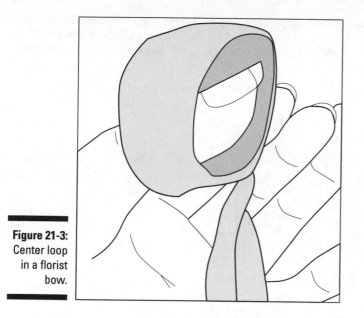

Figure 21-3:
Center loop
in a florist
bow.

2. Make another loop on the original piece of ribbon and twist the ribbon at the center, allowing the right side of the ribbon to show. Make another loop on the opposite side of the center of the bow. (See Figure 21-4.)

3. Continue making loops, alternating sides and making each loop longer than the previous one until the desired fullness is achieved.

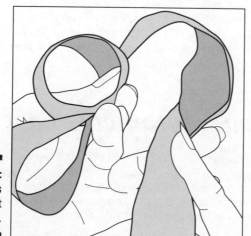

Figure 21-4:
First loops
in a florist
bow.

4. **Insert a chenille stem (pipe cleaner) or florist wire through the center of the bow and across the gathered loops. Wrap it around and twist tightly on the underside of the bow, tying all the loops together. (See Figure 21-5.)**

Use the remaining wire to attach the bow to an item.

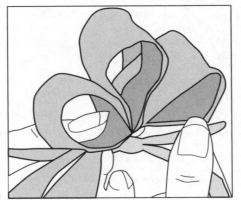

Figure 21-5:
Tying off a
florist bow.

Here are some designer tricks I use for florist bows:

✔ To prevent florist bows from getting crushed in storage, insert wadded tissue into each loop and store them loosely in a sturdy, noncollapsible box.

✔ If you need to make a lot of bows of the same size, or you're still intimidated by handling all that ribbon, try using a bow-making tool like the E-Z Bow bow maker. When you use one of these tools, bow making becomes a cinch (no pun intended).

Helping Flowers and Botanicals Last

You have many ways to preserve fresh flowers, weeds, and leaves for use in your holiday decorating and gifts. From gluing pressed flowers to invitations, candles, and place mats, to making a stunning window screen of waxed paper and autumn leaves, this section gives you the know-how to preserve, press, pound, and wax and wane over luscious, beautiful botanicals.

Preserving flowers, leaves, and weeds

You may want to try a couple of the techniques I give you in this chapter for preserving a fresh bouquet different ways to see which works best for you. These techniques are fun and inexpensive. And what's better than playing in a bunch of flowers, weeds, and leaves?

You can preserve flowers, leaves, and weeds with many different methods — such as by using corn meal and borax, or by sending them off to be freeze-dried — but the two methods that follow are the easiest and your best bet because they are the cheapest and most reliable and consistent in results.

Preserving your botanicals the old-fashioned way: Air-drying

If you have a rubber band and a ceiling, you can air-dry flowers, leaves, and herbs for your holiday decorating. It's easy.

To air-dry botanicals, you need

- Rubber bands, twine, or wire
- Scissors and/or clipping shears
- Hammer and nail (or a cup hook)
- Clothespins

To hang flowers individually, hammer a nail into a wall and use the clothespin to clip the stem to the nail, hanging the flower upside down.

To dry bunches of herbs, leaves, or flowers, divide them into small (less than a handful) bunches and then tie the stems with twine, wire, or rubber bands. (Remove the leaves from the flower stems before tying.) Hang the bunches upside down on nails or cup hooks that you screw into the ceiling. Most flowers will dry within a week.

Here are more tips for you to try:

- Hang the bunches in a cool, dry, dark area, such as a closet, pantry, or cellar.
- Feel free to use a good floral tint, such as Design Master Color Tool Just For Flowers aerosol spray (available in the floral or spray paint section in most craft stores), to bring a bit of color back to your dried flowers. The floral tint not only gives a nice natural tint of color, it also keeps the dried flowers from deteriorating too quickly.

Saving flowers with silica gel

Silica gel (which can be found at craft stores and some garden centers) is the quickest method for preserving flowers. With silica gel, most flowers in full bloom can be preserved in about five days; they also dry closer to their original color.

To preserve flowers in silica gel, you need

- Plastic airtight container
- Silica gel
- Flowers
- Floral wire
- Floral foam
- Scissors
- Knife
- Cutting board
- Packing tape

To dry flowers with silica gel, use the following directions:

1. **Cut a piece of floral foam the same size as the inside of your container. Cover the bottom of your container with a very thin layer of silica gel crystals and then place the floral foam on top of the crystals.**

2. **Cut flower stems and remove all leaves. Insert the stems into floral foam, making sure that the flowers do not touch each other.**

3. **Cover the flowers completely with silica gel and then close the container. Make sure that the container is airtight by taping the edges shut.**

   This step is important: If your container isn't airtight, it will absorb the moisture from the air instead of from the flowers.

4. **Check on the flowers every few days. The flowers are dry when their petals feel papery to the touch. Remove the silica gel and then gently remove the flowers from the floral foam. Brush the remaining silica gel from the petals with an artist brush (or just blow it off).**

For the best results, dry similar types of flowers at the same time so that the drying times will be close together.

Pressing flowers, leaves, and weeds

When you receive or pluck fresh botanicals, try pressing them just for fun. Flower presses are really nice, but they're not necessary for taking up this craft. You need nothing more than a nice, thick phone book and a few heavy items to place on top of it. Don't forget to press a few leaves from the stems of the flowers. Rose leaves work beautifully as a backdrop when doing a pressed floral arrangement. Opening a drawer of beautifully pressed blooms and adding them to little holiday items on a whim can be fun. Because the pressed botanicals are flat, you can file them away in a shoebox in plastic resealable bags. Pressing flowers or leaves is a beautiful way to preserve a bit of nature for a long time.

To press flowers, leaves, or weeds, you need

✔ Phone book or newspaper

✔ Flowers, weeds, or leaves

✔ Heavy items (such as tiles, books, bookends, and so on)

✔ Tweezers

Here's how you press flowers:

1. **Open the phone book about three-quarters of the way in. Start carefully placing flowers or leaves on the right page, making sure that the edges do not touch.**

   If you want to remove the stamen and pistils, you can do so with a pair of tweezers.

2. **Cover the botanicals by flipping several pages from the left side of the phone book over the flowers and leaves, making sure that the petals and leaves remain flat and intact. Continue placing flowers, weeds, and leaves in the phone book in this manner until you only have the first ¼ of the book's pages left.**

3. **Close the phone book and place it on a flat surface, preferably in a cool, dry, dark area such as a cupboard. Stack heavy objects on top of the phone book and allow it to press for three weeks.**

4. **Remove the heavy objects from the phone book and check to see if the flowers are crisply dried. Be careful not to bend or crease the petals or leaves.**

Try some of these ideas for pressing flowers:

✔ You may get better results if you pluck all the petals from a flower and press them individually. When assembling a collage or pressed flower arrangement, you can layer the individual petals to resemble a complete pressed flower. Remember, if you choose to do this, press the stem and center of the flower, as well.

✔ Speed up the leaf-drying process by placing the leaves between sheets of blank newsprint and then pressing them with an iron at medium setting. Avoid scorching the newsprint by keeping the iron moving in a constant motion, and never leave the project unattended or the iron flat on the pressing surface.

Pressing botanicals between wax paper

Pressing leaves and other botanicals between sheets of wax paper is an easy craft anyone can accomplish in a flash. This activity is especially fun for kids, even though it should only be done with adult supervision.

To press leaves or flowers between wax paper, you need the following items:

✔ Wax paper

✔ Fresh or pressed leaves, flowers, or flower petals

✔ Scissors

✔ Iron/ironing board

✔ Newsprint or brown paper bags

After you gather the materials, follow these instructions:

1. **Protect your ironing board with a few layers of blank newsprint or brown paper bags. Sandwich the leaves and/or flowers between two layers of wax paper and then cover them with more newsprint or another brown paper bag.**

2. **Press with a preheated warm iron (no steam!) until the wax paper fuses together. Allow the wax paper to cool.**

Here are more ideas you can use when pressing flowers and leaves with wax paper:

✔ Use this flower-pressing technique to make pretty gift wrap, place mats, or long sheets for table runners.

✔ Make a few extra sheets for wrapping quick breads (like pumpkin bread or zucchini nut bread) to pass out to your neighbors.

Fold and then staple or stitch the edges together to make tiny gift bags for cookies, candies, or other small trinkets or gift items. To seal the gift bags, fold the top edges under and punch two holes approximately 2 inches apart at the top. Thread a pretty ½-inch ribbon or strands of raffia through the holes and then tie it into a bow.

Dipping flowers and leaves in wax

Fresh flowers and leaves — especially autumn leaves — stay around a bit longer when you practice the Victorian art of dipping botanicals in hot wax. Waxed flowers, depending on how fresh they are at the time you dip them, can last for several days and give a porcelain effect when arranged in small clusters.

To wax flowers and leaves, you need the following items:

- Empty coffee can
- Large pan
- One pound of wax (beeswax or paraffin — available at craft stores)
- Bowl
- Empty cereal box
- Wax paper
- Knife (for cutting wax and flower stems)
- Cutting board
- Kitchen tongs

After you collect the materials you need, follow these instructions:

1. **Cut the wax into ½-inch squares and place them into a clean coffee can.**

2. **Place the can in a pan of cold water and slowly bring the water to a boil. Reduce the heat to simmer, and melt the wax completely.**

3. **While the wax is melting, prepare for the waxing process by collecting a bowl of cold tap water, laying out a sheet of wax paper, and punching holes, about three inches apart, in the side of a cereal box for drying the freshly waxed flowers.**

4. **Dip the leaves one at a time. Shake the excess wax off, and then immediately dip the leaf into the bowl of cold water.**

5. **Place the leaves flat on the sheet of wax paper and allow them to dry.**

6. **For flowers, cut the stems approximately 3 inches from the base of the flower. Dip the tip of the stem in wax to seal the flower's moisture in; allow the stem to dry.**

7. **Dip the bloom in the wax and then in the water.**

8. **Slip the stem of the flower into the holes in the cereal box and wait for the wax to harden.**

To make your waxed botanicals even more special, try using the following designer tips:

- ✔ Experiment with both paraffin and beeswax. I love beeswax because of the aroma and the beautiful golden color, but paraffin gives you a cleaner, more transparent look, and allows more of the colors to show through (plus, it's less expensive).

- ✔ Scent the wax by adding a few drops of essential oil in your favorite scent. (You may want to try cinnamon, vanilla, or spice.) If you use beeswax, you'll especially love the way the fragrances mix.

Don't place waxed leaves directly on an unprotected surface: The wax may damage the surface. Also, be careful not to place waxed botanicals in direct sunlight or near a heat source, because the heat may cause the wax to melt.

Chapter 22

Embracing Embossing

In This Chapter

▶ Making designs in velvet

▶ Creating paper, metal, and clay embossed art

*E*mbossing is a quick and easy, rewarding craft that produces exquisite results. You can easily emboss patterns, shapes, quotes, blessings, or other designs into metal, fabric, paper, and clay — materials that are all easy to find.

Embossing is simply a process of pressing a design into a particular craft medium with an embossing tool, giving your project a raised effect. It's beautiful because it's a subtle dimensional change on an otherwise smooth surface.

Have fun customizing velvet fabric and paper invitations. Create cool accents for your table in metal and clay. This chapter gives you the tools you need to quickly create fantastic décor for your holidays.

Embossing Velvet

Velvet is a fabric that's luxurious to the touch. Although this material is pretty enough when left alone, you can easily customize it for the holidays by embossing designs into it. Embossing adds patterns and texture to the fabric.

Don't fret if you don't know (or don't want to know) how to sew embossed velvet into items for your décor. Many prefabricated items (or velvet items you may already own), such as slipcovers, drapes, table runners, ribbons, and pillow covers, use this textural effect.

To emboss velvet, you need

- ✔ Rayon velvet
- ✔ Items for creating designs, such as
  - Rubber stamps
  - Armature wire
  - Cardboard
  - Metal caps or rings from jars
  - Glass candle holders (the bottom part)
  - Metal cookie cutters
  - Seashells
- ✔ Iron/ironing board (or the bottom of a metal pot or baking pan)
- ✔ Spray bottle filled with water

After you collect the items you need, follow these instructions:

1. **Preheat the iron to medium-high setting.**

2. **Place your design — stamp, wire shape, cookie cutter, or other item — right side up on your ironing surface. Place the fuzzy side of the velvet down on top of the design.**

3. **Spray the smooth side of the velvet with a small amount of water.**

4. **Press the iron on the velvet for only a few seconds at a time until the design is embossed into the fabric.**

Take care not to move the fabric when pressing, because if you do, you aren't going to get the design you're looking for. Also, don't leave the iron in one place for too long — rayon velvet can melt.

Embossing Metal

You can find embossed metal designs on everything from shower curtain rings to galvanized containers. You can introduce your own personally designed embossed metal art into your holiday décor by making a special ornament, covering a picture frame, or making napkin rings.

To emboss metal, you need

✔ Sheets of aluminum, copper, or brass tooling foil (available at your local craft supply store)

✔ Patterns for creating designs such as

  • Stencils

  • Stamped designs

  • Computer generated line art

  • Clip art

  • Freehand drawings

✔ Scissors

✔ Wooden stylus

✔ Hot glue gun (and hot glue)

✔ Steel wool

✔ Pencil

✔ Newspapers or sheets of craft foam

✔ Masking tape

To emboss metal, follow these simple instructions:

1. **Place a sheet of metal tooling foil right side down on newspapers or craft foam (you'll be embossing on the back side), and tape the foil in place on the edges with masking tape.**

2. **Lay the pattern on the metal tooling foil where you want to place the design, and tape it in place.**

3. **Use the wooden stylus to trace the design on the metal foil; remove the pattern and continue embossing the depth of design on metal by using the stylus to press harder in the embossed areas as desired.**

4. **Fill in the embossed areas with hot glue; allow the glue to harden.**

   The glue keeps your embossed designs raised and crinkle proof.

5. **Remove the metal from the newspaper or craft foam and cut it into the desired shape.**

6. **Turn the foil over and trace the outlines of the embossed design with the pointed end of the wooden stylus.**

7. **Scour the flat areas around the design with fine steel wool to mask any scratches and help remove any body oils that may tarnish the metal.**

You can use a faux finishing kit to paint or patinate your metal embossed project.

Embossing Paper

Embossing designs into paper gives an elegant look and feel to invitations, envelopes, and place cards. Besides embossing stationery, you may also want to try embossing a lampshade cover with the phrase "Happy Holidays." Use your imagination. You may find that many holiday paper items can use a pinch of panache.

To emboss paper, you need:

- Stencil bearing a decorative pattern
- Handmade or medium-weight paper
- Small light box or sunny window
- Wooden stylus or ball burnisher
- Removable tape

To emboss paper, follow these instructions:

1. **Position the stencil on the area of the paper where you want to emboss the design and secure it with removable tape.**

2. **Place the paper, with the stencil side down, on the light box or against a sunny window. Use the stylus or ball burnisher to rub the paper firmly where design is illuminated. Press the paper firmly against the edges of the stencil to make a crisp raised design.**

3. **When you're finished, remove the taped stencil and trace the outlines of the embossed design with the pointed end of the stylus.**

Try embossing paper with lockets, pennies, tin ceiling tiles, and other raised items. To reverse emboss, place the paper over the object, press down firmly, and then rub the burnishing end of the wooden stylus across the paper.

Embossing Clay

You don't have to be a sculptor or an artist to emboss clay. I prefer to work in polymer clay because it's super easy to work with, I can find it in many stores in virtually any color, and it stays soft and pliable until I decide to bake and harden it.

You can have fun using rubber stamps to create designer ornaments, gift tags, special buttons for pillows, plant pokes, flowerpot rims, and more. If you can wrap clay around an item or cut a shape out and stamp it, you can emboss clay to your heart's content. Try embossing clay with your kids; they'll love it . . . and you just may get hooked.

To emboss clay, you need

- ✔ Polymer clay (found at discount, art, and craft supply stores)
- ✔ Rubber stamps or other embossing designs (Use the list I provide in the velvet embossing section, earlier in this chapter.)
- ✔ Craft knife
- ✔ Baking sheet
- ✔ Rolling pin
- ✔ Baking parchment or piece of paper
- ✔ Cornstarch or talcum powder

After you collect the items you need, you can emboss clay by following these instructions:

1. **Soften the clay by warming it in your hands for a few minutes. Start kneading it to make it soft and pliable. Continue kneading it until it is the consistency you like.**

2. **Lightly dust a little cornstarch or talcum powder on your work surface and rolling pin to prevent sticking. Roll the clay flat with a rolling pin until it is the desired thickness.**

3. **Cut the clay into desired shapes with cookie cutters or a craft knife.**

4. **Gently place the clay onto a baking sheet covered with parchment paper or a plain sheet of white paper (this is so the clay won't scorch while baking). Poke holes into the ornaments, if applicable, to thread ribbon in them and hang after baking.**

5. **Preheat your oven according to polymer clay manufacturer's instructions (usually 275 degrees).**

6. **Dip the stamp (or embossing design) in cornstarch and blow off the excess. Stamp your designs on the clay shapes. Smooth any rough edges with your fingertips**

7. **Place the shapes in a preheated oven and bake 15 minutes for every ⅛ inch thickness of the shape.**

Dip your stamps in embossing powders (which are also available at craft stores) or pigment ink pads instead of cornstarch before pressing them into the clay. Your design will be in color, adding a very cool effect to the finished piece.

Chapter 23

Painting Decoratively

*P*aint is one of the easiest, most inexpensive ways to totally transform plain or outdated items. It's also one of the most fun and creative things you can do. Unfortunately, that means that it intimidates some when it comes to choosing color or deciding whether to freehand a design on your project, stencil, or stamp.

Don't worry. You don't have to paint the Sistine Chapel for the holidays. And I'm most certainly not going to give you something you can't do quickly and easily — you're going to be pressed for time anyway during the holidays.

All the techniques in this chapter are meant for the artistically, time-, budget-, or space-challenged person. If you fit into any of these categories, read on! You're sure to find something you want to at least try or experiment with (and because they're cheap and quick, why not!)

Grab your spouse's or roommate's clothes (to protect your own, of course), and a-painting we will go!

Prepping to Paint

You may have many surfaces you want to spiff up with a bit of paint, but don't go slapping a brush to them until you prep them properly to make the work worthwhile!

Proper preparation is the key to making a successful paint project last. The following list discusses how to prep common surfaces you may want to paint:

- **Metal:** Sand the surface with medium grit sandpaper (make sure that you scuff the surface) and use a wire brush to remove any rust. Clean the surface thoroughly with a mild detergent and water, and then rinse well. Allow the item to dry completely, and then prime it with a metal spray-on primer. After painting, seal the item with a rust-resistant metal sealant.

- **Wood:** Sand clean wood surfaces with sandpaper to smooth out any rough spots. Wipe the surface clean with a lint-free cloth and prime the surface of your wood, if desired, with a water-based primer; allow it to dry.

- **Glass or tile:** Remove dirt and oil from the surface of tile or glass with a quick swipe of a cotton ball or cosmetic pad soaked in rubbing alcohol. Check the label of the glass paint you're going to use for any special primers you may need to apply before painting.

- **Plastic:** Clean the surface with a mild detergent and water, and then rinse well. Wipe the surface with a lint-free cloth, and make sure that the surface is completely dry before proceeding. Check the labels on the paint you're going to use for suggestions on how to prime the surface before painting.

- **Styrofoam:** No preparation is necessary. Lightly brush any chipped or loose pieces from the item before painting. Test a tiny amount of paint on a small area of the item to see how the paint will react.

If the spray paint is not specifically formulated for use with Styrofoam, the solvents in the paint may melt your project. The paint may also ruin your project if you use it in excess and touch it before it dries.

Stenciling with Style

Stencils are wonderful for applying designs to surfaces without having to draw a thing! They come in just about any size and theme you can imagine, so hopefully, you can find something that will work for your holiday project.

I suggest starting with a relatively small stencil that can be used with only one color of paint. Try making snowflakes on a flat surface that's been painted powder blue. After you master stenciling, you can start to get creative. If stenciling still intimidates you, grab a poster board at your local discount store and try the technique in a couple of places. You'll get stenciling down pat in no time.

To stencil, you need the following materials:

- Paint or stencil cream (read manufacturer's suggestions to find out which surfaces each type of paint can be applied to)
- Stenciling brush (one for each color)
- Stencil
- Stencil adhesive or blue painter's tape
- Paper towels
- Paper plates (for squirting paint onto)
- Newsprint (for protecting work surface)
- Empty trash can with liner

After you gather the materials you need, follow these simple instructions:

1. **Cover your work surface with the newsprint.**

2. **Prepare the surface of the item you want to stencil according to the suggestions I list in the section, "Prepping to Paint," earlier in this chapter, or as recommended by a paint manufacturer.**

3. **Place the stencil inside the trash can (and liner) and spray a light coating of stencil adhesive to the back of the stencil.**

   If you don't want to use a spray adhesive, use blue painter's tape to secure the edges of your stencil.

4. **Position and place the stencil on the item as desired. Gently press the edges of the stencil where you're going to apply the paint to deter any seepage of paint under stencil.**

5. **Place a dime-sized amount of paint on a paper plate and then barely dab the tip of your stenciling brush into the paint. Tap and swirl the paint on a clean area of the paper plate to get an even coat of paint on the bristles and to remove any excess paint.**

   This process is called *offloading*. You can also use paper towels for this process.

6. **Keeping your paintbrush perpendicular to your surface, tap (pounce) or swirl the paint into the stencil design along the edges and then work your way to the center of the design.**

   When you reapply paint to your paintbrush, remember to offload before stenciling again.

7. **Remove the stencil by carefully peeling back the edge.**

   Use a paper towel to wipe off any seepage that may have leaked under the stencil before applying the stencil to another area.

8. **Continue following Steps 4–7 until you finish your project.**

Leaving Your Mark with Stamping

Stamps are great little (and sometimes big) items to have on hand during the holidays. You can use stamps in any holiday motif or design to accent place mats, napkins, gift wrap, invitations, place cards, and other home décor items. The beauty of having a stash of stamps is that you can quickly customize wood, fabric, metal, or ceramics to match any theme or special occasion.

Pigment pads (or rubber stamp pads) come in just about any color you can imagine and work well on most items. But you can use regular craft or latex paint, as well! Instead of pressing the stamp into a pigment pad, you can use a cosmetic sponge or your fingers to lightly coat the surface of the stamp with paint.

If you really get into using stamps, you may want to get more detailed information on such techniques as masking and layering. For the purposes of this book, though, I just stick to the basics.

To use stamps, you need the following items:

- Stamp (rubber or foam)
- Pigment pad or paint
- Item to be stamped
- Paper towels
- Sponge brush or cosmetic sponge
- Extra sheets of paper (for testing the stamp image)
- Stamp cleaner or mild detergent/water solution

Stamping is pretty self-explanatory, but you can follow these instructions to get the best results:

1. **Press the stamp onto the pigment pad several times to load it with ink.**

   To get an even coat of ink on the stamp, I prefer holding my stamp rubber side up and tapping the stamp pad against it. If you prefer to use paint, dip a sponge brush into a small amount of paint and coat the rubber side evenly.

2. **Test the stamp image by pressing three images in a row (without reloading the stamp) on a scrap piece of paper.**

   This step lets you to determine how dark you want the image to look on your item.

3. **Prepare your stamp again before pressing onto your item.**

   Press the stamp into the pigment pad again, or brush with another even coat of paint, and then stamp a number of images on scrap paper to get the level of color you desire.

4. **Position the stamp and press it firmly onto the item, making sure to press evenly on all parts of the stamp.**

   I prefer anchoring the stamp by pressing down in the center of stamp and then firmly pressing around the center.

5. **Lift the stamp straight up from the surface to prevent the image from blurring. You can then repeat the process until you're finished with your design.**

Be sure to clean each stamp immediately after every use to keep it in good shape and prolong its life.

If you want to stamp images on colored card stock or fabric, try using bleach as a paint alternative. Fold several layers of paper towels and place them in a plastic lid from a storage container. (Make sure that the lid has some depth to it, otherwise it won't work.) Pour straight liquid bleach onto the paper towels until they're completely saturated. Use these paper towels as your stamp pad and follow the instructions for stamping that I provide in this section. Wear protective clothing.

Embellishing Items with Decorative Painting

Decorative painting is one of the most rewarding pastimes I've found. You don't have to go all out to decoratively paint items for holidays unless you want to.

Decoratively painted items can have a few embellishments or many embellishments. If you're a beginner, you may want to try painting a random selection of geometric shapes. Use a few tools to help you along. Here are some examples to help get you started:

- Make polka dots by dipping new pencil erasers in paint and then stamping them onto the surface of the item you want to paint.

- Use a toothpick to make smaller dots or do detail work. Dab a little bit of paint on the tip and then press it onto the item.

- Create circles by dipping one end of a piece of macaroni (or any other round, hollow-shaped pasta) in paint and dabbing it onto the surface of the item.

When you think that you just don't have the right tools or a steady hand for the job, a little creativity can help you along.

Most of the decorative painting projects I suggest in this book can be done by using clip art or coloring books for your patterns so that you don't have to worry about drawing things to scale or proportion. You can enlarge or reduce these patterns on a photocopier and then trace them onto your item. To trace smaller pieces of art onto an object, use the graphite paper technique I cover in Chapter 24.

After you trace the outlines of your design onto an area or object, you can paint the project just like you color a coloring page. Depending on the size of your project, you may want to use a #1 or #2 liner brush to outline and define the images, but for larger items, you can just use a paint pen for easy outlining and better control.

Try to keep your holiday projects simple so that you won't have to worry about shading, blending colors, or trying to show dimension. If you discover that you want to really get into decorative painting, contact local arts and craft stores, cooperative extension services, community colleges, or other teaching centers in your area and find out if they offer a class that will fit into your budget and schedule.

Putting on Other Finishing Touches

You can apply simple finishing techniques, such as spattering and gilding, to decorate your holiday items. These techniques don't take a long time to do. Try the ones I list here, and if you find that you're really good at them, you may try researching and picking up other techniques to expand on your talents.

Spattering

Who knew that items from your bathroom could come in handy for a painting technique? Leave the toilet, but grab an old comb and toothbrush. You can spatter white paint on items like Christmas villages to make it look like snow came to town, and you can spatter small blue flecks on Easter eggs to make them look freshly laid.

To perform the spattering technique, you need the following items:

- ✔ Old toothbrush and comb
- ✔ Paint
- ✔ Items to spatter with paint
- ✔ Paper plate
- ✔ Newsprint to protect work surface.

After you collect all the necessary items, follow these simple steps:

1. **Place a small amount of paint on a paper plate. Dip the bristles of the toothbrush into a small amount of paint for light spatters, or a large amount of paint for bigger spatters.**

2. **Hold the comb over the item to be painted and then wipe the paint-dipped toothbrush over the tines of the comb using a quick motion.**

   Imagine that you're grating Parmesan cheese. Continue moving the comb and toothbrush combo over your item as needed, spattering paint where desired.

Gilding

You can *gild* (or apply gold leaf to) almost any surface — such as fruits, vegetables, wood items, or glass. You name it, and I've tried to put gold leaf on it. I refer to gold leaf in the directions, but you can also find copper or silver leaf sheets that may give you the look you're after. You can find these copper or silver leaf sheets in the same section of the art and craft store that you find the gold leaf.

Gather the following materials together to start gilding:

- ✔ Item to gild
- ✔ Paint for base coat
- ✔ School glue
- ✔ Sponge brush
- ✔ Paper plate
- ✔ Soft-bristled brush
- ✔ Clear-coat spray

Making faux finishing easy with kits

If you want to make an item look like stone, or like it's been weathered and rusted, you don't have to worry about trying to practice a technique or getting a combination of paint colors just right. You can find several paint kits on the market (both brush-on and spray-on) that will help you quickly and easily achieve an authentic look.

Your local home improvement center or craft store should have a wide selection of kits for you to choose from. Look for colors and finishes that mimic the surface you have in mind. You may find that even skeptics are wowed by the results.

My favorite is a line called Modern Options; it offers faux-effect solutions in kits or open stock so that you can buy only what you need. Within this line, you can find iron, rust, verdigris, pewter, bronze, and other magnificent faux finishes that give plain items an authentic or aged look.

To gild your craft item, use the following instructions:

1. **After you paint your surface with a base-coat color (one that you don't mind showing through the cracks of the gold leaf), brush on a thinned-out layer of school glue with a sponge brush.**

   Thin your glue by adding a tiny amount of water to a generous amount of glue.

2. **Carefully separate and place a sheet of gold leaf onto the item and then gently press it into the glue.**

3. **Use a soft-bristled brush; tap gold leaf onto surface to adhere. Gently move the brush in a swirling motion over the gold leaf and then remove any nonadhered areas by brushing them gently away.**

If you're painting the item the same general shade as the gold leaf, you can save time by brushing the item with paint and then pressing the sheet of gold leaf onto the surface. After you apply the gold leaf, brush and remove any of the excess. Seal the surface with a couple of coats of clear-coat spray.

Chapter 24

Working With Transfers

C ustom holiday accents that compare to pricey department store furnish-ings can be yours for about the price of a color photocopy or two. You can transfer noncopyrighted images of motifs, photos, flags, and even bless-ings or poems to many of the items you incorporate into your holiday décor. You can transfer images to finished items, such as vases, platters, or furni-ture, or you can transfer them to raw materials, such as fabric, clay, or metal tooling foil that you can fashion into objects later on. Reproducing fantastic artwork is effortless with today's transfer mediums. You don't need much time or talent to produce lovely works from the heart.

Tinkering with Transfer Mediums

Most transfers start as a color copy, or a full-color inkjet-printed page. Following are some of the most popular techniques, products, and tools for transferring images onto many surfaces:

- **Iron-on:** Many of the first transfer papers I tried were iron-ons. With iron-ons, you print your image directly onto a specialty paper with a color copier or an inkjet printer, and then you iron it onto a fabric.

- **Waterslide decals:** A waterslide transfer medium, such as Lazertran, allows you to print full-color images onto special transfer paper. Lazertran works well at transferring images to canvas, fabric, wax, ceramic tiles, glass, metals/foils, plaster, wood, and stone. It also offers other specialty papers for use with inkjet printers.

✔ **Printables:** You can find many items, such as ties, cotton fabrics, and other novelties, that you can run through your color inkjet printer or copier. These printable items work really well for transferring images instantly.

✔ **Gel mediums:** You can transfer color or black-and-white copies of images by using artist's gel mediums, such as Liquitex Gel Medium or Heavy Gel Medium.

Transferring Images onto Fabric

Quilts, pillow tops, stockings, and kitschy items (such as gift bags) are some of the wonderful holiday items you can make by transferring photos or images to fabrics.

Some iron-on transfer papers leave a waxy residue, causing your fabric to stiffen. One product, Lazertran Silk, works well on woven silk, satin, and ribbons. After the image has been transferred, this medium allows the fabric to flow, stiffening it very little if at all.

You can transfer images to fabric by using iron-on, waterslide, or printable-type transfer mediums. You can also use pure turpentine to transfer a color copy to a 100 percent natural fiber fabric item, such as cotton, linen, or silk. You're probably thinking that turpentine will ruin the piece of fabric. Not so. Just follow these simple instructions:

1. **Copy your image in reverse, and then place it face down on your fabric.**

2. **Use a disposable sponge brush to soak the back of the paper with pure turpentine.**

   Let the paper sit for a few minutes.

3. **Burnish the back of the transfer with the back of a spoon and then remove the paper.**

   The chemicals in the turpentine release the colors from the copy and adhere them to the fabric.

4. **Hand wash the fabric and allow it to dry.**

Transferring Designs onto Wood

If you want to transfer designs onto wood to complete a wood-burning or painting project, using graphite paper is your best bet. Just follow these instructions:

1. Tape a piece of graphite paper to the wood surface (with the graphite side facing the wood), and then tape a pattern or drawing over the graphite paper.

2. Use a ballpoint pen to retrace over the pattern outlines, pressing firmly on the paper.

   Check under the graphite paper occasionally to make sure that you're using the right amount of pressure to transfer your design.

3. Remove the pattern and the graphite paper.

   You can use the graphite paper as much as you like.

Transferring Images onto Clay

Polymer clay is one of the most versatile crafting mediums. You can use it to make napkin rings, ornaments, beads, candleholders, and more for the holidays.

Lazertran Silk is the only transfer paper I've been able to use to successfully transfer images to polymer clay before baking it. To transfer images to polymer clay, follow these instructions:

1. Press the image onto the clay and then roll it into the surface by using a brayer or rolling pin or inserting it into a pasta maker.

2. Leave the image on the clay for 10 minutes and then wet the paper backing sheet; let it soak for one minute and then carefully peel the paper backing off.

3. Let the clay set for 30 minutes before bending or shaping it. Bake the clay according to the manufacturer's instructions.

Transferring Designs onto Glass, Ceramic, or Porcelain

You can make custom coasters, decorative platters, or gifts by transferring holiday designs or other images to ceramic tiles, pottery, glass, or porcelain.

One easy way is to transfer images to these items is to use Lazertran. Here's how:

1. Trim the color-copied transfer paper close to the image and then soak it in water for about a minute.

2. Place the transfer on the tile (or pottery, glass, or porcelain) and then slide the paper backing off.

3. Squeegee any air bubbles out from under the decal and wipe off any wet residue.

4. Place the item in a domestic oven set at 100 degrees Fahrenheit to dry it out, and then increase the temperature gradually (to 400 degrees Fahrenheit) over about a 30 to 45 minute period until the decal melts and all the bubbles smooth out.

The finish should have a shiny, glazed appearance. Let the glossiness (rather than the temperature) be your guide when trying to determine whether or not the transfer is finished.

Transferring Designs onto Metal

Plain metal items, such as galvanized containers, brass, or silver-plated flea market finds, can be transformed to chic by using a transfer medium to apply photos, architectural images, patterns from fabric prints, and other images. You can also transfer an image to a plain sheet of tooling foil before crafting it into something else.

You can use Lazertran to transfer a color image onto any type of metal. Follow these instructions:

1. Iron the color-copied transfer (with the image side down) onto the foil.

2. Turn the foil over and iron the back of the metal to make sure that it's well fused.

3. Immerse the entire metal sheet in water and allow the paper backing sheet to slide off.

4. Shake the metal to remove any excess water and then pat it dry with a soft, absorbent cloth.

5. When the metal is completely dry, reheat it to make sure that the image fully adheres to the surface.

6. Spray with a clear-coat spray to seal the surface.

Chapter 25

Creating Luminarias

• •

• •

*T*raditionally, *luminarias* are made of votive candles set in paper bags weighted with sand, and placed in rows along walkways, driveways, and even rooftops. In this chapter, you find other creative ideas and materials for creating and using luminarias inside and outside the house. They can light paths, a mantel, or a staircase, and they can be made with traditional materials with no embellishment whatsoever or turned into works of art. Because they're so simple to make, you can use them as projects for children. You can light up your nights for the holidays by making some luminarias for your home and customizing them for a specific holiday.

Creating Paper Bag Luminarias

You can decorate, punch, or cut designs from lunch-size paper bags to make holiday luminarias quickly and easily. Try using bags in holiday colors (you can find them at party supply stores) to give your luminarias a holiday look. For instant decorating — no embellishments required — try using the preprinted themed bags that are often used for holding goodies.

Place one to two inches of sand in the bottom of each paper bag. Nestle a tealight or votive candle into the center of the sand. When you're ready to use your luminaria, just light the wick of the tealight or candle.

For other unique paper bag luminaria designs, try using some of the design techniques I describe in the following sections.

Stamping, stenciling, or drawing designs

You can customize plain bags by stamping, stenciling, or drawing designs on them with craft paint or markers. Stencil stars for the Fourth of July, or stamp shamrocks for St. Patrick's Day. A simple drawing of a jack-o'-lantern for Halloween or a stenciled Star of David for a dusk celebration can provide a beautiful way to welcome guests and make any occasion special. For specific instructions on how to stencil or stamp designs, refer to Chapter 23.

For a simple way to make a luminaria with a complex design, print clip art in black ink on plain copy paper. Trim the copy down to fit just inside one side of the plain brown bag, and then glue or tape it into place. When the luminaria is lit, the black lines of the design will show up on the outside of the bag. With this little trick, you can quickly make luminarias that look like you spent lots of artistic energy on them.

Try to find designs that look like silhouettes or are completely black: They show up better when the luminaria is lit.

Perforating designs

When you perforate outlines of designs in your paper bag luminaria, bright pinpricks of light shine through the paper. Perforating outlines of designs in paper is easy. Just follow these steps:

1. **Place several layers of folded newspaper on a cutting board.**

2. **Tape your paper bag, with the bottom flap unfolded, to the newspaper with pieces of masking tape or removable tape.**

3. **Refer to the pinpricking instructions (for using a thumbtack) in Chapter 20 to punch designs into your paper luminarias.**

Cutting out designs

Cutting small designs out of the paper bag will allow a little more light to shine through your luminaria. But remember, when you cut more paper from the bag, you also allow more wind in, making the candle flame more likely to go out.

When cutting out designs, use shapes that are 1 to 1½ inches in size. Anything larger will weaken the structure of the bag, making it more likely to sag.

1. **Place several layers of folded newspaper on a cutting board. Tape your paper bag, with the bottom flap unfolded, to the newspaper with masking tape or removable tape.**

2. **Draw or trace the outline of the design on the bag.**

3. **Cut out shapes with a craft knife.**

If you want to use cookie cutters for patterns or larger motifs, you can use two bags (with one serving as a liner) to give the cut bag strength. This layered effect is very pretty when you use a contrasting colored bag for the inner liner.

A scrapbook supply store may have a die cutter, such as an Ellison or Accu-Cut system, for cutting out shapes. See if you can use these systems to cut out your luminarias. Or the store may cut the shapes out for you for only a few cents a bag.

Making Metal Luminarias

You can recycle metal containers, such as soup or coffee cans, or use metal foil or mesh to make luminarias. The following sections give you some ideas to help get you started designing luminarias with metal.

Using cans

Empty, clean cans with the label and glue removed are great for making informal or whimsical luminarias. They're sturdy, and they can be used several times for years of holiday decorating. You can leave them in their silvery state, or you can spray paint them with holiday colors.

The cans will rust if left out in the elements, so be sure to bring them in when you're not using them. Or, if you like the look of rust, you may want to make your metal luminarias well in advance and then leave them outside for at least three weeks, wetting them down occasionally to accelerate the corrosion.

Metal can get hot! Keep your luminarias out of the reach of young children, and be careful not to touch them when they're lit.

To punch a pattern into your cans, you need the following materials:

- ✔ Paper pattern (a piece of paper with a design printed on it)
- ✔ Metal can
- ✔ Tape
- ✔ Scissors
- ✔ Hammer
- ✔ Awl
- ✔ Large nail

After you collect the materials you need, you can follow these instructions to create your metal luminaria:

1. **Cut approximately 2 inches from all sides of the printed design. Position the pattern on the can as desired and tape it down on all sides.**

2. **Place the awl on the center of the design (near the top of the design) and then tap the handle end of the awl with the hammer until you punch the sharp end of the awl through the can.**

3. **Following the outlines of the design, punch holes into the can with the awl approximately every ¼ inch, adjusting the punches as necessary to completely outline the design. Pull your pattern up on one side to check your progress as necessary. Realign the holes in the pattern with the finished punches to secure the pattern back into place.**

4. **Remove the pattern and repeat as desired, or spray paint the can with your preferred color. Be sure not to clog up your punched design with paint!**

5. **To hang your luminaria, punch two holes approximately ½ inch from the top edge of can on opposite sides. Thread 18 inches of sturdy wire (a cut-up coat hanger will do) through the punched holes at the edges of the can and bend the ends up at least ½ inch to secure the handle in place.**

6. **Fill standing luminarias with about 1 inch of sand or rocks, and insert a tealight or votive candle inside the metal container.**

   Light the wick of the tealight or candle when you're ready to use the luminaria.

Using metal mesh

Metal mesh is perfect for making luminarias, because the mesh is made of either a weave of wire or is cut into perforated designs already. The small chicken wire, radiator grill mesh, window screen mesh, and other durable mesh that you find at home improvement centers are great for luminarias. You can also try armature mesh or the tightly woven mesh that resembles a metallic fabric; both of these items can be found at craft stores.

To make a metal mesh luminaria, you need:

- Metal mesh
- Tin snips or sharp scissors
- Thin wire in a complementing color
- Needle nose pliers

To create a luminaria with metal mesh, follow these instructions:

1. **Cut a length of metal mesh big enough to wrap around a coffee can.**

2. **Roll the piece of metal mesh around the can to form it; thread thin wire through the side edges to join them together. Use needle nose pliers to help twist the wire several times to secure and snip the excess wire with scissors or tin snips.**

3. **Slip the can out from the metal mesh and then place the mesh on top of a candle. Beautiful!**

 Use vases, cartons, or other odd-shaped containers to form your metal mesh luminarias. Wrap the mesh around the container and then sculpt and crease the mesh with your gloved hands to help form it to the shape of the container. Use a felt-tip pen to mark the spot on the mesh where the cut line should be. Cut the mesh and continue joining the side edges as I suggest in the previous list.

Creating designs with metal foil

Metal foil comes in many colors and *gauges* (thicknesses), and it can be found at craft stores everywhere. To make sturdier luminarias, you need to stay away from the metal foil that is manufactured especially for embossing. These foils crease and tear easily — sometimes more easily than paper — and they're too lightweight to withstand even the slightest breeze.

Choose a heavy-duty tin, copper, or brass. If you want to punch or cut a design out of thin metal tooling foil, follow the instructions I give for punching designs out of cans in the section "Using cans," earlier in this chapter. To form the luminarias, refer to "Using metal mesh" earlier in this chapter.

Choosing Other Mediums

Believe it or not, you can make incredible luminarias by using materials other than paper bags and metal. Simple items found at flea markets, in basements, or in the garden can also be used. Try some of the starter ideas I provide in the following sections. They may shed new light on unique items you may already own.

Canning jars

Vintage or new Mason jars, which are used for canning fruits and vegetables, make wonderful luminarias. Weigh them down with rock salt, sand, berries, or nuts, and then place a candle inside. These luminarias are good for use inside and outside the home.

Cheese graters

Vintage or new metal cheese graters are great conversation pieces for just the right occasion. Just light a tealight candle and place a grater over it — the light shines through. To be safe, place the candles and graters on a tile or other scorch-proof surface. Metal graters can get hot and damage furniture surfaces; they can also be hot to the touch. Make sure that the candles have been blown out for a while before moving the luminarias.

Pumpkins

The hollowed out, carved pumpkin that you normally see at Halloween is the most famous luminaria of all. These luminarias can be used, in any shape or size, throughout all the fall season months and holidays. If you want to find out more about carving pumpkins, see Chapter 12.

Ice

Ice luminarias give you an easy way to make beautiful luminarias for a special occasion during the cold weather months.

You can make ice luminarias easily by reusing plastic two-liter bottles or other deep, plastic cylindrical vases. Milk cartons also work well for a nice square shape. Just slice off the top of the carton with a serrated kitchen knife and you're ready to go!

1. **Fill the container, half full, with water. Insert a smaller cylindrical container, weighted with pebbles or rocks, into the first container.**

   I've found that empty, clean frozen juice containers work best for the inside container.

   Make sure that the water doesn't completely come up to the top of the inside container. You then set the containers on a level surface inside your freezer and wait until the water freezes. If it's 32 degrees or colder outside, you won't even need a freezer for this project, you can just stick the containers outside.

2. **A simple, clear ice luminaria is beautiful on it's own. You don't need to float materials in your ice luminaria, but if you want to, go right ahead. Insert flowers (fresh or faux), greenery, or berries for a natural look, or suspend metallic stars or other festive materials in the water between the two containers.**

   If the materials float, that's okay. Empty enough water to make the floating contents even with the top of the inside container. Allow the water to freeze, and then fill the container the rest of the way up and freeze it again.

3. **To remove the ice luminaria from the containers, empty the pebbles or rocks from the inside container. Run hot water into the container inside the luminaria until the ice melts away enough to remove it. After you remove the inside container, run hot water on the outside to loosen and remove the outside container.**

4. **Keep ice luminarias in a freezer until you're ready to illuminate your paths or walkways. Place a tealight or votive candle inside your luminaria, and light the wick when you're ready to use it.**

Candle safety tips

I sprinkle tips for using candles to decorate for the holidays throughout this book. According to the National Candle Association (`www.candles.org`), candles are safe when burned properly, responsibly, and according to manufacturers' directions. When burning candles, you should always follow these basic safety rules:

- Lighted candles should always be within sight. Never leave a burning candle unattended.

- Never burn a candle on or near anything that can catch fire.

- Keep candles out of the reach of children and pets.

- Read and follow all manufacturer instructions carefully.

- Trim the wick to a ¼ inch before lighting it.

- Always use an appropriate candleholder placed on a stable, heat-resistant surface.

- Keep burning candles away from drafts, vents, and air currents.

- Extinguish a candle if it smokes, flickers repeatedly, or its flame burns too high. Let the candle cool, trim the wick, check for drafts, and then relight it.

- Keep the wax pool free of wick trimmings, matches, and debris at all times.

- Do not burn a candle for longer than the manufacturer recommends.

- Always burn candles in a well-ventilated room (or outside).

- Extinguish the flame if it comes too close to the holder or container. For a margin of safety, discontinue burning a candle when 2 inches of wax remains (½ inch if in a container).

- Never touch or move a votive or container candle when the wax is liquid.

- Extinguish pillar candles if the wax pool approaches the outer edge.

- Place lighted candles at least 3 inches apart from each other.

If you follow these safety tips, you can make sure that your holidays remain happy and bright.

Chapter 26

Beading Beautifully

● ●

● ●

*B*eads, beautiful beads, are hot. Adding them to holiday cards, table linens, and other home décor accents is one of the easiest things to do. They add just the right touch of elegance and sparkle.

Whether you use plastic, glass, crystal, or clay beads, begin thinking of how you can add little bits of color and texture to everyday items. After you tackle your first few beadwork projects, you can get into more-complex beadwork designs that will add an heirloom quality to home furnishings, cards, and holiday decorations. You can transform ordinary items that you can pick up for a song into pricey-looking holiday accents for your home.

Beading Fabric

You can add texture, drama, patterns, and designs to fabric by using beads. Beads can help make plain textiles look fabulous, and beading fabric is like sewing on buttons — super easy.

With today's selection of beads, you can make your own color combinations and styles with ease. When selecting the type of bead you're going to work with and the technique you're going to use to adhere or stitch the beadwork to your project, consider what the bead is going to be used for:

  ✔ If you plan on washing the item several times, you may want to use a small glass seed bead to stitch your beaded design, sewing the beads on individually. You can find stitching instructions in the "Using thread" section later in this chapter.

✔ If you're going to be using or displaying your beadwork design (for example, a throw pillow or table topper), you can string long strands of beads — made out of plastic, glass, or other material — that range from tiny to medium size, and then stitch them to your item.

✔ For items that will be used once or seldom washed, you can fuse or glue the beads to your fabric. (See the "Adhering beads" section, later in this chapter, for best products to use.) You can also find beautiful premade beadwork appliqués that can be glued or ironed on just like a patch. These appliqués work well for seldom-used items, as well.

You may want to add a beaded fringe to the end of a table runner, or monogram a napkin with a vintage strand of faux pearls. Adding beadwork to fabric items is a simple process that yields beautiful results. To find out how to add beadwork to fabric items, see the "Attaching Your Beads" section, later in this chapter.

Adding Beads to a Variety of Items

You've probably seen gowns, wedding dresses, shoes, and handbags with beading, so why not add beads to photo frames, place cards, invitations, candlesticks, and other accessory items?

My favorite holiday items to add beads to are Christmas stockings, ornaments, Easter eggs, and romantic objects of affection for Valentine's Day. Napkin rings can be made of wired beads or embellished with a few loops of beads in festive colors. Adding a rim of brightly colored beads to a simple clear glass vase creates something special. Beaded faux pearls wrapped around the base of a candle, or Swarovski crystals wired together and dangled on a candelabrum reflect the flicker of soft candlelight like a prism.

Still don't know where to add beads? If you were a glitter fanatic as a kid, you can easily find hard-surfaced items to add beads to. After all, beads are like glitter for grown-ups.

I tell you how to adhere beadwork designs to hard surfaces in the section, "Attaching Your Beads," later in this chapter.

Stringing Beads

If you're going to use a large amount of the same kind of bead to complete a design, stringing them together before laying them out and attaching them to fabric or other items can be helpful. You have a couple of ways to do this.

Using thread

The quickest way to string a beaded design for textiles is to use a heavy-duty thread in a coordinating color. You should try to use cotton, nylon, or monofilament beading thread (which is different than sewing thread) to string your design, but because you may just be starting out, you can go ahead and use the heavy-duty sewing thread you may already have in your mending kit.

Before you string your beads, you need to first choose a beading needle that's thin enough to pass through the center of the beads. When you're ready to start stringing the beads, follow these instructions:

1. **Thread a long length of thread through the eye of the needle and knot the ends together to form a double strand of thread.**

   Trim the loose ends close to the knot.

2. **Thread the first bead, being careful not to let it slip off the knotted end.**

3. **Holding the knotted end in one hand and the needle in the other, slide the bead almost to the knot.**

4. **Thread the needle through the looped thread just inside the knot, pulling the thread taut to secure the bead.**

   The bead should now act as an anchor for all the other beads to slide to.

5. **Continue threading beads until you get enough for your project.**

The easiest way to thread beads is to dump them into a shallow plastic bowl or glass dish. I like using a resealable plastic container because I can close it when I'm finished and keep my beads from scattering. If you have trouble getting tiny beads onto your needle, wrap a piece of double-sided tape on your finger and then dip it into the beads and start threading them that way. You may find that bringing the bead to you is easier than chasing a rogue bead across a shallow dish.

To tie off your strand of threaded beads, thread your needle through the last few beads several times and then knot the thread before cutting it close to the fabric. When you attach the beads to fabric, you can place any thread that is showing to the garment side.

Using wire

I often string beads onto wire because I don't have to knot thread, use a beading needle, or worry about tangling large strands of beads like I do when I use a needle and thread. You may also want to use wire when stringing beads for sewing projects, because the wire easily holds its shape.

The option of using wire beading on fabric is not widely accepted, because the wire can rust and harm the fabric when washed, or it can poke holes into the fabric. But I've found that plastic-coated copper wire works for just about any beadwork project. The protective coating on the wire prevents discoloration and corrosion from the natural oils in your hands, chemicals, or environments and protects fabrics well. Also, wire-strung beads can be glued to other accent items, such as photo frames, vases, or any other hard object — even furniture.

Before you string beads with wire, you need to select a gauge of wire that's thin enough to pass through the center of your bead. After you chose your wire, follow these simple instructions:

1. **Cut the desired length of wire with scissors and loop one end into a curled hook. (You can shape it with your fingers or needle nose pliers.) On the other end, straighten the wire to resemble a long needle.**

2. **Thread the beads onto the wire as desired.**

3. **To finish the strand, cut the wire close to the last bead you threaded onto the wire. Wrap or kink the wire into a knot to secure it, or bend it up and over the last bead and then twist wrap the end around the wire between the last and next-to-last bead.**

Jewelry wire in sterling silver, brass, or copper is great to use with beads if you know that it's going to be adhered to surfaces with glue. You can find wire in many colors to match any holiday or bead. Also, look for wireworking tools with special attachments to help you bend wire into special holiday designs.

TIP

Gauging differences in metal and wire

When shopping for wire or metal, check the package to determine the *gauge,* or thickness, of the product. Remember that the higher the number, the smaller the thickness of the wire or metal. For example, 24-gauge wire is thinner than 18-gauge wire.

I know, I know — it seems like it should be the other way around. If you see wire or metal in person, determining the difference in thickness is easy — but when you purchase these items online or from mail-order sources, you want to be sure that you know what you're getting.

If you start to get confused, just remember — big number, little size.

Attaching Your Beads

Just as you can find many items to add beads to, you can also find many ways to attach beads to items. Here are my best techniques for adding beads that are loose, strung, or in appliqués.

Attaching bead appliqués

As I mention earlier in this chapter, you can find a number of premade beaded appliqués at fabric stores and craft stores. Look in the special-occasion fabric aisles for a rack of these displays or ask a clerk to help you find them. Specialty trim and beading stores have a wealth of different patterns and designs and sometimes implement other materials in beaded appliqués, such as lace, sequins, or crystals.

Beaded appliqués come in two different kinds: one that you can fuse to fabric just by ironing it on, and another that you sew on just like a patch. Most likely, the manufacturer will provide recommendations for how to attach the appliqué to your selected item.

To attach an appliqué by sewing it on, follow these instructions:

1. **Place your beadwork appliqué on your item and baste around the edges, using a running stitch or a basting glue adhesive.**

2. **Use a small *whipstitch* (see Chapter 19 for instructions and an illustration of this stitch) to go back and secure all the edges of the appliqué, or use a satin stitch on your sewing machine to sew around the edges.**

3. **Remove the basting threads.**

You can use a special fabric glue to adhere the appliqué to your textile — no sewing required! If you prefer to sew on your appliqué, you may want to try using a basting glue to save a bit of time.

You can also stitch or sew your solid beaded design onto nonfusible webbing instead of directly onto your item. After you finish sewing the design onto the nonfusible webbing, trim the webbing close to the design and glue or sew it onto the item as desired.

Sewing on beads

Sewing beads onto fabric is simple. After you transfer or draw a beading pattern onto your fabric, you may find that stretching the fabric taut in a wooden hoop is helpful. Make sure that if you use a hoop, you use a fabric with a noncrushable pile — in other words, velvet is out.

Sewing strings of beads

Sewing on strings of beads — wired or threaded — is easy. Just follow these instructions:

1. **Secure the first bead to sew on your design by coming up through the fabric next to the bead and crossing over to the bead next to it, securing it to the fabric.**

    I like to perform this technique a couple of times for the beginning stitch.

2. **Continue to come up every few beads and go down across the threaded wire or string, securing the beads in place (see Figure 26-1).**

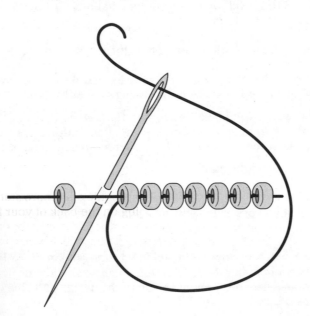

Figure 26-1:
Couching strands of beads to fabric.

Sewing individual beads

If you anticipate that the fabric you're beading is going to need to withstand handwashing several times, you may want to come up through your fabric, thread a bead, and then come back down through the fabric, making sure that you sew each and every bead on as you go (see Figure 26-2).

Figure 26-2: Stitching each bead individually, following pattern lines.

If you don't think that your fabric is going to have to withstand much wear and tear, here's a quick way to sew individual beads onto your fabric: Come up through a starting point in your design, thread a few beads onto your needle and thread, and then go down back through your fabric. With this technique, you sew as you go. After you become acquainted with how beads lay out on fabric, you may find this to be the quickest way to sew on beads.

If your fabric is lightweight, you may want to provide a bit more stability for the weight beads add. Use lightweight webbing on the back of your fabric — basted along the outside edges of the design — as additional support for your beaded design. After you completely stitch your piece, you can remove the basting threads and trim the webbing close to the edges of the design so that it doesn't show through.

Adhering beads

How do you sew a bead to a picture frame? Well, you can't. That's why it's always good to know what to do in case of a beading emergency . . . as if beading emergencies actually exist.

Cleaning your beadwork

Dust your beaded gems occasionally with a soft, damp cloth. Use a soft-bristled brush to gently go over areas where dirt has settled, and then vacuum as necessary.

For fabric pieces, a gentle handwashing in a mild detergent is sufficient. Hang the item to dry, or press it, bead side down, on a white towel until dry.

Several adhesives on the market today promise ultimate bonding properties for gluing beads to many surfaces. To glue individual beads to any surface, including fabrics, you can use Crafter's Pick Jewel Bond, Beacon Adhesive's Gem Tac, or Aleene's Jewel-It Embellishing Glue. You may also want to use fusible tape as an alternative.

Chapter 27

Etching Glass

● ●

In This Chapter

▶ Preparing to etch glass

▶ Cutting patterns and etching your design

● ●

*E*tching glass may sound intimidating if you've never tried it before. Surprisingly, it's super easy and quick to do. The supplies you need are minimal, so it's also one of the most inexpensive crafts you can do.

If you can't find a particular holiday motif you like in accessories that you want, you can create your own with etching. Etch glass items such as cake domes, glasses, ornaments, vases, and plates to coordinate themes and table settings. Virtually any glass item is game to receive your own special holiday touch. Try practicing on a few empty wine bottles or clean glass jars before putting them into the recycling bin. It will help you gain confidence and allow you to try out the techniques I cover in this chapter.

Getting Started

Traditionally, glass etching is done by frosting the surface of the glass with a sandblaster. Thank goodness you don't have to go industrial to do this craft these days! You can have beautifully etched items in a jiffy by using a few items at your kitchen sink.

You can find several materials for frosting glass items at your local craft store. You can use a spray paint by Krylon that comes in several colors or a few other paint-based products that are available out on the market, but I find that it's just as easy and quick to get an authentic etch by using an etching cream or a premixed etching bath solution.

Before you begin etching your glass, you need to choose an etching pattern. You can often find an assortment of rub-on etching patterns at your local craft store, and you can also get peel-and-stick patterns that are made especially for etching. You can also make your own pattern (more about that later in this chapter).

Choosing your etching product

If you want to etch small areas, use an *etching cream*. You apply this cream (which is the consistency of mayonnaise) with a craft stick. It's easier to control.

If you want to etch most of the surface of an item (like an ornament) or the outside surface of a glass, an *etch bath solution* is your best bet. You just soak the item in the solution and let it work its magic. All you have to do is follow the manufacturer's instructions for the proper technique, because each manufacturer has its own recommendations and guidelines. Using an etch bath solution is a little more cost-effective for etching larger surfaces.

If you haven't etched glass before, I suggest starting out with a small bottle of etching cream so that you can get comfortable using this technique first, doing a few pieces at a time. Etching is one of those instant gratification projects — one that looks very custom, very hard to do, and very expensive. (Of course, it's quite the opposite.)

Finding an etching pattern

If you can't find exactly what you're looking for in the premade patterns, try making your own patterns with the following ideas.

Clip art books

Clip art books can be found in book, craft, and graphic arts supply stores. They contain black-and-white, reproducible, copyright-free art that is usually grouped together in themes. You can find clip art books in just about every theme imaginable; make sure you look for holiday specific books.

Pick a design for etching and then cut or copy the design from the book. Place the design up to a light source, like a window or a light box, and then place a piece of vinyl adhesive paper on top of it. Trace the design onto the vinyl adhesive paper with a permanent marker. After you trace your design onto the adhesive paper, you can cut your pattern and follow the basic etching instructions (both are discussed in the "Itching to Etch" section, later in this chapter).

Computer art

If you're good on the computer, and you have software that can help you incorporate graphics into a document, you can make your own computer art designs.

Start by selecting the design you're going to use. Search clip art files, check out symbols, or play with text fonts to find something you like.

Decide how big you want the design to be on your glass object and then enlarge or reduce the design on your computer to fit your specifications. The design itself needs to be a relatively solid pattern so that you can cut out the printed part easily.

Print out your pattern and place it on a light source, such as a window or a light box. Place a piece of vinyl adhesive paper on top of it, with the paper backing in place, and trace the outlines onto the adhesive paper. After you trace your design onto the vinyl adhesive paper, you're ready to attach your pattern and start etching (see the instructions in the "Etching the glass" section, later in this chapter).

Stamps

To make designs with stamps, you need to select stamps with large designs and solid patterns. You can find these stamps in the home-decorating section of a craft store.

Stamp the design onto vinyl adhesive paper and allow the ink to dry. If you have trouble getting the ink to set, outline the design with a permanent marker and blot the excess ink off with a paper towel. Cut out your etching pattern approximately 2 inches from the edge of the design and then attach the pattern to your glass. Now, you're ready to start etching (see the "Etching the glass" section, later in this chapter).

Stencils

Stencils are one of the best resources for making etching patterns. You can cut design an etching pattern with stencils by using one of two techniques:

- Apply vinyl adhesive paper to your glass surface and then trace the stencil onto the paper. When you're finished tracing, cut out the design with a craft knife.
- Trace the design onto a piece of adhesive paper and then follow the instructions for cutting patterns and etching glass that I provide in the "Itching to Etch" section, later in this chapter.

TIP

Making etching patterns with other materials

You can use creativity and your imagination when trying to find unusual patterns or designs to etch into glass. Here are a few ideas to get you going:

✔ At office supply, art, and craft stores, you can find a number of different shapes and sizes of adhesive vinyl lettering. These stick-on letters, symbols, and shapes, which are normally used to make large reports on poster board or signify names and addresses on mailboxes, can be used to etch monograms or sayings onto glass items.

Press the vinyl adhesive letters to the glass and burnish the edges with a spoon to make sure that none of the etching cream seeps underneath. You can use an etch bath, etching cream, or a faux etching spray paint to create your etched design on glass. Refer to the basic etching instructions in the "Etching the glass" section of this chapter Remove your lettering, and *voilà!*

For a designer look, try mixing up styles of lettering for cute holiday sayings. Use cursive for the first letter of each word, and then use straight sans serif lettering for the rest of the word.

✔ You can find a selection of paper punches in the scrapbook or paper crafting section of craft stores. Purchase paper punches that have interesting designs or geometric shapes. Use these punches to make your own adhesive art; punch the shapes out of vinyl adhesive paper. You can use the designs that you punch out of the adhesive paper as your pattern, or you can use the sheet of adhesive paper that you punched the designs out of.

Carefully remove the paper backing, making sure that you don't rip or tear the edges of the cutout design. If you happen to rip the design, just adhere the design to the glass as usual, making sure that you connect the torn or separated edges as well as possible. Place a small piece of adhesive paper or tape over the torn or separated vinyl.

Itching to Etch

Okay. You have your glass, your etching product, and your chosen pattern, and now you're just itching to get started!

Cutting the pattern

If you don't already have a pattern cut, you've come to the right place. First, you need the following materials:

✔ Glass cleaner

✔ Paper towels

✔ Craft knife

Now that you have what you need, follow these instructions:

1. **Remove any oils or residue from the glass surface by cleaning it with glass cleaner and paper towels.**

   Make sure that your glass item is dry before proceeding.

2. **Peel the paper backing from the vinyl adhesive paper and then position and apply it to the glass item as desired.**

   Minimize any air bubbles that may appear between the glass and vinyl adhesive by pressing and smoothing them with your fingers.

3. **Use a craft knife to cut out the design by following your drawn lines; remove the pieces of adhesive paper that you want to etch.**

4. **Burnish the remaining vinyl adhesive on the glass by using the back side of a spoon. Press the edges of design firmly so that no etching cream can seep under the adhesive paper.**

Now you're ready to etch.

Etching the glass

To get the best results when etching glass, you need the following materials:

✔ Etching cream

✔ Glass item with cut pattern adhered

✔ Rubber gloves

✔ Craft stick

✔ Newsprint (to protect work surface)

✔ Sink

✔ Glass cleaner

✔ Paper towels

If you have your materials ready, follow these instructions:

1. **Cover and protect your work surface with newsprint. Wear rubber gloves to protect your skin from coming in contact with the etching cream.**

2. **Using a craft stick as an applicator, apply a thick layer of etching cream onto the glass item, covering the design completely. Wait five minutes for the etching cream to react.**

3. **Rinse off the etching cream under tap water and rub off any stubborn areas with your finger. Remove the vinyl adhesive paper pattern and rinse the glass thoroughly again.**

4. **Clean the glass surface with glass cleaner and paper towels. You're done! (And you thought that it was going to be hard.)**

Part V
The Part of Tens

The 5th Wave   By Rich Tennant

"Let's see, where can I hang this good luck shamrock
garland? How about on one of your casts?"

In this part . . .

Looking for some quick and easy tips? The "top ten" format provides you with great lists for ways to add holiday sparkle to your home. And although no one may be able to stop Aunt Zelda from guzzling too much eggnog and doing a table dance on Christmas Eve, you can make the holidays easier by checking out the tips for making your holiday decorating less hectic.

Chapter 28

Ten Quick and Easy Ways to Decorate for the Holidays

- -

In This Chapter

▶ Decorating on your own

▶ Hiring a professional

- -

Decorating for the holidays can be as easy as 1-2-3. If you're running low on time or just need a quick reminder of things you can do to add a little holiday sparkle to your home, try a few of these ideas.

Decorate Your Door

Holidays begin at your front door, so that's where you should begin your decorating. Hang a holiday or seasonal wreath, outline the door frame with creative garlands or swags, or set potted plants beside the entry to welcome your guests (and impress the neighbors to boot).

Let the kids get crafty and make something to dangle in the door window, if applicable. Hey, with this solution, you don't have to do anything but supply the tape!

Turn to Chapter 20 for many paper crafting activities, such as making paper garlands, paper snowflakes, or pretty cut-out holiday motifs taped to string for hanging or taped directly to the door. You can even press seasonal botanicals, such as autumn leaves, between wax paper to tape to every pane of glass (see Chapter 21 for instructions).

Hang Something

Don't limit yourself to wreaths and garlands. Look for banners or flags to hang inside or out. Often, changing up a banner or flag is enough to give the exterior of your home a wonderful holiday touch without having to go to extremes.

Hanging banners on the inside of your home can welcome a happy Hanukkah or Easter. Get creative and make your own by familiarizing yourself with the sewing suggestions given in Chapter 19. You can follow the how-to-make-a-table-runner instructions there, and then instead of placing it on a table, hang it on the wall! Of course, you can always make it even easier on yourself — buy a cool banner at a party supply store.

Light Something

Light the menorah or kinara, turn on some twinkle lights, shoot some fireworks — whatever your holiday calls for. Add a few more light sources here and there to light it up, baby, yeah!

Purchase various shapes and sizes of candles in holiday colors to replace boring white or cream tapers. Group them together on a mantle or serving area to add instant sparkle to an evening holiday gathering.

Rearrange Something

Shake things up for the holidays and move your furniture or furnishings around. Make way for the Christmas tree or rearrange your patio for a festive Fourth of July party.

Sometimes, just moving things around refreshes a stale setting and gives you new surfaces or places to decorate (and did I mention clean?). The new scenery may also inspire you to get creative.

Color Your Home Festive

Give your holiday home a punch of color. Just about every holiday has a certain standard color palette or combo already assigned to it, so deciding what colors to use is easy. If you don't want a bunch of schmaltzy holiday shapes, motifs, or other holiday-patterned designs, just accent your home with a color that corresponds to the holiday. Bright red napkins and a lush arrangement of red roses on a white tablecloth can say Valentine's Day beautifully. Add a few stems of red ware and you're set.

Deck One Hall (or Room)

If decorating the whole house seems to overwhelm you, or you just don't have the time or budget to do everything you want, commit to doing just one room beautifully! If you're having a party, only decorate the living space that you'll have your guests in. That space may be the dining room, the living room, your game room — whatever space you decide to decorate, invest your time and energy in making it pretty.

You don't have to go over the top to impress friends or family. If you have one room decorated to the hilt, you'll still wow everyone with your sense of style.

Accentuate a Focal Point

If you just want to add a bit of holiday touches to a room, choose your *focal point* and dress it up! A focal point can be a fireplace (decorate the mantel), a picture window (add holiday swags, switch out drapes seasonally, and so on), a filled-to-the-brim bookcase (add holiday accent items or add a few holiday picks here and there), or anything you want.

Whatever you choose as a focal point, you can add a few holiday items to accentuate it for any festive occasion.

Make a Centerpiece

Adding a centerpiece to a table is an easy way to add holiday style. Think of items that are out of the ordinary to make up your centerpiece. Stack pumpkins; tier cake plate stands in various sizes adding layers of seasonal flowers and fruit; pile vegetables and fruit in large baskets or bowls. When in doubt, stack or pile. Ornaments piled into a crystal bowl are pretty. A basket stacked high with colorful Easter eggs is also a beautiful centerpiece. Dreidels and gelts gathered together on a decorative platter are as pretty as a flower arrangement.

Stack and pile, pile and stack. It's an easy way to make a centerpiece without arranging flower one.

Now, if you want to make your own floral arrangement, or for other creative centerpiece ideas, refer to Chapter 21. But in a pinch, keep your favorite florist on speed dial.

Place a Plant

Easter lilies say Easter (duh); poinsettias say Christmas. Often, just by placing a plant in a room, you effectively make a holiday statement. Place plants on a coffee table, mantel, fireplace hearth, or buffet.

I list a variety of botanicals in each holiday section for you to choose from, but there are an infinite number of plants, flowers, and other botanicals available that I couldn't fit in. Need ideas? Visit your local garden center to see what's in stock. Usually, they have an ample supply of botanicals that are appropriate for a particular holiday or season.

Hire Me

So, I tried. Seriously, though, if you find that you're running out of time, energy, and ideas, hiring a decorating professional can help you out in a jiff. Decorating pros are good at giving you a helping hand at the holidays, especially if you've hit your stress limit and need to unwind while you watch the help try to untangle your mess of Christmas lights. Sometimes, just getting a third-party opinion on what looks good and what you should chuck is also beneficial.

Interior designers and decorators usually advertise whether holiday decorating is a service that they offer, so check your local newspaper or phone book listings for a professional in your area. Also, visit a local garden center to see if they have staff to decorate your home. Often, places that make fresh wreaths and garlands, as well as places that offer a good selection of holiday merchandise, have salespeople on staff that are really good at adding holiday pizzazz. They may even offer these services for free if you purchase your holiday decorations from their store.

Chapter 29

Ten Tips to Make Your Holiday Decorating Less Hectic

In This Chapter

▶ Beating stress with preparation and organization

▶ Keeping things in perspective

- -

The one word most often associated with holidays is stress! Why? You only have so many days and hours to get everything done for the holidays; plus, you have to add these tasks to your normal, everyday, hectic life.

I'm sure I don't have to tell you, but let me remind you anyway of the best tip for keeping your holidays less hectic: Less is more; keep your decorating *simple*. You can have a wonderfully impressive holiday decorating scheme without working yourself into a frenzy. If you're still stressed, though, here are more of my best tips for keeping your holidays, and your holiday decorating, as hassle free as possible.

Planning Wisely

If you haven't been preparing for the holidays year-round (who does?), take your planning cues from retail stores — they do plan for them year-round, and they stock their merchandise accordingly. As soon as you see the seasonal or holiday displays go up — even in the grocery stores — take it as your cue to start planning your holiday and decorations.

Being Realistic

Before finalizing any plans for the holidays, go through the list and ask yourself if your plans are realistic. As cool as it sounds, do you really need a Christmas tree in *every* room or a wreath on *every* door? Do you really have to host your own Halloween bash or put together 20 handmade gift baskets (shalach manot) for Purim?

Finding ways to keep your holidays less hectic may mean paring down what you've planned. Remember that for every thing you add, you tack on more time, energy, and money as well. Make sure that you go through a reality check for the things you've planned. You may need to make a few minor (or major) adjustments, but look at how much richer your holiday will be when you're refreshed, rested, and organized. Plus, the holiday decorating you'll do will look better because you had the time to do it right.

Using Organizational Tools

A day planner (paper or electronic), a decorating notebook, a monthly calendar — whatever you choose as your organizational weapon, wield it fiercely at the holidays.

In this book, I show you how to create a decorating notebook, project forms, and more. Use them. If you don't, create your own organizational system for planning your holidays. Note when invitations, cards, and shopping have to be done and preplan as much as possible, using the sections in each holiday chapter as your idea starter from which you can make accurate lists.

Keep your organizational planner handy. You'll find yourself being less stressed and worn out if you don't have to remember everything off the top of your head. You'll have everything you need, including notes, at your fingertips.

Multi-Tasking for Efficiency

Try to multi-task as much as possible. When you sit down and list all the things you need to do for the holidays, go back through the list and match up the tasks that can be done at the same time.

For example, you can clean the house or hang some garland while you're baking cookies for a party. You can shop for more than one holiday or occasion at a time. You can have your presents gift-wrapped for just a few dollars (sometimes, the money goes to charity) while you continue shopping, and on and on. You can accomplish any number of tasks simultaneously; all you need to do is look at your task list. You probably already multi-task on a daily basis anyway (folding laundry while watching TV or talking on the phone with dinner in the oven), so multi-tasking your holiday chores should be a no-brainer.

Having a Plan B

Perhaps Murphy's Law will skip your house and go on to the next, but Murphy never takes a day off. Things can go wrong. I'm not trying to sound pessimistic here, but you need to have contingency plans in place just in case the turkey burns, is raw inside, or the fire department has to be called because the garland goes up in smoke.

Keep emergency numbers by the phone, make plans in case you have to move a feast to a different room, keep extra food in the freezer should the family get snowed in a few extra days (or if the turkey's too far gone to even bother carving it), and figure out how to change the fuse in your Christmas tree lights *before* stringing them up so that you won't have to take down the tree just to figure it out in the middle of your holiday.

Think of anything that's ever gone wrong in the past and list what you could've done to help prevent it or make it better. Without going through additional stress, just add these few things to your list in the planning portion of your holiday without getting all neurotic about it. You'll breathe a sigh of relief if, after the holidays have come and gone, you never needed that extra entrée or box of fuses. Eat the entrée some other evening and save the box of fuses for next year!

Getting a Little Help from Your Friends (or the Pros)

You may not get your own live-in maid or butler for the holidays, but don't nix the idea of getting *some* help.

You can accomplish many holiday tasks without stressing over everything by cutting a few corners, delegating, hiring professional help, and enlisting your family and friends.

Cutting a few corners means that you order fresh bread from the bakery instead of growing your own flour, beating it against a rock, raising hens to gather their wonderful blue-hued eggs from your own chicken coop, and spending two days to knead and rise bread before baking this golden-crusted loaf on designer parchment paper. Cutting corners also means that you can feel guilt free when decorating by buying many premade decorating items instead of crafting them yourself. (Who's gonna know the difference anyway?)

Give yourself a break: Craft only what you want, cook only what you want, and feel free to buy everything else from the store. Also keep in mind that the holidays aren't necessarily a good time for starting something new. Sure, you may have instructions in this book for making many holiday items by hand, but just make sure that you've planned on making them plenty of time in advance.

Cleaning is another one of those things for which you may want to get additional help. Even if you don't have a regular maid and never considered hiring one, perhaps a holiday is a good time to justify the expense. Hire someone from a cleaning service for one day and let him or her clean your house from top to bottom concentrating on doing those tedious chores such as baseboards, crevice cleaning, and blinds or draperies. This way you have one less thing to worry about, and you just picked up extra well-needed time to do other holiday tasks.

Shopping Smarter

One of the things I both love and hate about the holidays is the unbelievable amount of shopping one must do to get things done. After running to the bakery and deli to get special orders and going to the post office, mall, specialty stores, and card shops, you have little time to breathe — much less decorate.

Catalog orders and Internet shopping can save you time (as you know, time = money) at the holidays. Shopping from home is pretty reliable and quick, plus you can comparison shop more easily and sometimes have a better selection of merchandise to choose from. Save the elbow-to-elbow combat for the local sales you want to catch or the buggy bumper wars for the supermarket. You'll still have plenty of opportunities to get in on all that fun.

Oh, and speaking of sales: If you have room, shop the sales at the end of the season when you're far less stressed and buy only the things that you truly deeply want — not just the leftover junk that's at a great deal. You should already have a list of your wants and needs in your decorating notebook; use that as your guide.

Make sure that you list in your holiday planner all the new items you've bought, so that you don't overbuy next year, and store items according to my suggestions in Chapter 7.

When the holiday rolls around the next time, you'll be relieved to remember that you've done lots of your shopping in advance, so you don't have to fight with other shoppers for decorative items or overpay for merchandise that puts a strain on your pocketbook and your stress level.

Taking Breaks

In the midst of your holiday decorating days, remember to take breaks often to enjoy the process.

I've seen many people rush, rush, rush to beat the neighbors in getting things up or spend Thanksgiving trying to decorate for Christmas. Relax. Who are you trying to beat?

When you find yourself working up a sweat, stop and admire what you've done. Then relax and take a breather. Have a fresh cup of coffee or tea, take a snooze, read a book to a child — do whatever you like when you normally take some downtime. Sure, I know it's not good to just draw things out, but you want to make holiday decorating an enjoyable experience, not a test of your endurance.

Not Sweating the Small Stuff

Take it from me, the ultimate planner: I *hate* it when I take the time to make a plan, and then nothing goes as it seems. Flowers ordered in plenty of time come in with buds half opened instead of in full bloom, Kiddush cups ordered for special Seder table settings never make it and can't be tracked down, or people who RSVP to come to your four-course meal suddenly cancel because the kids got sick. All these unexpected occurrences can be quite frustrating for the "planaholic."

Don't let your stress level on the stress-o-meter burst. Flowers, cups, people — all are important. What's *not* important, however, is hanging on to the why. When my stress level hits an all-time high, I have to step back and go, "Why am I really upset?" I usually find that it's my frustration that things didn't go as I planned them.

Occasionally, plans have to change because of budget shifts in the household. No problem. You can easily edit or pare down any specific decorations as needed.

Drop the unimportant details and don't dwell on them. Concentrate on what did go right, and just go with the flow. Although I love paying attention to detail, it's not worth getting upset over the little things. Be able to step back and look at the big picture. You'll see your heart rate and stress level go down, and you'll be able to enjoy a more fulfilling holiday. Take a deep breath, adjust, and work with what you have.

Realizing What the Holidays Are All About

Ultimately, the goal for decorating any holiday is to celebrate a wonderful occasion with family and friends. Never let any decorating, shopping, or other stressor interfere with the reason for the season. Even if you're simply celebrating Valentine's Day or a lighthearted St. Patrick's Day, know that you're paying tribute on a special day to honor a momentous occasion that was made into a holiday to commemorate it. That truly is special any way you look at it.

When you feel yourself getting overwhelmed, just stop for a moment, take one of those breaks I mentioned earlier in this chapter, and reflect or rejoice for the reason that you're decorating. You're celebrating! May you enjoy every single moment of it, and never, ever let stress override your pleasure.

Appendix

Holiday Resources

● ●

In This Chapter

▶ Locating craft or decorating supplies online
▶ Finding more free holiday craft projects
▶ Finding out more about the history of holidays

● ●

Many of the items, companies, and resources mentioned in this book are listed in this chapter. You can find where to get the following:

✔ Free holiday craft projects

✔ Product recall information

✔ Products mentioned in each chapter

✔ Special stores for merchandise

✔ History for each holiday

✔ And much more

Dive in to see what else you can do for the holidays. Search here for more great ideas.

Helpful Holiday Contacts

To locate a tree recycling program in your area:

Earth 911
Phone: 1-800-CLEANUP
Internet: www.earth911.org

For household cleaning tips and hints:

Heloise
P O Box 795000
San Antonio, TX 78279-5000
Internet: www.heloise.com/
E-mail: Heloise@compuserve.com
Fax: (210) HELOISE (435-6473)

To find the history of a particular holiday:

HistoryChannel.com
Internet: www.historychannel.com

For free holiday safety reports on candle safety, fireworks, Halloween safety, Christmas tree fires, and more:

National Fire Protection Association
1 Batterymarch Park
P.O. Box 9101
Quincy, MA 02269-9101
Phone: (617) 770-3000
Internet: www.nfpa.org

For product recall, holiday safety tips, and more:

U.S. Consumer Product Safety Commission (Main office)
4330 East-West Highway
Bethesda, Maryland 20814-4408
Phone: (301) 504-6816 or 1-800-638-2772 (TTY 800-638-8270)
Internet: www.cpsc.gov
E-mail: info@cpsc.gov

U.S Consumer Product Safety Commission (Eastern office)
201 Varick Street, Room 903
New York, NY 10014-4811
Phone: (212) 620-4120
Fax: (212) 620-5338

U.S. Consumer Product Safety Commission (Central office)
230 South Dearborn Street, Room 2944
Chicago, IL 60604-8260
Phone: (312) 353-8260
Fax: (312) 353-5013

U.S. Consumer Product Safety Commission (Western office)
1301 Clay Street, Suite 610-N
Oakland, CA 94612-5217
Phone: (510) 637-4050
Fax: (510) 637-4060

For a searchable database of holidays broken down into categories of religion, country, and more:

Worldwide Holiday & Festival Site
Internet: www.holidayfestival.com

Free Online Holiday Craft Projects

- Better Homes and Gardens (www.bhg.com)
- Chadis Crafts and Kippot (www.chadiscrafts.com/)
- Crafts Magazine (www.craftsmag.com)
- Creating Home Décor (www.creatinghomedecor.com)
- Home and Garden Television (www.hgtv.com)
- Ivillage.com (www.ivillage.com)
- Make-Stuff.com (www.make-stuff.com/hollidays/index.html)

Craft Supplies

Most of the products mentioned can be found locally at craft, fabric, and home improvement stores. In this section, I list major online craft stores and specialty Web sites that sell merchandise specifically mentioned in this book.

- Dick Blick (www.dickblick.com)
- Beverly's Craft and Fabric Stores (www.save-on-crafts.com)
- Create For Less (www.createforless.com)
- Joann Fabric and Crafts (www.joann.com)
- Creating Home Décor (www.creatinghomedecor.com)

REMEMBER

Each site has different product offerings, shipping and privacy policies, and so on, so be sure to check these things out before placing an order.

Holiday Decorating Catalogues and Online Resources

For decorations and supplies for Jewish holidays:

> Ahuva.com
> Internet: www.ahuva.com
> E-mail: sales@ahuva.com

> Alljudaica.com
> 2906 West Devon Ave.
> Chicago, IL 60659
> Phone: 1-800-626-6536 or (773) 262-1700
> Internet: www.alljudaica.com

For decorations and supplies for Christmas:

> Christmas Mouse
> Williamsburg, Virginia
> Norge, Virginia
> Nags Head, North Carolina
> North Myrtle Beach, South Carolina
> Myrtle Beach, South Carolina
> Virginia Beach, Virginia
> Phone: 1-888-437-5635
> Internet: www.christmasmouse.com/

For decorations and supplies for Kwanzaa:

> HBS Kwanzaa Shop
> Phone: (718) 379-9291
> Internet: www.tike.com/kwanzaaitem.htm

For storage containers and organizers for holiday decorating items:

> The Container Store
> 2000 Valwood Parkway
> Dallas, TX 75234
> Phone: 1-888-CONTAIN or (214) 654-2000
> Internet: www.containerstore.com

For craft supplies, decorating kits, and holiday merchandise:

Creating Home Décor
105 Dawson Avenue
West Haven, CT 06516
Phone: 1-866-931-9417
Internet: www.creatinghomedecor.com

Lillian Vernon Corporation
100 Lillian Vernon Drive
Virginia Beach, VA 23479-0002
Phone: 1-800-545-5426 or 1-800-285-5536 (TDD)
Internet: www.lillianvernon.com

For special holiday lighting, timers, and outdoor yard ornaments:

Novelty Lights, Inc.
1630 W. Evans Ave. Suite K
Englewood, CO 80110
Phone: 1-800-209-6122 or (303) 671-0533
Internet: www.noveltylights.com/holiday_lighting.htm

Index

Notes

Notes

Notes

Notes

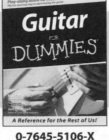

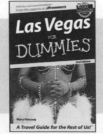

FOR DUMMIES®

Plain-English solutions for everyday challenges

COMPUTER BASICS

0-7645-0838-5

0-7645-1663-9

0-7645-1548-9

BUSINESS SOFTWARE

0-7645-0822-9

0-7645-0839-3

0-7645-0819-9

FOR DUMMIES

Helping you expand your horizons and realize your potential

INTERNET

The Internet FOR DUMMIES
0-7645-0894-6

The Internet ALL-IN-ONE DESK REFERENCE FOR DUMMIES
0-7645-1659-0

eBay FOR DUMMIES
0-7645-1642-6

Also available:

America Online 7.0 For Dummies
(0-7645-1624-8)

Genealogy Online For Dummies
(0-7645-0807-5)

The Internet All-in-One Desk Reference For Dummies
(0-7645-1659-0)

Internet Explorer 6 For Dummies
(0-7645-1344-3)

The Internet For Dummies Quick Reference
(0-7645-1645-0)

Internet Privacy For Dummies
(0-7645-0846-6)

Researching Online For Dummies
(0-7645-0546-7)

Starting an Online Business For Dummies
(0-7645-1655-8)

DIGITAL MEDIA

Digital Photography FOR DUMMIES
0-7645-1664-7

Photoshop Elements 2 FOR DUMMIES
0-7645-1675-2

Digital Video FOR DUMMIES
0-7645-0806-7

Also available:

CD and DVD Recording For Dummies
(0-7645-1627-2)

Digital Photography All-in-One Desk Reference For Dummies
(0-7645-1800-3)

Digital Photography For Dummies Quick Reference
(0-7645-0750-8)

Home Recording for Musicians For Dummies
(0-7645-1634-5)

MP3 For Dummies
(0-7645-0858-X)

Paint Shop Pro "X" For Dummies
(0-7645-2440-2)

Photo Retouching & Restoration For Dummies
(0-7645-1662-0)

Scanners For Dummies
(0-7645-0783-4)

GRAPHICS

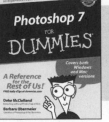

PowerPoint 2002 FOR DUMMIES
0-7645-0817-2

Photoshop 7 FOR DUMMIES
0-7645-1651-5

Macromedia Flash MX FOR DUMMIES
0-7645-0895-4

Also available:

Adobe Acrobat 5 PDF For Dummies
(0-7645-1652-3)

Fireworks 4 For Dummies
(0-7645-0804-0)

Illustrator 10 For Dummies
(0-7645-3636-2)

QuarkXPress 5 For Dummies
(0-7645-0643-9)

Visio 2000 For Dummies
(0-7645-0635-8)

FOR DUMMIES®

The advice and explanations you need to succeed

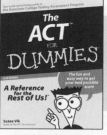